David F. Salisbury is a science journalist with *The Christian Science Monitor*. He has won numerous awards for articles he has written on nuclear energy, water pollution, and earthquake prediction.

David F. Salisbury

MONEY MATTERS

Personal Financial Decision Making with the Pocket Calculator

A SPECTRUM BOOK

Prentice-Hall, Inc., Englewood Cliffs, New Jersey 07632

Library of Congress Cataloging in Publication Data

Salisbury, David F.
   Money Matters.

    "A Spectrum Book."
    Includes index.
    1. Finance, Personal–Data processing.   2. Mini-
computers.   I. Title.
HG179.S235   1982   332.024'0028'54   82-11198
ISBN 0-13-600528-4
ISBN 0-13-600510-1 (pbk.)

This Spectrum Book can be made available to
businesses and organizations at a special discount
when ordered in large quantities. For more information,
contact: Prentice-Hall, Inc., General Book Marketing,
Special Sales Division, Englewood Cliffs, New Jersey 07632

ISBN 0-13-600528-4

ISBN 0-13-600510-1 (PBK.)

10 9 8 7 6 5 4 3 2 1

Editorial/production supervision
and interior design by Alberta Boddy
Cover design by Ira Shapiro
Manufacturing buyer: Barbara A. Frick

Prentice-Hall International, Inc., *London*
Prentice-Hall of Australia Pty. Limited, *Sydney*
Prentice-Hall Canada, Inc., *Toronto*
Prentice-Hall of India Private Limited, *New Delhi*
Prentice-Hall of Japan, Inc., *Tokyo*
Prentice-Hall of Southeast Asia Pte. Ltd., *Singapore*
Whitehall Books Limited, *Wellington, New Zealand*

To Robert Cowen who, like Archimedes,
gets his best ideas while in the bath.

Contents

Preface

Many people these days have a calculator, but what do they do with it? Most of them are content to use it merely to balance their checkbooks. This is unfortunate, yet perfectly understandable: It is much easier to buy a calculator than it is to put its capabilities to work. Advanced calculators are really small handheld computers, and like their big brother, the computer, they are dumb machines; they can only do what their operator instructs them to do.

Calculators have a tremendous capacity to help you put your entire financial house in order, even if you heartily dislike the rigors of arithmetic. To do this, however, requires more than simply owning an intriguing little plastic box that, with its keys and winking lights, can add, subtract, multiply, and divide with such phenomenal ease, provided the batteries are charged. The *software* of computer technology—the procedures, the equations, and the basic numbers— is needed to put these modern "magic boxes" to work. Software also consists of programs and logical routines, without which even the most expensive computer is nothing more than a complicated tangle of wires and magnets.

This book, then, is a software package on money matters for your calculator: It provides the information you need to employ your calculator far beyond checkbook balancing. It brings together in one textbook, in a simple and straightforward manner, all the formulas you need to deal with personal finances.

This book concentrates entirely on financial concerns, not on such esoteric matters as how to compute gas mileage or the area of a triangle, or how to make your calculator spell "Shell Oil," or how to understand the magic of fibonnaci numbers. In the realm of personal finance, we are forced to use numbers. We must know how much change to expect from the checkout clerk or risk being cheated, whether we loved or hated arithmetic and algebra in school. Of course, if counting change were all there is to our financial lives, no one would need a calculator. But, alas, the modern world of personal finance is much more complicated than this—and is getting more and more confusing all the time.

For many years now banks and big businesses have used computers to cope with the ever-increasing tangle of numbers, which all of us must back our way through from adulthood to the grave. It is only in recent times—since calculators have become available for less than $10—that there is any computational relief for the average individual.

We can compare the calculator to the Colt-45 of the Old West. The six-shooter enabled the 90-pound weakling to stand up against the 220-pound bruiser, as legend has it. For this reason it was called the "equalizer." In a similar fashion, the 4-function calculator equalizes the abilities of those people who without paper and pencil, would have to add and subtract on their fingers to compute complex money matters, with the abilities of those who can add, subtract, multiply, and divide 6 digits in their head. To take advantage of this new equalizer, however, the arithmetic hater must become proficient with the calculator just as the 90-pound weakling on the old frontier had to master the use of the six-shooter.

Along a similar vein, calculators having the computational power of a sub-machine gun are becoming available. These *business-analyst* models are now available for as little as $20. Wired into these models are a number of financial functions, such as compound interest and installment buying formulas, that make even complicated personal finance problems almost as easy as adding and subtracting.

New technologies, such as six-shooters and calculators, reshape society in ways that demand new survival skills. Even though calculators make arithmetic easy, they require a new sophistication in applying mathematics to daily living. This is a process that is just beginning; calculators are only the tip of the iceberg. Beyond them are home computers, which hover on the horizon. Now primarily the domain of hobbyists, they will be revolutionizing family living within the foreseeable future. Individuals who make an effort to understand and utilize the capabilities of calculators and home computers today are preparing themselves for the future. They are gaining valuable capabilities that those who make no effort will not have, giving them a number of advantages, particularly in the world of high and low finance.

Learning to operate a 4-function calculator is the place to start in understanding and utilizing the electronics revolution. As an immediate benefit, this skill will enable you to make better and more informed financial decisions. It will give you added insight into the mechanics of banks and other financial institutions. Even the simplest calculator, when used with the proper software, is sufficient to simplify relatively complicated financial problems, such as calculating interest compounded on a savings account. As a less immediate benefit, your skill with a calculator will provide a stepping stone from which you can advance to home computers as they come within your price range.

MONEY MATTERS

1

Buying a Calculator

Calculators come in a wide variety of shapes, sizes, functions, and characteristics. They are mounted in wrist watches and pens, inserted in checkbook holders, manufactured the size of business cards, plated with sterling silver or 14-carat gold, and mated with alarm clocks and stop watches. The vast majority of calculators on the market are the 4-function type. This means that they perform the 4 basic mathematical operations or functions: addition, subtraction, multiplication, and division. They sell for less than $10.

If you already have a calculator, it is probably a 4-function model. All the problems in this text can be done on such a calculator. Unfortunately, this simplest of calculators is not well suited for the more complicated financial operations, such as computing compound interest, installment borrowing, and inflationary effects. Whenever possible, I have attempted to give methods and approximations that will allow you to make these calculations with minimal effort.

ADVANCED CALCULATORS

Nevertheless, it is worth considering the more advanced types of calculators, the 2 basic categories of which are the electronic slide rule and the business analyst. The electronic slide rule is primarily designed for the engineering and science student or professional. It includes a large number of functions that are of little use in personal-finance computations. But it does have functions that greatly simplify the financial calculations in this book, particularly the ability to raise a number to a power. An electronic slide rule is adequate for the task of personal finances. The business analyst calculator, however, is tailored to handle money matters. It is endowed with a number of financial functions that make quick work of the problems presented in this text, such as, for example, computing the future value of a savings account. Readers who do not have a calculator or who are dissatisfied with the one they have should seriously consider a business-analyst model. These range in price from $20 to $150.

PROGRAMMABILITY

The more expensive business and scientific models have a feature called *programmability*. This simply means that you can instruct the device to automatically execute a series of operations. For instance, to find the amount of sales tax on a number of different products, simply toggle the calculator into the *programming* mode, key through the steps involved, switch back into the *operational* mode, enter the first price, push the *execute* key, and the calculator automatically determines the tax. For each subsequent product, you simply enter the price and push the execute key to obtain the amount of tax. Programmability, then, is extremely useful for repetitive operations. It is also of value in "what if" financial explorations. For example, what if you want to buy a parcel of real estate, but you first wish to compare various mortgage options? The advanced calculator can be programmed to do this with a minimum of effort. Or, what if you wish to determine the monthly payments and the equity after 5 years for a certain priced property, as well as the interest rate on down payments of different amounts? You can program the calculator to automatically compute the payments and equity by entering a down payment amount and then pushing the execute key. A more detailed examination of the programmability of advanced calculators is given in Chapter 13.

Most advanced calculators are of good quality, as befits their high price tags. However, some 4-function calculators on the market are of questionable quality. One good way to judge the quality of a calculator is by its instruction manual. Some come with only a long strip of paper containing instructions for the company's 5 different models printed in 4 languages. Such instructions are inadequate, and the calculators are often improperly assembled. Others, however, come with pamphlets describing their complete operation. These are the best kind, especially for those unfamiliar with calculators.

Calculators, like digital watches, have 2 different types of number displays. One is the liquid-crystal display (LCD), with silver- or bluish-colored numbers. This display type uses only a little electricity, and thus is preferred for calculators without rechargeable batteries. LCDs are clearly visible in bright light, but they are not as visible in dim light. They also have a slow response time: It is possible to push the buttons faster than the numbers can appear on the display.

The alternative to the LCD is the light-emitting diode (LED) display, with its distinctive red glow. These are being used on a number of products ranging from watches to stereo equipment. They require more current than do LCDs; they drain a hearing aid battery in no time at all. Therefore, it is better to use them with rechargeable batteries. They can be difficult to see in direct light, but they are clearly visible in filtered light or even in the dark.

FIXED AND FLOATING
POINT DECIMAL

In calculators, the decimal point is positioned in 2 different and very important ways: (1) the decimal point is in a fixed position set by the electronic circuitry (fixed point); and (2) the decimal is free to move about (floating point). Let us consider the difference between 2 8-digit calculators, one fixed point and the other floating. In a fixed-point calculator, the decimal point is typically frozen between the third and fourth decimal places from the right, giving the calculator 3 decimal places. The numbers are built from right to left. Thus, if you enter 1 in a fixed-point machine, you get

$$1.000$$

Push a second number, 5, for instance, and you get

$$15.000$$

Enter a decimal point and 125, and the result is

$$15.125$$

A drawback to the fixed-point calculator is that it limits the accuracy of the calculations. If 1.113 is multiplied by itself, the correct result is 1.2388. But because the fixed-point calculator has only 3 decimal places, it will round off this number to 1.239. This seemingly small error may prove significant in certain instances.

Machines with floating-point architecture build up numbers from left to right, much as you would write a multi-digited number on a piece of paper. In this case, when you punch a 1, it appears as

$$1.0000000$$

Add a 5, and the result is

$$15.000000$$

Then, entering 0.125 results in

$$15.125000$$

Squaring this number gives

$$228.76563$$

In this case the number was rounded off at the fifth decimal place rather than at the third, giving a much smaller rounding-off error.

The floating-point number system is the most natural and accurate system for calculators. The calculations, illustrative examples, and answers to questions in this text are all done using a floating-point machine. Readers

3

working with a fixed-point machine may obtain significantly different results in a number of cases, even if they do all the computations correctly.

EXPONENTIAL NOTATION

The capability for exponential notation also greatly expands a calculator's capacity. When an operation results in a number larger or smaller than the capacity of the display, the calculator automatically expresses it as a number between 0 and 10 multiplied by a power of 10. To tell whether an 8-digit calculator has this feature, enter the number 99999999 into the machine, and then add 1. If it does not have this feature, all you will get is an overflow indicator. If it does, it will give a readout similar to

$$1. \qquad 08$$

This is calculator shorthand for 1×10^8, or 100,000,000. The two digits displayed at right are the proper power of ten.

The exponential-notation capability enables the calculator to deal with numbers as large as 10^{99} (1 followed by 99 zeros) and as small as 10^{-99} (a decimal point followed by 98 zeros and a 1).[1] Unless you are a business tycoon, it is unlikely that your calculations will exceed the capacity of an 8- to 12-digit calculator, but if double digit inflation continues much longer this may not be the case.

CALCULATOR LOGIC

Another fundamental difference between calculators is the way they perform their arithmetic functions. Most use familiar *arithmetic logic*: Enter the first number, the operation (add, subtract, multiply, or divide), the second number, and then, when you push the equal-sign key, the operation is performed on the 2 numbers. Several manufacturers, however, offer calculators employing what is known as *reverse Polish logic*—a name that, unfortunately, has given rise to a number of "reverse Polish" jokes by devotees of the arithmetic approach. Its odd name not withstanding, this logic system has more flexibility than the arithmetic approach, especially when extremely complex calculations are concerned. One disadvantage is that it is more difficult to learn.

To use the reverse-logic system, you first enter the 2 numbers, then punch the operation. Instead of an equal key, an enter key is used to store the first number in a special set of memories called the "stack" until an operation key is depressed. The difference between the arithmetic-logic and the reverse-logic systems is mainly a matter of taste. Both types of calculators do exactly the same job. Hewlett-Packard, the primary exponent of the reverse-logic approach, makes the "Cadillac" line of the calculator world, giving the reverse-logic system a distinct status. But for most people arithmetic-logic calculators are sufficient.

---

[1] Negative exponents are defined in Chapter 2.

While shopping for a calculator, don't overlook the practicalities. For instance, pick one that fits in your hand comfortably. Consider the size of the keys: A calculator with small buttons may be fine for an indoor-type person, but hopeless for a ham-fisted athlete studying for a degree in accounting. Also, a person with a light touch will probably prefer a model with a pressure-sensitive keyboard. But those who enjoy rapping out numbers (perhaps pretending they are pounding Uncle Sam or their friendly banker on the top of the head) will want a sturdy calculator with keys that depress significantly.

Some calculators are a pleasure to use; others are just a means to an end. If your calculator has features you find irritating, you probably will not use it very much, at least if you are like me.

CHECKLIST
FOR PURCHASING A CALCULATOR

Display

1. *Type* — Is it an LCD or an LED? If the latter, rechargeable batteries are preferable.
2. *Architecture* — Floating-point is far better than fixed-point.
3. *Rounding Off* — Models that round off numbers without truncating them are preferable.
4. *Digits* — A display should have at least 8 digits; a display of 12 is preferable. The ability to handle exponential notation greatly expands a calculator's capacity.

Logic

1. *Arithmetic* — If a calculator has an equal-sign key $\boxed{=}$, it uses arithmetic logic. In this system, parentheses keys $\boxed{()}$ are extremely helpful because they allow computation of complicated mathematical expressions without first having to arrange the numbers, record intermediate values on paper, or keep them in one's memory.
2. *Reverse Polish Notation (RPN)* — If a calculator has an enter key $\boxed{\blacktriangle}$, it employs RPN. While more difficult to learn, this system has more flexibility in solving complex mathematical expressions. RPN calculators with a 4-memory stack are considerably better than those with only 2 or 3.

Basic Functions

1. *Constant* — Some 4-function calculators without an accessible memory have other ways of performing repeated operations using the same number. While better than nothing, they are not nearly as useful as those with addressable memories.
2. *Memory* — An addressable memory is extremely valuable, particularly in calculators with arithmetic logic, because it stores intermediate re-

sults. Several memories give even greater flexibility and reduce the amount of scratch pad work involved. A large number of memories, called storage registers, are particularly valuable on programmable calculators.

3. *Register Arithmetic* — This enables one to add, subtract, multiply, and divide numbers in memory with those in the display. In its simplest form, register arithmetic is represented by memory plus $\boxed{M+}$ and memory minus $\boxed{M-}$ keys. It is handy but not essential.

4. *Last X* — This key makes recovery from entry errors easy. The last number in the display is automatically saved in a special register. It can be recalled by pushing the $\boxed{\text{LAST X}}$ key.

5. *Percent* — Percent keys come in handy for a number of financial calculations. They come in several varieties: Some simply divide the number in the display by 100, converting it into a percentage; others have *percent of* keys that compute a given percentage of a number. Another version is the *percent difference* key, sometimes symbolized by $\boxed{\triangle\%}$, which determines the percent difference between 2 numbers.

6. *Number-to-a-Power* — Designated by $\boxed{y^x}$, this extremely valuable key for financial calculations allows direct calculation of inflationary effects, compound interest, and installment buying formulas.

7. *Logarithm* — This function is necessary for a limited number of financial computations. It can substitute for the number-to-a-power function as well, although most calculators that have the y^x function also have logarithms. There are 2 types of logarithms; common and natural. They are interchangeable in most financial equations.

8. *Square/Square Root* — Although commonly included on calculators, these functions have a very limited utility because they do not take much computational power.

Financial Functions
(Business-Analyst Models)

1. *Simple Interest* — Special keys allow you to enter a given principal, interest rate, and maturity. By pushing a single key the interest accrued is computed.

2. *Compound Interest/Installment Buying* — This function is extremely valuable. The mathematics involved in compound interest, installment buying, and inflation are closely related. Therefore, this built-in function can be used for a whole range of financial applications.

3. *Days between Dates* — An internal "calendar" allows one to enter 2 dates, using a calculator convention, to determine the number of days in between them. Some calculators can determine the date a given number of days before or after a specified date. This is useful in determining when payments are due and in checking the interest on passbook savings accounts, to mention just a few.

Instruction Manual

Is the instruction manual complete? This is an important indication of the quality of the calculator itself. A good instruction manual with illustrative problems is essential to understand how the device works, especially the more advanced calculators.

Aesthetics

Do the keys fit your fingers? Are they easy to punch? Can you read the display easily?

2

Some Common-sense Rules for Calculator Operation

A properly operating calculator adds, subtracts, multiplies, and divides infallibly; yet it is only as accurate as the fingers punching the buttons. Computer programmers have an apt saying: "Garbage in, garbage out." If erroneous data are fed into a computer, the results will be worthless. This holds just as true for calculators. It is unrealistic to expect to go through hundreds of computations perfectly no matter how strenuously one concentrates. However, there are some common-sense rules that a calculator operator can follow to minimize problems.

CHECK EACH ENTRY

Each time you enter a number, look at it on the display to make sure you have properly keyed it in. Once you become proficient with a calculator there is a great temptation—especially when adding long columns or going through complicated computations—to punch in numbers and operations without taking your eyes off the paper on which the figures are written. This makes it almost impossible to catch mistakes immediately. Train yourself to glance at the display after each entry.

REDUCE KEYSTROKES AND SCRATCH PAD WORK

Each time you touch a key or write down a number you risk making a mistake. Therefore, keep to a minimum the number of keystrokes and the amount of transcribing needed to solve a problem. For the efficiency experts among us, this also reduces the time it takes to do computations. Sometimes a little thinking ahead may help. Take the case of adding

$$55.20 + 89.70 + \frac{(125.00 + 132.00 + 45.00 + 15.00)}{4.00}$$

If, in using a 4-function calculator, you start at the left and work to the right as is natural, you add 55.20 + 89.70 and get 144.90. Now you are stuck. In order to continue, this sum has to be written down. If, however, you had worked the other way, starting with the sums in the parentheses, you could have computed straight through without having to write anything down

$$(125.00 + 132.00 + 45.00 + 15.00) \div 4.00 + 89.70 + 55.20$$

which, incidentally, equals 224.15. In other words, problems can be organized to cut down on the number of steps it takes to solve them.

Another way to eliminate keystrokes is to enter only the necessary decimals. Thus, in adding $15.70 + $23.00 + $14.79, simply enter 15.7 and push the + key. The calculator will automatically add the zero. Similarly, for the next amount, key in only 23. The calculator will add the decimal point and the 2 zeros for you.

An accessible memory also considerably reduces the number of key-strokes and the amount of scratch pad work involved in computations.[1] In checking the addition of a column of figures without a calculator with a memory key, you either have to commit the number to memory or write it down before re-adding. A calculator with a memory key can store the total, add the figures again, and then recall the total to verify the answer. A memory can also help in solving involved calculations. Take again the case of

$$55.20 + 89.70 + \frac{(125.00 + 132.00 + 45.00 + 15.00)}{4.00}$$

Now you can start at the left. After you have added 55.20 and 89.70 and obtained 144.90, you can store this in memory and proceed to average the remaining 4 numbers.

$$(125.00 + 132.00 + 45.00 + 15.00) \div 4.00 = 79.25$$

Now add the 144.90 recalled from memory to the 79.25 to get the correct answer of 224.15.

In using a calculator without a memory there are many cases when there is no other alternative than to write down some numbers. For instance, you want to calculate your grocery bills for a quarter of a year, and you want to calculate both a monthly total and a quarterly average. The receipts show

---

[1] All calculators have memories, but the simplest models have only those required for adding, subtracting, multiplying, and dividing. They do not have a memory set aside for storing and recalling numbers.

JANUARY	FEBRUARY	MARCH
$142.70	$14.19	$77.07
23.65	48.81	35.05
6.03	37.99	48.55
12.12	2.08	58.06
	11.17	23.13
	5.54	18.42

Using a memory-less calculator, you would have to write down 2 of the sums and rekey them to come up with the quarterly total.

Using a calculator with a memory eliminates writing down numbers. Adding up January, the sum is $184.50. Store this value in the memory and then go on to February. For this month the grocery bills add up to $119.78. Add $184.50 recalled from memory to this and put the total, $304.28, back into the memory.[2] For March, the total is $260.28. Adding the $304.28 to this gives a grand total of $564.56 for the quarter. Now to calculate the monthly average for the quarter, divide by 3 to obtain $188.19 per month.

If you stored the quarterly total in the memory just prior to dividing by 3, you can now use it in other calculations, such as computing the weekly average of $43.43 by dividing by 13 weeks. Some of the more costly calculators have several accessible memories that can be used to store numbers for future use.

DOUBLE CHECK
EACH COMPUTATION

Even when you have taken all these steps, errors may creep in. If your calculator is equipped with a paper tape, you can check the numbers and operations recorded on the tape. Otherwise, it is a good idea to do each computation twice. Even if you have to go through a column of figures several times with the calculator, it takes only a fraction of the time longhand arithmetic would take. It is usually a good idea to do computations in a different order the second time. This cuts down on the probability that you will make the same keying error twice. For instance, add a column of figures from top to bottom, record the sum, and then add from bottom to top. If the 2 sums are the same, it is almost certainly correct. If you get 2 different answers, simply go through the process another time. The third sum should agree with one of the first 2 answers, and it will probably be the correct one.

USE OR APPROXIMATIONS
AND INEQUALITIES

While "number crunching" with your calculator, there is a strong temptation to succumb to punch-button hypnosis. Your mind disengages as your fingers fly over the buttons. You wake up a few minutes later with a number glowing

[2] Some calculators have keys that automatically add the number in the register to the one that is stored in the memory. These keys are usually marked with the symbol Σ (the Greek letter *sigma*).

on the display and you have no idea whether it is right or wrong. To assume it is okay is dangerous. When in the grip of this mental malady, you may add instead of subtract, multiply instead of divide, add a few extra zeros to a number, or unwittingly make other disastrous mistakes.

To ward off punch-button hypnosis, think concretely about what is being done. For instance, in adding a column of 10 figures all under $5, common sense tells you that the correct answer must be less than $50. If you get $67.67, you know you made a mistake somewhere along the line. This simple example illustrates what is known by the cognoscenti as the inequality theory. This is a powerful mathematical approach, which is used a great deal by mathematicians and scientists, perhaps because many mathematicians and scientists are notoriously bad at simple arithmetic.

The inequality theory in its rudimentary form is very useful in keeping a continual mental check on the accuracy of your computations. It takes a little practice before it becomes second nature. The basis of the theory is the simple concept of *greater than* and *less than*. The symbol for *greater than* is $>$, and the symbol for *less than* is $<$. For instance, $5 > 4$ and $277.43 < 478.02$. Look at the following column of figures:

$$1.25$$
$$1.54$$
$$1.43$$
$$1.78$$
$$4.99$$
$$2.34$$
$$3.55$$
$$4.34$$
$$2.27$$
$$1.02$$

Notice that all of them are less than 5.00. It is obvious, then, that if you replace each number by 5.00 and add up the column this sum will be greater than the sum of the actual numbers

$$1.25 < 5.00$$
$$1.54 < 5.00$$
$$1.43 < 5.00$$
$$1.78 < 5.00$$
$$4.99 < 5.00$$
$$2.34 < 5.00$$
$$3.55 < 5.00$$
$$4.34 < 5.00$$
$$2.27 < 5.00$$
$$1.02 < 5.00$$
$$24.51 < 50.00$$

Similarly, since all the numbers are greater than 1.00, the correct answer must be greater than 10.00. What we have done is to determine the upper and lower bounds for the correct answer: The sum must lie somewhere between 10.00 and 50.00. If you mistakenly enter 49.9 instead of 4.99 for the fifth entry, the result would be 69.42, a figure that is obviously too large. Because of the inexactness of our upper bound, however, keying 12.5 instead of 1.25 would not result in a sum that is obviously wrong.

Smaller mistakes can be detected by mentally applying approximations and inequalities on a step-by-step basis. Looking at the column of 10 numbers used previously, first add 1.25 and 1.54. You know the sum will be greater than 2 and less than 4, so when you get 2.79 it seems about right. Then, in adding 1.43 to 2.79, you figure the sum will be greater than 3 and less than 5, and so on. So, then, in using the inequality theory we are looking for unreasonable numbers.

The inequality theory may be applied as well to more complicated arithmetic and mathematical situations. Let us look at a slightly more involved case. Compute

$$(5 \times 1.69) + 9.99 + (3 \times 3.78)$$

Using the step-by-step approach, you see that 5×1.69 is greater than $5 \times 1.00 = 5.00$ and less than $5 \times 2.00 = 10.00$. So you feel comfortable when you compute 8.45. Similarly, 3×3.78 is greater than $3 \times 3.00 = 9.00$ and less than $3 \times 4.00 = 12.00$. If you were to slip and absentmindedly key 6.78 instead of 3.78, the product, 20.34, would indicate an error.

Going through the addition, note that $8.45 + 9.99$ is 0.01 less than $8.45 + 10.00$. Therefore, the sum must be 18.44. Then $18.44 + (3 \times 3.78)$ is greater than $18.00 + 11.00 = 29.00$ and less than $19.00 + 12.00 = 31.00$. The final answer is 29.78. Writing all this out may make it seem difficult, but after some practice it will be much easier to do in your head.

There are countless variations of the inequality theory. Some people like to approximate the final answer before they begin. Take again

$$(5 \times 1.69) + 9.99 + (3 \times 3.78)$$

This can be approximated as

$$(5 \times 2) + 10 + (3 \times 4)$$

or

$$10 + 10 + 12 = 32$$

Since both approximated numbers (2 for 1.69 and 4 for 3.78) are larger than the actual numbers, 32 is the upper bound. The lower bound may be obtained in the same way.

The mental use of approximations and inequality theory to minimize computational errors illustrates one way the calculator can deepen a person's arithmetic intuition, especially in the case of school children.

The question of how calculators should be used in public schools has become a matter of intense debate. The mindless use of calculators does present a very real threat to the basic arithmetic skills of students. However, studies indicate that many students cannot balance a checkbook correctly, and they suggest that present approaches to teaching the third "R" have not been effective. Teaching the inequality theory would do much to offset this trend.

On the one hand, calculators can create an illusory sense of mathematical well-being. Blind acceptance of the 8-digit numbers on a calculator's read-out can result in incorrect financial decisions. On the other hand, the calculator makes it possible for the average man and woman to handle very difficult problems that only CPAs and accountants have been willing to handle in the past. But even with a calculator, this increased proficiency is not obtained without cost.

PROBLEMS

1 Rearrange the following calculations so that they can be done without writing down an intermediate result:

a. $215.7 + \dfrac{17 \times 24}{5.5} - 16.6$

b. $(66 + 57 - 102 + 33.4) \times 55.7$

c. $2{,}100 \times 44.7 \times (44 + 55)$

d. $(11 + 22) \times (33 + 44)$

2 Mentally determine upper and lower limits for the following calculations, and compare them with the computed answer:

a. $107 + 112 + 155 + 108 + 99$

b. $1 \times 2 \times 3 \times 4 \times 5$

c. $1 \times 20 \times 0.3 \times 400 \times 0.05$

d. $\dfrac{125}{9 + 24 + 22 + 16 + 11}$

e. $100 - 12 - 8 - 14 - 6$

3

A Brief Mathematics Review

This chapter is included for those readers who feel their basic math skills are extremely rusty. It covers the topics of basic algebra, percentage, percentage difference, fractions, significant figures, and rounding off. The reader who is confident of his or her grasp of these subjects should skip this chapter. For the person who feels the need to brush up on any of these topics, however, they are covered here.

ALGEBRA

Algebra is the branch of mathematics that uses symbols instead of numbers. An example of an algebraic expression is

$$\frac{a \times b}{c}$$

The symbols a, b, and c are called variables because they may stand for a variety of different numbers. If we let $a = 1$, $b = 2$, and $c = 3$, for instance, then

$$\frac{a \times b}{c} = \frac{1 \times 2}{3} = 0.6666667$$

But if $a = 25.57$, $b = 2.24$, and $c = 2$, then the value of $(a \times b)/c$ is totally different:

$$\frac{a \times b}{c} = \frac{25.57 \times 2.24}{2} = 28.638400$$

The advantage of using symbols instead of numbers is that the symbols allow one to express the relationship between different types of quantities, such as principal, interest, and time. Let us look at the algebraic formula for simple interest as an illustration. It is

$$INT = P \times i \times T \qquad \text{(Equation 3-1)}$$

where INT is the interest, P is the principal, i is the interest rate, and T is the length of time. With this formula one can calculate the amount of simple interest for any principal, interest rate, and length of time. Simply substitute the appropriate value of each variable into the equation.

EXAMPLE: Calculate the simple interest on a principal of $1,000 with an interest rate of 0.10 per year for 5 years. P = $1,000; i = 0.10; and T = 5 years. (Note that i is given per year and T is in years. If i were given per month, then T would have to be given in months also.) We substitute these numbers into Equation 3-1.

$$INT = P \times i \times T = \$1,000 \times 0.10 \times 5 = \$500$$

The simple interest is $500.

As most people will remember from algebra in junior high and high school, mathematicians have created an elaborate and complex set of rules and theories based on algebra. For our purposes, however, it is enough to understand how to substitute specific numeric values in mathematical formulas.

PERCENTAGES

Percentages is an age-old game, and it can be confusing. Percentages are simply a convenient way to write very small numbers. To convert an ordinary number p to a percent P, multiply p by 100,

$$P = p \times 100 \qquad \text{(Equation 3-2)}$$

and to convert a percentage to an ordinary number, divide it by 100.

$$p = \frac{P}{100} \qquad \text{(Equation 3-3)}$$

EXAMPLE: How is the decimal 0.111 expressed as a percentage? Using Equation 3-2, we get

$$0.111 \times 100 = 11.1\%$$

How is the decimal 0.00075 expressed as a percentage?

$$0.00075 \times 100 = 0.075\%$$

It is obviously easier to write 0.075% than .00075.

EXAMPLE: At present mortgage interest rates are about 12½%. How is this expressed as an ordinary number?

In this case $P = 12½ = 12.5$. Using equation 3-3, we get

$$\frac{12.5}{100} = .1250$$

How is 100% expressed as an ordinary number?

$$\frac{100\%}{100} = 1.00$$

The common expression "percentage of" is shorthand for 2 mathematical operations. The first is converting the specified percentage into a decimal. The second is multiplying the decimal times a given quantity.

EXAMPLE: What is 12% of $1,200?

First, convert 12% into a decimal using Equation 3-3.

$$\frac{12}{100} = 0.12$$

Next, multiply 0.12 times $1,200.

$$0.12 \times \$1,200 = \$144$$

Thus 12% of $1,200 is $144.

In general, then, $X\%$ of Y can be expressed as

$$X\% \text{ of } Y = Y \times \frac{X}{100} \qquad \textbf{(Equation 3-4)}$$

EXAMPLE: What is 500% of $40,000?

$X = 500$ and $Y = \$40,000$. Using Equation 3-4 gives

$$500\% \text{ of } \$40,000 = \$40,000 \times \frac{500}{100} = \$200,000$$

In this text we follow the general convention that percentages are designated by capital letters and their decimal equivalents by the same lower case letter. For instance, an interest rate expressed as *APR* in a sentence or equation indicates the percentage form. If it is written as *apr*, however, it signifies a decimal form. Similarly, *R* is used as the percentage inflation rate, whereas *r* is its decimal equivalent.

PERCENTAGE DIFFERENCE

Many people who have no trouble at all with straight percentages find the concept of percentage difference extremely confusing. Understanding percentage difference is important because it is widely used to measure change. Merchants use percentage differences to advertise sales or special discounts. Inflation is measured in these terms. All sorts of statistics such as changes in the crime, marriage, annual income, energy supplies, and employment rates are also quoted as percentage differences. Because these numbers indicate how well or how poorly our society is functioning, it is crucial to understand what they imply.

Understanding percentage differences is also important because they tend to make changes sound different from what they actually are. For instance, a merchant discounts a $2.00 item to $1.80 and advertises this as a 10% saving. This sounds much more attractive than it actually is. Percentage difference is a relative measure. For small quantities it tends to exaggerate the magnitude of the change. On the other hand, for very large quantities it tends to understate the difference. In the latter case, salesmen will use the actual discount rather than the percentage difference to attract customers.

Take, for instance, an area with an extremely low but increasing crime rate. The percentage increase in the crime rate tends to be large even though the actual increase in the incidence of crime may be quite modest. Therefore, a politician trying to get elected might use the percentage increase in crime to discredit an incumbent and get the votes of those afraid of increasing crime.

What, then, is the percentage difference between 2 numbers? If the first number is *A* and the second number is *B*, then

$$Percentage\ Difference\ (A\ :\ B) = \frac{B - A}{A} \times 100 \quad \textbf{(Equation 3-5)}$$

EXAMPLE: Ham's TV is having a 5-day sale on Super Pan Galactic color television sets. The normal price is $447.50. The sale price is $403.25. What is the percentage difference (or discount) from the normal price?

In this case, *A* = $447.50 and *B* = $403.25. Using these values in Equation 3-5 gives

$$Percentage\ Difference = \frac{\$403.25 - \$447.50}{\$447.50} \times 100$$

$$= \frac{-\$44.25}{\$447.50} \times 100$$

$$= -0.0988827 \times 100$$

$$= -9.88827\%$$

A $44 reduction in the price of these television sets is a percentage difference of 9.9. Ham would probably advertise this as a 10% discount.

EXAMPLE: The Udder Delight Dairy has just raised the cost of milk from $1.51 to $1.71 per gal. What is the percentage difference in the cost of milk?

Here A = $1.51 and B = $1.71, so

$$Percentage\ Difference = \frac{\$1.71 - \$1.51}{\$1.51} \times 100$$

$$= \frac{\$0.20}{\$1.51} \times 100$$

$$= 0.1324503 \times 100$$

$$= 13.25\%$$

The price of milk has risen by 13¼%.

As can be seen from the examples above, a positive percentage difference is an increase and a negative percentage difference is a percentage decrease or discount. It is often handy to be able to determine how much money a percentage increase or decrease corresponds to. To do this we must know the original price, call it A, and the percentage difference, which we will designate as D. If we call the actual sum the absolute difference, then

$$Absolute\ Difference\ (A : D) = A \times \frac{D}{100} \qquad \textbf{(Equation 3-6)}$$

EXAMPLE: Given an original price of $2,447 what is the absolute difference for a percentage difference of 11%, and for a percentage difference of −5.5%?

In the first case, A = $2,447 and D is 11%. Using Equation 3-6, we get

$$Absolute\ Difference\ (\$2,447 : 11\%) = \$2,447 \times \frac{11}{100}$$

$$= \$2,447 \times 0.11$$

$$= \$269.17$$

and with $D = -5.5\%$, we get

$$\textit{Absolute Difference}\ (\$2{,}447 : -5.5\%) = \$2{,}447 \times \frac{-5.5}{100}$$

$$= \$2{,}447 \times 0.055$$

$$= -\$134.59$$

Sometimes it is the value of an item that results in a percentage increase or decrease that is wanted. If A is the initial value and D is the percentage difference, then the resultant value, B is

$$B = A \times \left(1 + \frac{D}{100}\right) \qquad \textbf{(Equation 3-7)}$$

EXAMPLE: The Bon Appetit Restaurant raised all its prices 5%. The stuffed flounder was $7.98, and the filet mignon was $11.98. What are the new prices for these 2 items?
For the flounder A = $7.98 and D = 5.

$$\textit{New Price}\ \text{(flounder)} = \$7.98\left(1 + \frac{5}{100}\right)$$

$$= \$7.98 \times 1.05$$

$$= \$8.38$$

For the filet mignon A = $11.98 and D remains the same, so

$$\textit{New Price}\ \text{(filet mignon)} = \$11.98 \times 1.05$$

$$= \$12.58$$

EXAMPLE: The Tin Ear stereo store is discounting its Magnificat stereo system, which normally sells for $515, by 45% (and is still making a profit). What is the discount price?
In this case A = $525 and D = −45. Therefore,

$$\textit{Sale Price} = \$525\left(1 + \frac{-45}{100}\right)$$

$$= \$525\ (1 - 0.45)$$

$$= \$525 \times 0.55$$

$$= \$288.75$$

FRACTIONS AND DECIMALS

The thought of adding, subtracting, multiplying, and dividing fractions may bring to mind the rigors of grade school. Yet even though decimals are gradually pushing fractions out of everyday life, they still appear every so often. Stock-market prices are typically quoted in halves, quarters, and eighths. Interest rates and yardsticks continue the fraction tradition. Calculators, however, are inseparably united to the decimal system, and their Universal acceptance will probably help hasten the fraction's demise. Nevertheless, the calculator can assist us in dealing with and understanding fractions.

Let us briefly review here what the relationship is between fractions and decimals. Fractions are closely related to division. Dividing 152 by 7 using the old method gives

$$
\begin{array}{r}
21 \\
7\overline{\smash{)}152} \\
-14 \\
\hline
12 \\
-7 \\
\hline
5
\end{array}
$$

The number 5 is the remainder, and 147 is the number closest to 152 into which 7 divides evenly (21 times). The remainder is the difference between 152 and 147. Put another way, 7 divides into 152 a little bit more than 21 times and a little bit less than 22 times.

Somewhere in the dim dawning of civilization, our ancestors were first confronted with the problem of how to express quantities that fall between whole or integer numbers such as 21 and 22. The earliest historical records indicate that the Babylonians charted these unknown waters almost 5,000 years ago. The method they first used to visualize fractional numbers is not known, but it could well have been the number line. Imagine all the integer numbers inscribed in order on an infinitely long yardstick with the distance between adjacent numbers always equal.

Concentrating on the distance between two integers,

it is apparent that this length can be divided into a number of equal pieces: 2, 3, 4, 5, 6, 7, 8, and so on. In fact, there is no limit to the number of pieces this length can be chopped into.

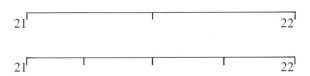

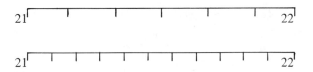

This system has some interesting implications for uneven division. Somewhere between 21 and 22 there must be a point or number that, when multiplied by 7, gives 152. Because we are dividing by 7, it makes sense to partition the distance between 21 and 22 into 7 equal lengths. Since the remainder is 5, counting over 5 divisions from 21 should give us the number we seek. Multiplying 7 times 1 gives 7 and multiplying 7 times a number less than 1 should logically produce a number less than 7. Postulating that the product of 7 and 5/7 is 5, it follows that if we multiply 7 times 21 5/7, we get 147 plus 5, or 152. Now it is necessary to develop a shorthand fashion for writing fractional numbers. What develops is the familiar fraction notation with numerator (number of parts) over denominator (number of divisions) such as 5/7.

Since people have 10 fingers and 10 toes, and all arithmetic derives historically from counting and commerce, it is not surprising that the number 10 is given a special role. This is certainly the case in the world of fractions. Tenths, hundredths, thousandths, and the rest of the family of tenths are called by a special name—decimals—and have been given a special notation system, the decimal system. The decimal system is used almost exclusively in all pocket calculators. Some advanced models can operate in the octal, or base 8, system, which is useful in computer programming.

Ten thousands | Thousands | Hundreds | Tens | Ones | Tenths | Hundredths | Thousandths | Ten thousandths | Hundred thousandths

Any fraction can be approximated in the decimal system. For instance, 5/7 can be expressed as the sum of a series of decimal fractions: 0.7 (seven tenths) plus 0.01 (one hundredths) plus 0.004 (four thousandths) plus 0.0002 (two ten thousandths), and so forth. This can be seen by dividing 5 by 7 on your calculator. The result is an 8-digit approximation of the fraction—0.71428571. This approximation is accurate to 8 places. The difference between 5/7 and 0.71428571 is less than 0.00000001 (one one hundred millionth). Some fractions such as 5/7 require an infinite number of decimal places to express exactly. Others need only a few. An example of the latter is 1/8, which is just 0.125.

It is easy to convert from fractions to decimals on a calculator. Simply divide the numerator by the denominator. This makes it possible to add and subtract fractions without worrying about common denominators and the other rules of fractional arithmetic.

$$\frac{1}{2} + \frac{1}{3} + \frac{1}{4} + \frac{1}{5} + \frac{1}{7} + \frac{1}{11} + \frac{1}{13}$$

With a calculator it is a straightforward operation.

$$1 \div 2 = 0.5$$

$$1 \div 3 = 0.33333333$$

$$1 \div 4 = 0.25$$

$$1 \div 5 = 0.2$$

$$1 \div 7 = 0.14285714$$

$$1 \div 11 = 0.09090909$$

$$1 \div 13 = 0.07692308$$

The total is 1.5940226.

Now compare this to the alternative method. First, you must find a common denominator. In this case it is $3 \times 4 \times 5 \times 7 \times 11 \times 13 = 60060$. Before adding, you must change all the denominators to 60060, by multiplying both numerator and denominator by an appropriate factor.

$$\frac{1}{2} \times \frac{30,030}{30,030} = \frac{30,030}{60,060}$$

$$\frac{1}{3} \times \frac{20,020}{20,020} = \frac{20,020}{60,060}$$

$$\frac{1}{4} \times \frac{15,015}{15,015} = \frac{15,015}{60,060}$$

$$\frac{1}{5} \times \frac{12,012}{12,012} = \frac{12,012}{60,060}$$

$$\frac{1}{7} \times \frac{8,580}{8,580} = \frac{8,580}{60,060}$$

$$\frac{1}{11} \times \frac{5,460}{5,460} = \frac{5,460}{60,060}$$

$$\frac{1}{13} \times \frac{4,620}{4,620} = \frac{4,620}{60,060}$$

Now we can add the numerators

$$\frac{30,030 + 20,020 + 15,015 + 12,012 + 8,580 + 5,460 + 4,620}{60,060} = \frac{95,737}{60,060}$$

Convert this to decimal form by dividing 95,737 by 60,060. This gives us 1.5940226, which is the same as using the decimal approach.

Although it is a simple matter to convert from fraction to decimal, there is no easy way to go from decimals like 1.5940226 back to fractions like 95,737/60,060. In most cases you probably won't have any reason to return to fractional form. Nevertheless, a table of common decimals and their fractional equivalents is included below. Looking it over may help further clarify the relationship between them.

Table 3-1 Decimal Equivalents of Common Fractions

		1/64 = 0.015625	1/2	16/32	32/64 = 0.5
	1/32	2/64 = 0.03125			33/64 = 0.515625
		3/64 = 0.046875	17/32		34/64 = 0.53125
1/16	2/32	4/64 = 0.0625			35/64 = 0.546875
		5/64 = 0.078125	9/16	18/32	36/64 = 0.5625
	3/32	6/64 = 0.09375			37/64 = 0.578125
		7/64 = 0.109375	19/32		38/64 = 0.59375
1/8	4/32	8/64 = 0.125			39/64 = 0.609375
		9/64 = 0.140625	5/8	20/32	40/64 = 0.625
	5/32	10/64 = 0.15625			41/64 = 0.640625
		11/64 = 0.171875	21/32		42/64 = 0.65625
3/16	6/32	12/64 = 0.1875			43/64 = 0.671875
		13/64 = 0.203125	11/16	22/32	44/64 = 0.6875
	7/32	14/64 = 0.21875			45/64 = 0.703125
		15/64 = 0.234275	23/32		46/64 = 0.718750
1/4	8/32	16/64 = 0.25			47/64 = 0.734375
		17/64 = 0.265625	3/4	24/32	48/64 = 0.75
	9/32	18/64 = 0.28125			49/64 = 0.765625
		19/64 = 0.296875	25/32		50/64 = 0.78125
5/16	10/32	20/64 = 0.3125			51/64 = 0.796875
		21/64 = 0.328125	13/16	26/32	52/64 = 0.812500
	11/32	22/64 = 0.34375			53/64 = 0.828125
		23/64 = 0.359375	27/32		54/64 = 0.843750
3/8	12/32	24/64 = 0.375			55/64 = 0.859375
		25/64 = 0.390625	7/8	28/32	56/64 = 0.875
	13/32	26/64 = 0.406250			57/64 = 0.890625
		27/64 = 0.421875	29/32		58/64 = 0.90625
7/16	14/32	28/64 = 0.4375			59/64 = 0.921875
		29/64 = 0.453125	15/16	30/32	60/64 = 0.9375
	15/32	30/64 = 0.46870			61/64 = 0.953125
		31/64 = 0.484375		31/32	62/64 = 0.968750
					63/64 = 0.984375

ROUNDING OFF
AND SIGNIFICANT FIGURES

As mentioned previously, calculators use the language of decimals. However, it is a language of approximations, whose accuracy is determined by the number of digits used. Calculators with 8 to 12 digits are usually quite accurate. But there are circumstances when they are not.

To understand just how accurate calculators are, the first concept we need is that of rounding off. How do we go about shortening an 8-digit number to a 4-digit one? By simply dropping off the last 4 digits? This is one way to proceed, but in certain cases it leads to a large error. For instance, suppose you want to shorten 43,259,999. If you just dropped the last 4 digits, it would amount to an error of .0002311.

$$\frac{9,999}{43,259,999} = 0.0002311$$

If, then, you use 43,250,000 as an approximation for 43,259,999, and multiply it by a large number such as 1,200,000, the error would be appreciable.

43,250,000 × 1,200,000 = 51,900,000,000,000 (Approximation)

43,259,999 × 1,200,000 = 51,911,998,000,000 (Right Answer)

The difference, or error, between the two is 11,998,000,000. And, as you can see, the fourth digit in the correct answer is 1 different than that of the approximation.

If you use 43,260,000 instead, the error due to the rounding-off process is considerably less. In this case the difference between the approximation and the actual value is only 00000001, instead of 00009999,

$$\frac{00000001}{43,259,999} = 0.00000002$$

and the error is only 0.00000002, and

43,260,000 × 1,200,000 = 51,912,000,000,000

43,259,999 × 1,200,000 = 51,911,998,000,000

Following this logic further, we find that the way to minimize the error resulting from rounding off is to follow a fairly simple rule. If the digits being dropped are less than 5,000, we simply drop them off. If they are greater than or equal to 5,000, we add one to the last digit of the rounded-off number. To illustrate this point, consider the following series of 8-digit numbers:

43252222
43254999
43255000
43256777
43259999

Rounding off these numbers to 4 digits following the procedure just detailed gives

43252222 → 4325   (2222 < 5000)

43254999 → 4325   (4999 < 5000)

43255000 → 4326   (5000 ≥ 5000)

$$43256777 \rightarrow 4326 \quad (6777 \geqslant 5000)$$

$$43259999 \rightarrow 4326 \quad (9999 \geqslant 5000)$$

Now let's look at the difference between the original numbers and the rounded-off ones:

$$43252222 - 43250000 = 00002222$$

$$43254999 - 43250000 = 00004999$$

$$43255000 - 43260000 = -00005000$$

$$43256777 - 43260000 = -00001777$$

$$43259999 - 43260000 = -00004999$$

As you can see, the rounding-off rule keeps the difference at less than ± 00005000. Thus, the resulting error is minimal.

Some calculators automatically round off the last digit in the display. Others simply drop them off. To tell which way a machine works, divide 3 into 2. If the final digit is 7, the calculator automatically rounds off, if it is 6, the calculator does not.

PROBLEMS

1   Evaluate the following algebraic formula

$$a + \left(\frac{b \times c}{d} \times 100 \right)$$

when $a = 177.5, b = 22.12, c = 2.55, d = 2.0$
when $a = 17,650, b = 0.0075, c = 6.455, d = 85.775$
when $a - 1, b - 2, c - 3, d - 1$

2   If d is the distance traveled, s is the speed traveled, and t is the time, then

$$d = s \times t$$

Determine d, given the following values for s and t:

a. $s = 60$ mi per hr
    $t = 5.5$ hrs
b. $s = 170$ km per hr
    $t = 20$ hr
c. $s = 5.6$ ft per sec
    $t = 2$ hr $= 7,200$ sec

3 Convert the following decimals into percentages:

110.0

0.055

0.001

1.550

4 Convert the following percentages into decimals:

4%

12.5%

100%

0.03%

5 What is 15% of $345?

6 What is 125% of $15,000?

7 What is the percentage difference between $1,200 and $1,400?

8 A gas stove originally priced at $275 is on sale for $250. What is the percentage different between the 2 prices?

9 Due to inflation, the price of a Japanese-imported automobile increases by 2%. If the original price is $4,283.00, how much will this increase the price? What will be the new price?

10 Use your calculator to evaluate the following fractions:

a. $\dfrac{13}{27} \times \left(\dfrac{7}{153} + \dfrac{113}{479}\right)$

b. $\dfrac{1}{2} + \left(\dfrac{25}{3} \times 15\right) + \left(\dfrac{17}{4} \times 45\right)$

11 Round off the following 8-digit numbers to 4 digits:

12,345,678

87,654,321

150.49494

.00555001

13,435,125

2,256.7890

12 Round off the following 5-digit numbers to 3 digits:

99,999

456.44

.00777

5.0475

75.757

1,414,1

4

Checking Accounts

RECONCILING
YOUR CHECKBOOK

One of the most vexing experiences in a person's life is being unable to reconcile a checking account balance with a bank statement. Each time you run through the numbers and come up with the wrong answer, the days before checks were invented look more and more appealing. How much easier it is to count currency and coin than to handle all those figures! Unfortunately, today there is almost no way to survive without figures, but at least the calculator helps. Despite the aid and succor of the calculator, checkbook balancers are not yet out of the woods. Even though errors in addition and subtraction can be cut to an absolute minimum, making improper entries in the checkbook register is a potential source of error.

A methodical approach to this monthly duty can keep such difficulties to a minimum. First, consider the following sources of possible error in the bank statement:

1. Addition or subtraction error in computing the balance.
2. Entry of incorrect amount for check or deposit.
3. Failure to credit a deposit.
4. Subtracting a check you did not write.
5. Improper service or finance charge.

and in the checkbook register:

1. Arithmetic error in calculating the balance.
2. Adding instead of subtracting a check.
3. Subtracting instead of adding a deposit.

4. Failure to enter a check or a deposit.

5. Entering an incorrect amount for a check or deposit.

It is not often the bank that makes a mistake, but it does happen.

There was a case of computer theft a few years ago that was uncovered because of action taken by a checking-account customer. The customer discovered that the balance on his statement was consistently a few pennies short. When he brought this fact to the attention of the bank, they investigated and discovered that one of their computer programmers was skimming a few pennies from hundreds of different accounts and transferring them to fictitious accounts he had set up. The computer thief evidently reasoned that all the customers would assume the slight discrepancy was their mistake and not the bank's. Except for one customer, this assumption seemed right, for the thief managed to transfer thousands of dollars into his accounts before he was caught.

There are several steps you can take to see if your bank—or one of its employees—is tampering with your account. First, compare each cancelled check with the statement to make sure the amounts agree. This will verify each entry. By putting a mark on the statement next to every check as you verify them, you can spot any additional entries that may have been subtracted from your account in error. Next, check your deposit receipts for the period against the statement to make sure all deposits were credited to your account.

It is difficult to generalize about the steps that should be taken to verify charges. Service charges vary widely from checking account to checking account. Some accounts charge for every check, others charge only when the account drops below a minimum balance, and others are free unless they are overdrawn. Make sure you understand all charges, check them, and subtract valid charges from the balance in your checkbook. Most bank managers are more than willing to answer any questions you might have.

Now you check the arithmetic of the bank's computer and its programmers. Beginning with the starting balance on the statement, subtract all the checks, add all the deposits, and, hopefully, come up with the same final balance as the bank did. If you do this several times and consistently come up with a different final balance, or if you discover any other errors in the statement, don't hestitate to take the statement, cancelled checks, deposit slips, and checkbook to the bank to go over the problem. You may be wrong, but even so, the time you spend will increase your understanding of bank operations. Or if you are right, you may save a little money or perhaps even help catch a white-collar thief. Either way, you have met the bank's officers and can begin to build a personal relationship with them. This can prove to be a benefit if you apply for a loan or if unexpected financial difficulties arise.

Let us now tackle checkbook errors. First, there are some procedures that serve to minimize certain common errors.

1. Always compute your balance with a calculator. This does not mean you must always have a calculator with you, although there are models the size of a business card and even some built into a checkbook case. Checkbook arithmetic should not be done while at a supermarket checkout counter or in a busy department store. People often make arithmetic errors in such distracting and pressured surroundings. The

alternative is to enter the check amounts and then at some convenient time, sit down with the checkbook and calculator and bring the balance up to date. This is practical unless your balance is very low.

2. Prenumbered checks are an excellent safety precaution. With the unnumbered variety it is very easy to write a check, neglect to enter it in the register, and totally forget about it until the next statement comes, or, more traumatically, an unexpected notice that the account is overdrawn. With numbered checks, such an oversight is more easily noticed the very next time you write a check, because there will be a number missing in the register.

Even when these steps are taken, mistakes may creep in. Most are easily detected when reconciling the checkbook balance with the bank statement. First, we compare the cancelled checks with the bank statement, comparing them against the entries in the checkbook register at the same time. This should indicate any incorrect entries. By putting an X or other notation in the register opposite each entry, outstanding checks are easy to spot. Next, we reconcile the checkbook register and the bank statement by beginning with the final balance on the statement. We subtract outstanding checks, add outstanding deposits, and the result should equal the final balance in the register. Most bank statements have a form on the back to use when reconciling. You can either use this form—which involves a lot of transcribing—or do it directly from the register, which is quicker but more difficult to spot errors should there be a discrepancy.

Reconciling a checkbook can be described mathematically. If FB is the final checkbook balance, SB the final bank statement, D_i the ith outstanding deposit, and C_i the ith outstanding check (when there are m outstanding deposits and n outstanding checks), and

$$\sum_{i=1}^{p}$$

is the mathematical symbol for the sum from 1 to any number, p, then

$$FB = SB + \sum_{i=1}^{m} D_i - \sum_{i=1}^{n} C_i \qquad \text{(Equation 4-1)}$$

EXAMPLE: Consider a case in which the statement balance is $1,206.59. The final checkbook balance is $1,058.64. There are 8 outstanding checks and 2 outstanding deposits

Outstanding Checks	*Outstanding Deposits*
$ 30.06	$450.00
52.29	425.85
48.34	
31.00	
532.83	
50.00	
29.28	
250.00	

Since SB = \$1,206.59, then

$$\sum_{i=1}^{2} D_i = \$450.00 + \$425.85 = \$875.85$$

$$\sum_{i=1}^{8} C_i = \text{sum of all the checks} = \$1,023.80$$

Therefore the final balance, FB, should be

$$\$1,206.59 + \$875.85 - \$1,023.80$$

which, as it should, equals \$1,058.64.

Figure 4-1 Note this Sample Checkbook Register

ITEM NO. OR TRANSACTION CODE	DATE	DESCRIPTION OF TRANSACTION	AMOUNT OF PAYMENT/WITHDRAWAL (−)	√ TAX	FEE OR OTHER DEDUCT	AMOUNT OF DEPOSIT OR INTEREST(+)	BALANCE FORWARD 479 90
223	4/3	TO Gas Company / FOR	8 22				471 68
224	4/11	TO Electric Company / FOR	47 53				424 15
	4/16	TO Deposit / FOR Paycheck				405 50	829 65
225	4/17	TO Supermarket / FOR	127 86				701 79
226	4/19	TO Bookstore / FOR	23 91				725 70
227	4/22	TO John Doe / FOR	15 —				710 70
228	4/22	TO Cash / FOR	50 —				660 70
229	4/29	TO Rent / FOR	210 —				450 70
230	4/30	TO Deposit / FOR Paycheck				405 50	856 20
231	4/30	TO Bank Credit Card / FOR	325 49				530 71
232	5/2	TO Theatre / FOR	22 —				508 71
		TO FOR					
		TO FOR					

BE SURE TO DEDUCT FEES OR SERVICE CHARGES — DEBITS — CREDITS

There is a sense of relief when the 2 sides of the equation balance, only because sometimes they do not. When there is a discrepancy, first go through the arithmetic again. If you repeatedly calculate a different final balance from the one in your checkbook, you must hunt for the error or errors. First, see if you have included all outstanding checks. Often a check will go unprocessed for a considerable period and, if overlooked, it will make the computed balance too large. If they have all been included, then the difference between the computed balance and the one in the register may indicate the error. If, for instance, the final balance in the register is $1,058.64, and you have computed $958.64, the difference is $100. Perhaps you added a check somewhere instead of subtracting it. This type of error doubles the value of the check in the incorrect balance.

Divide the difference in the balances by 2—in our example this equals $50—and look for checks of this value. If there are any, a quick inspection should reveal whether they are the source of the problem. If not, then the difficulty must lie in the checkbook arithmetic.

For those readers who, for their own peace of mind, must track down the offending error and exorcize it, this means reading the pertinent section of the checkbook register. However, if you have gone to the trouble of verifying the accuracy of the bank statement, then the computed balance should be the correct balance. The easiest course, then, is to correct the checkbook register and not worry exactly where the mistake came in. Because errors in the bank statement, if uncorrected, actually affect the amount of money you have in your account, it is more productive to spend your time checking the statement rather than trying to track down a will-o'-the-wisp checkbook error.

Xs in the date column indicate that the checks have been processed, returned, and compared with the register entry. Note that the check to the bookstore was accidentally added instead of subtracted. Thus, instead of $725.70, the balance at that point should have been $677.88—a difference of $47.82 and twice the value of the check.

SHOPPING
FOR A CHECKING ACCOUNT

Despite extensive federal regulations, banking is an extremely competitive business in most areas. Following the example of Manhattan's Madison Avenue, this once staid profession has become increasingly concerned with packaging and advertising. Sleek brochures accentuate the positive, giving the impression that various services are free. Giveaways ranging from calculators to stuffed animals are standard lures to get people to open new accounts. But nothing is really free. Furthermore, it is often difficult to pry beneath the pretty frills and to get bank officers to reveal the important details about banking services—details that represent a significant difference in what it costs to write checks.

While most people will shop around for the best price in a television set or an automobile, few shop comparatively for a bank. The primary determinant seems to be the most convenient location, probably because most people mistakenly think that all banks are about the same. Actually, there is a considerable variation in charges and services offered. Exactly which combination of services and prices is best for an individual will, of course, depend on his or her financial situation and spending patterns. The following analysis is intended to help the reader weigh the financial pros and cons of different types of accounts.

One important aspect of your spending is the average number of checks written per month. If you have never had a checking account before, various banks estimate that the average customer writes between 10 and 20 checks per month. If you have maintained a checking account for a while, this average is easy to determine. One way to do this is to look up in your checkbook register the length of time it took you to write the last 100 checks. For example, let us say that the last check you wrote was numbered 307. Flipping back you find that you wrote number 207 about 8 months ago. Thus your monthly average is

$$100 \div 8 = 12.5 \text{ checks per mo}$$

An alternate approach is to go back 12 months and find the last check you wrote a year ago. If this is 189, then the average is

$$(307 - 189) \div 12 = 9.8 \text{ checks per mo}$$

Notice that we have obtained 2 different results, since check writing is such an irregular process. The difference between the 2 averages gives us an idea of the degree of irregularity in the determination. An intermediate value may be used in the following analysis.

Knowing the approximate number of checks you write every month is important when choosing from the 2 major types of checking accounts—those with "free" checks (a minimum balance required) and those with a set charge per check.

MINIMUM-BALANCE ACCOUNTS

A typical minimum-balance account allows you to write as many checks as you wish provided you maintain a minimum balance of $500. Bank brochures seldom tell you exactly what they mean by a minimum balance. This could mean an average minimum balance: The amount of money in the account each day is added together and divided by the number of days. Or it could mean the level below which your balance can never drop without incurring a stiff fee. If your balance will be well over the limit most, but perhaps not all, of the time, the averaging scheme is the best one.

Whereas it may appear that the minimum-balance account offers free checking, this is not really the case. The bank invests the $500 and earns interest on it during the entire period you maintain the account. Of course you cannot get the same high interest rates the bank gets if you invested the $500 instead of keeping it locked up in a checking account. However, if you took this amount and deposited it in a savings and loan, the money would earn 5¼% interest. Thus, maintaining such a balance translates into $2.25 per month in lost interest, using the methods fully described in Chapter 8. This is just a minimum figure because you could easily put your money into a time deposit that yields more than the lower-interest passbook account mentioned above.

For the typical minimum balances required by banks, the following table lists the monthly loss in interest that you absorb.

MONTHLY INTEREST AT 5¼%*

Amount	Interest
$200	$0.90
300	1.35
400	1.80
500	2.25

*Compounded daily for 1 year (360 days per year). The annual interest is then divided by 12.

If B_{min} is the minimum balance and *APR* the annual interest rate of the savings account (as a percentage) that would otherwise be deposited as the minimum balance, then the following expression approximates the monthly cost of a minimum-balance account:

$$COST\,(Min\,Bal) \cong \frac{B_{min} \times 0.088 \times APR}{100} \qquad \textbf{(Equation 4-2)}$$

EXAMPLE: Using the $500 minimum balance with a 5¼% account yields

$$COST\,(Min\,Bal) \cong \frac{\$500 \times 0.088 \times 5.25}{100} = \$2.31$$

Comparing this with the calculations above, it is a few cents off. These calculations are only accurate to the nearest dime. They are simple compared with those required for compound interest used in savings accounts.

EXAMPLE: Suppose, instead, you put this $500 in a one-year savings certificate with a 6½% annual interest rate.
Then,

$$COST\,(Min\,Bal) = \frac{\$500 \times 0.088 \times 6.5}{100} = \$2.86$$

What if the minimum balance were only $300?

$$COST\,(Min\,Bal) = \frac{\$300 \times 0.088 \times 6.5}{100} = \$1.72$$

PER-CHECK CHARGE ACCOUNTS

Now compare minimum-balance accounts with those that levy per-check charges. These typically have monthly service charges ranging up to $0.75 and per-check charges up to $0.15. The basic cost of this type of account is simply the monthly charge plus the product of the per-check charge times the average number of checks written. To formalize this, let C_M be the monthly service charge, C_C the per-check charge, and N the average number of checks written per month. Then the monthly cost is

$$COST\,(Chk\ Chg) = C_M + (C_C \times N) \qquad \text{(Equation 4-3)}$$

EXAMPLE: You have an account with a monthly charge of $0.50 and a per-check charge of $0.10. The average number of checks per month is 12.

$$COST\,(Chk\ Chg) = \$0.50 + (\$0.10 \times 12) = \$1.70$$

Thus, other things being equal, this account would be cheaper than an account with a minimum balance of $400 or more (using the 5¼% annual interest rate for savings).

Now let us look at an expensive account of this sort—a monthly charge of $0.75 and a $0.15 per-check charge. For 12 checks per month

$$COST\,(Chk\ Chg) = \$0.75 + (\$0.15 \times 12) = \$2.55$$

This is 50% more expensive than the charges in the previous example—a difference of $10.20 per year.

It is now possible to compare the relative cost of the per-check charge account with that of the minimum-balance account. Simply evaluate the expressions for COST (Min Bal) and COST (Chk Chg) given previously. The one that is lower probably represents the most economical account. While these two types of accounts are the most popular, there are some variations that include elements of both and so are slightly more difficult to evaluate.

INTEREST ON CHECKING-ACCOUNT BALANCE

One variation extremely beneficial to the checking-account holder is the arrangement in which the bank pays interest on the balance of the checking account. This began several years ago in Massachusetts and has now spread to the rest of the country. These accounts are either the minimum-balance type or per-check charge variety. While in the account, your money earns interest for you instead of just lying idle. Because of the fluctuations in most people's checking accounts, the exact amount that this will save is difficult to calculate precisely. But by averaging your checking balance, you can get a fairly good idea. The best way to do this is to get out your bank statements from the last few months. These will contain the balance of your account at various dates during each period. For example,

Date	Balance
6/19	$ 994.63
6/21	971.23
6/23	953.23
6/26	899.49
6/28	825.33
6/29	1,285.03
7/06	1,035.03
7/07	985.03
7/10	969.53
7/12	919.53
7/14	1,395.38
7/17	1,210.38
7/18	1,206.59

The daily average is the sum of each day's balance divided by the total number of days. This is not the same as the sum of the balances on the statement divided by 30, because some of the balances listed on the statement remain for more than 1 day. The beginning amount of $994.63, for instance, is in your account on the 19th and on the 20th. Therefore, multiply $994.63 by 2 before adding it to the summation. Thus, the average balance, B_{av} is

$$B_{av} = \frac{\sum\limits_{i=1}^{n} B_i \times D_i}{D_t} \qquad \text{(Equation 4-4)}$$

when B_i is each successive balance on the statement, D_i is the number of days each balance remains, D_t is the total number of days in the period, and n is the total number of balances listed on the statement.

For the statement just detailed, then, the numerator (upper part) of this equation becomes

B_i		D_i		$B_i \times D_i$
$ 994.63	×	2	=	$1,989.26
+ 971.23	×	2	=	1,942.46
+ 953.23	×	3	=	2,859.69
+ 899.49	×	2	=	1,798.98
+ 825.33	×	1	=	825.33
+ 1,285.03	×	7	=	8,995.21
+ 1,035.03	×	1	=	1,035.03
+ 985.03	×	3	=	2,955.09
+ 969.53	×	2	=	1,939.06
+ 919.53	×	2	=	1,839.06
+ 1,395.38	×	3	=	4,186.14
+ 1,210.38	×	1	=	1,210.38
+ 1,206.59	×	1	=	1,206.59

$$\sum_{i=1}^{13} B_i \times D_i = \$32,782.28$$

So B_{av} for the month is $\$32,782.28/30 = \$1,092.74$.

Such calculations are tedious even with a pocket calculator, and it is easy to make mistakes. You may want to round off to the nearest dollar to make it easier. One safety check to bear in mind is that the sum of the D_i's should equal D_t, in this case 30 days. The longer the period over which you calculate your average balance, the more representative it is likely to be. However, there is a definite point of diminishing return for the amount of work involved. I suggest you use a fairly representative 30-day period and follow the procedures outlined.

Now that we have an average balance, we can estimate what the advantage will be of a checking account that pays interest. Adapting the approximation developed to estimate the cost of a minimum-balance account, the yield is expressed as

$$YIELD = \frac{B_{av} \times 0.088 \times APR}{100} \qquad \textbf{(Equation 4-5)}$$

EXAMPLE: Using the average balance previously calculated and an annual interest rate (*APR*) of 5%, which is typical, we find

$$YIELD \text{ (per mo)} = \frac{\$1,092.74 \times 0.088 \times 5}{100}$$

$$= \$4.81$$

In this case such an account would earn about $58 per year.[1]

So you can see that receiving interest on the balance is a practice which can be profitable for the customer, particularly when he or she has a tendency to keep a fairly large balance in the account.

With a certain amount of extra work, you can regularly transfer money back and forth between a checking and savings account with about the same results. Some banks allow such transfers by telephone, which makes this juggling act much easier than going to the bank each time. If you intend to do this, however, find out whether or not the bank charges for these transfers. Most do not, but some do levy a charge equivalent to check cashing, which can eat into the extra interest you are earning.

Besides charging for transferring money between accounts, some banks charge for various other services. This may be important to you. One charge

---

[1]Using the more complicated compounding formula introduced in Chapter 10 this comes out to be $56.

about which bank officers seldom volunteer information about is the over-draft charge. The gifted few never overdraw their account, but for most of us this happens every so often due to arithmetic errors, a deposit failing to clear, or temporary cash-flow problems. Obviously, the more prone you are to over-drafting the more concerned you should be about the charges that result. They vary widely.

Because of the embarrassment and the difficulties overdrafting causes, accounts with overdraft protection have become popular. They are not only popular with customers, but with banks as well, because in most cases over-draft protection is simply a disguise for an automatic, high-interest loan. These loans are usually activated when your balance drops below zero, al-though in some minimum-balance accounts they are activated when the balance drops below the minimum. For the money the bank lends, it usually charges a hefty 18% annual interest rate. Some banks increase their profits from such a service by advancing you money in lump sums only: $100, $200, and so on. In this case, if you overdraw your account by $0.10, $1.66, or $53.85 you must pay interest on $100 until you discover the situation and rectify it. For an overdraft of a penny you can end up paying 5 cents a day interest. Thus, it is important to understand the overdraft protection feature should you desire it. The best service, of course, is the one in which the bank loans you only the amount overdrawn. In many minimum-balance accounts a similar charge is levied when your balance falls below the minimum. Typi-cally, this is about $1 per $100. As previously mentioned, the manner in which the bank determines your minimum balance can be important.

Often accounts drop below the minimum or the account is overdrawn without your knowledge, because you have no idea how long it takes to clear deposits. While it takes less than two days to verify most checks, it may take as many as eight working days to credit a local check to an account. For out-of-state checks, this period may be as long as twenty days. If the checks you write on this deposit come to the bank before the deposit has cleared, your account may be overdrawn.

Another way banks make money on checking accounts is to charge you if a deposited check does not clear. So the bank's policy on deposits that "bounce" is worth understanding.

If you frequently use certified, cashier's, or traveler's checks, you should find out what the bank charges. Traveler's checks are often thrown in for free.

A safe-deposit box is another convenient feature that banks maintain, usually at a financial loss. Read the fine print, for you might just find out they are not as "safe" as you think.

Now that you have read through the preceding discussion, and, hope-fully, understood it, if you are like me, you will have vowed to put this knowledge into practice. But just step into the hushed and teak-appointed interior of your local bank, sit down with an officer, and 50% of this material flies right out of your head. For this reason, the contents of this chapter are summarized in a "grocery list" form that may be taken to the bank. Once filled out, the form represents a handy summary of the services and charges that a bank offers. By using it with the procedures explained in this chapter, you can estimate the real cost of different accounts at the same bank and at different banks. A copy of this form is in Appendix 1.

PROBLEMS

1 Spot the checkbook register error.

ITEM NO. OR TRANSACTION CODE	DATE	DESCRIPTION OF TRANSACTION	AMOUNT OF PAYMENT/WITHDRAWAL (−)	✓ TAX	FEE OR OTHER DEDUCT	AMOUNT OF DEPOSIT OR INTEREST(+)	BALANCE FORWARD 1257.17
177		TO Cleaner Joe's / FOR	12 34				BAL 1244 83
178		TO Mortgage / FOR	313.99				BAL 930 84
		TO Deposit / FOR				250 00	BAL 1180 84
179		TO Ideal Market / FOR	59 50				BAL 1124 94
180		TO Chic Clothiers / FOR	227 45				BAL 897 49
181		TO Ma Bell Tel & Tel / FOR	67 12				BAL 830 37

BE SURE TO DEDUCT FEES OR SERVICE CHARGES — DEBITS — CREDITS

2 One bank offers a checking account with a $2.00 monthly service charge and a $0.05 per-check charge. Another bank has a $1.00 monthly charge and levies $0.15 per check. If Nora James writes about 25 checks per month, which account would be the cheapest? At what number of checks per month are the 2 accounts equal in cost?

3 Following is a list of dates and balances for a checking account. Find the average balance. With an *APR* of 5.25% what would be the monthly yield of this account if the bank pays interest on it?

Date	Balance
1/01	$1,023.45
1/09	773.55
1/11	547.12
1/14	502.02
1/18	1,052.02
1/24	855.55
1/26	476.02
1/27	410.12
1/30	960.12

4 John Beaumont is checking his latest bank statement. The balance on the statement is $404.56. Here is the last page in his checkbook register with all outstanding checks and deposits. Deposit entries with an X in the check number column are included in the statement. Is his register balance correct? If not, what should it be?

ITEM NO. OR TRANSACTION CODE	DATE	DESCRIPTION OF TRANSACTION	AMOUNT OF PAYMENT/WITHDRAWAL (–)	✓ TAX	FEE OR OTHER DEDUCT	AMOUNT OF DEPOSIT OR INTEREST(+)	BALANCE FORWARD 212 62
333	TO XXX / FOR		15.50				197 12
X	TO Deposit / FOR					544.50	741.62
334	TO XXX / FOR		125.00				616.62
335	TO VOID / FOR						616 62
336	TO XXX / FOR		12.57				604 05
337	TO XXX / FOR		250.00				354 05
338	TO XXX / FOR		70.07				283 98
339	TO XXX / FOR		102.56				181 42
	TO Deposit / FOR					275.00	456 42
340	TO XXX / FOR		21 01				435 41
341	TO XXX / FOR		55 00				380 41
342	TO XXX / FOR		318 00				62 41
	TO / FOR						

BE SURE TO DEDUCT FEES OR SERVICE CHARGES   DEBITS   CREDITS

5

Budgeting

HAVE YOU EVER WONDERED WHERE YOUR MONEY GOES?

Some years ago I started my career in journalism. It was my first full-time job, and I was simultaneously attempting to learn a challenging trade and to work out the procedures needed to cope with bills, taxes, and the other unavoidable complications of being totally "on your own." This was made all the more difficult because while I was a university student I had cultivated an attitude of indifference toward things financial. Due to my low salary, the high cost of living in Boston, the demands of a job, and my unfamiliarity with finances, paying bills and keeping records rapidly became an unpleasant and oft procrastinated chore. Being basically an orderly person this disorganized state of affairs was in itself an irritation. I struggled a number of times to put my financial house in order, with minimal success.

This went on for several years. During this time I got a number of raises. Despite my increased salary, however, I was unable to save any more money. When I realized this fact, another question struck me. Just where was all my money going? I had only the haziest idea. At about this time calculators were dropping steadily in price, although they had not yet reached the $10 mark. Thinking the matter through I realized that with a calculator I could end the disorderly financial state that was plaguing me. So I went out and bought a calculator. With it, I went through all my financial records for the previous 3 years. It was even kind of fun. It took only 2 evenings. Even though my records were incomplete, they revealed some interesting things. For instance, I was spending much more on clothes than I had thought, simply replacing things as they wore out. I realized that buying clothes at yearly sales instead of haphazardly would give me considerably more for my money.

Despite the steps I had taken, the question of where my money was going was still not adequately answered. Too many of my expenses were cash and unrecorded. To shed some light on how much I was spending on dining out, entertainment, and other out-of-pocket expenses, I began carrying around a small vest calendar. Each time I spent some money I wrote down the amount and what it was for. It was difficult to discipline myself at first. The minute or two it took to fish out the little book and a pen and make the proper notation was often annoying. But my curiosity about where my money was going was stronger than the annoyance, so I kept at it. Meanwhile I noticed an interesting fact. This new financial awareness was directly affecting my spending. By recording each expenditure, I became more careful about how I was spending my money. It was now much easier to evaluate each item I wanted or needed. This was not a mechanical cost-benefit analysis but a mental and often intuitive process.

About the time this record-keeping was becoming natural, I discovered an invaluable aid: the Pocket Daytimer record-keeping system, a well-thought-out approach developed for the businessperson. It consists of a wallet with pen and monthly binders and has plenty of room to record appointments, expenses, and each day's activities. It is particularly good for recording tax-deductible expenses. Although it may be too elaborate for some people, it is always better to have too much space rather than too little. Those interested can get more information by writing: Day-Timers, Allentown, Pennsylvania 18001.

HOW TO ASCERTAIN
WHERE YOUR MONEY IS GOING

Following are the steps to use to determine how you are spending your money:

1. List the categories of your expenses, such as house payments or rent, utilities, telephone, insurance (life, home, medical, auto), income tax and social security, finance charges, savings, food, household, furnishings, clothing, transportation, medical and dental, business, recreation, contributions, gifts, and miscellaneous.

2. Get out your financial records: Checkbook register, credit-card statements, and so forth. Decide how many years you want to go back. A three-year period makes it possible to see trends in your spending patterns and makes it easier to pick out unusual expenses.

3. Under each expense category, rule off a column for each year. Make sure there is plenty of room; there is nothing worse than running out of space three-quarters of the way through.

4. Go through the records, listing each expense under the proper category and year. There is no need to keep track of every penny; round off each expense to the nearest dollar. Everything from $.50 to $1.49 is rounded off to $1; everything from $1.50 to $2.49 is rounded to $2, and so forth.

5. You will probably find that some categories, such as rent and telephone, are easy to fill in correctly. Others, such as entertainment and recre-

ation, are more difficult if not impossible. For these difficult categories the best you can do is to make an estimate.

6. Once you have gone through all your records, you will have hundreds of numbers to add. The calculator comes in handy to "buzz-saw" through all these computations.

7. When you have totaled these myriad numbers, you might want to put them all on a single sheet of paper and ponder them a while. Are there any surprises? Any trends in your spending that you did not realize?

8. There is a good check on the accuracy of these figures. Each year's sum should be a fair approximation of your income for that year. If your expenses exceed your income for a given year, either your savings will have dropped by an equivalent amount or your expenditures are in error. If your totals are significantly lower than your income, your estimates are too low or you have other out-of-pocket expenses that have not been included.

9. You may want to start recording all your expenditures, particularly if your expenditures are substantially lower than your income. You can do this either for a set period of time, 1 or 2 months, or you can do it indefinitely. In a few months you will have a much better idea of how you are spending your money. You can use this knowledge to better estimate those categories in which you had no previous records.

PUTTING YOURSELF ON A BUDGET

Having discovered where your money is going, you have done almost all the groundwork needed to set up a budget. Many people—particularly those who have not put themselves on a budget—consider budgeting to be rigid, inflexible, and distasteful. There are distinct disadvantages to a budget: It is more difficult to live in a financial fantasy world: it is harder to run up large balances on charge cards that typically use the almost usurious interest rate of 18% per annum on the unpaid balance; it forces a person to weigh the trade-offs between different purchases. In short, a budget is not for those who prefer to live beyond their means and who are content to suffer the financial penalties. Rather, it is for those who are trying to stretch their dollars as far as possible and who are attempting to set their own financial priorities.

Budgets can be designed to meet a multitude of life styles: They can be extremely rigid or extremely flexible, very complicated or extraordinarily simple. Some individuals have come up with ingenious variations. With a little thought and some experimentation, you will be able to put together a budget that will work for you.

In the past, budgeting has demanded a tremendous amount of tedious arithmetic. The calculator has changed all this. It is now possible to draw up a budget and maintain it without exceptional effort and with less time per month than is spent paying bills and reconciling the checking account. Budgets are a good thing, too, in light of the nation's economic difficulties.

They are rapidly becoming popular for the first time in several generations. Not only people with limited means, but also those in the middle- and even upper-income brackets are returning to budgeting as a valuable tool for achieving their material aspirations.

These budgets vary as widely as do the individuals who prepare and use them. Here are some illustrative examples. Ann Meyer, a young woman working in an office in Manhattan, just beginning her career, and living in an expensive location, finds that budgeting is essential.

Of her $215-per-week salary, her take-home pay is only $620 per month. Her fixed, monthly expenses include:

Rent	$230
Gas, electricity	20
Telephone	25
Installment debt	45
	$320

The installment debt is the result of buying furniture and housewares on credit when she moved from her parents' home into New York City. Her fixed expenses amount to $320, 52% of her available income. Of course there are also variable expenses. These include:

Food	$120
Clothing	80
Laundry	17
Newspapers	5
Books	3
Cosmetics	18
Gifts	15
Entertainment	30
Medical, dental	35
Vacation	50
	$373

These total $373, putting Ann's expenses about $73 higher than her income. Currently she copes by carrying over balances on charge cards and by arranging monthly payments with obliging creditors.

However, Ann's budget is flashing a bright red warning: Cut down on spending or face bankruptcy. (Budgeting experts recommend that a person not go into debt more than 20% of their gross income, $2,400 in Ann's case.)

Now let us consider Jennifer Wayland's case. She lives in Connecticut, and when her husband died their estate amounted to $140,000. Mrs. Wayland's income before taxes is $15,340 per year. Most of this, about $13,000, comes from high-grade corporate bonds and a government annuity. Social sercurity amounts to $2,200 per year and is tax free. It just covers her income tax. Thus she has about $13,200 to cover yearly expenses. From this she must pay out the following fixed expenses:

Municipal taxes	$80
Sewage charge	12
Gas, water, electricity	30
Fuel oil	15
Telephone	18
Insurance	27
	$182

Jennifer Wayland's fixed expenses come to $182 per month. This leaves her $11,000 per year for the rest of her expenses. She spends this in a way that reflects her personal interests, mainly traveling and doing things for her 2 adult children. Therefore, she budgets the remaining money as follows:

Travel fund	$180
Food, cosmetics	150
Charity	90
Clothes	60
House maintenance	60
Cleaning	5
Books, newspapers	16
Auto operation	50
Entertainment	10
Miscellaneous	10
Gifts	Variable
	$631

Excluding gifts, this adds up to $631 per month, or $7,560 annually. This means that she has about $3,440 for gifts and savings, $2,200 of which she uses for a yearly trip. Mrs. Wayland manages to do those things that mean the most to her, but to do so, she lives fairly modestly.

Although her income is comfortable at present, each year inflation takes its toll. Her budgets for years past give a clear picture of the extent of the inflationary bite. Using techniques that will be explained later, she can get a rough idea of what the future might hold. This could spark Mrs. Wayland to consider ways to hedge against inflation, such as placing a certain percentage of her investments in high-yielding stocks rather than bonds, which she might not have otherwise considered.

Of course many retired people live on a much smaller income than Jennifer Wayland. For them, inflation represents a much more immediate problem. Typical of those in such a situation are Herbert and Rosemary Hardcastle. A retired postal worker in New Jersey, Mr. Hardcastle and his spouse live on his federal retirement, social security, and a retirement allowance from the state for his work as a night guard at a community college. The Hardcastles' total income amounts to $12,300 tax free.

Although they live fairly well, making ends meet is a problem. Their fixed expenses per month are as follows:

Second mortgage	$190
Gas, electricity	23
Water	5
Fuel oil	33
Telephone	25
Installment debt	46
Insurance	85
Property tax	75
	$482

These expenses total $482 per month, 47% of their income. The second mortgage and the installment debt resulted from the Hardcastles' putting their 2 children through private colleges. The Hardcastles' remaining expenses quickly consume the rest of their income:

Food	$120
Clothing	60
Laundry	13
Automobile	100
Entertainment	8
Haircuts, cosmetics	43
Gifts	150
Donations	100
	$594

These total $594, making a total of $1,076 per month, $51 per month over their income. The Hardcastles are also getting a warning from their budget to reduce their spending, and they have been attempting to cut down their food costs by shopping for sales and clipping coupons. When the television went out, they decided not to spend the $60 to fix it. Their children agree that their parents should cut down on the money spent on them. Also the amount they spend on clothing could also be reduced. Still the situation that the Hardcastles and others face raises an important question that society needs to answer. How can the retired and other people on fixed incomes live out their lives in dignity?

In many ways young adults (even those with several children) tend to be in a much stronger financial position than are retired people. Although the expenses involved in bringing up children are high and getting higher, young wage earners can look forward to salary increases that will keep pace with inflation more than retirement incomes will. Nevertheless a budget can also prove invaluable to young adults. Take the case of a Chicago couple, Tom and Jane Reger, with three young children. Tom is a professional, a partner in an engineering firm, and makes a very good salary. His monthly take-home pay is $1,310. While this is an income many would consider affluent, it is a 25% reduction from his salary in 1974. So the Regers find that budgeting is a necessity to keep their expenses within their income. The Regers live in a large, expensive home in the suburbs. With their high mortgage, their fixed expenses amount to over 60% of their income:

Mortgage	$353
Home improvement loan	208
Gas, electricity	60
Water	13
Fuel oil	45
Telephone	30
Insurance	110
	$819

Another 23%, or $300 per month, is budgeted for food, household supplies, and toilet articles. Thus about 80% of Tom's paycheck goes for food, living expenses, and rent.

The remaing amount is divided as follows:

Clothes	$100
Gifts	50
Automobile	51
Entertainment	50
Education	55
Household maint.	35
Haircuts, cosmetics	35
Savings bonds	56
Total	$432

The $60 that remains goes for vacations, donations, Boy Scouting, dry cleaning, and other expenses. There is very little left after they get through paying all the bills. As a result, the Regers are economizing: buying less meat, no longer dining out, making clothes for the children, making gifts instead of buying them, and insulating the house to cut down on heating bills. Although the Regers are not saving much money, neither do they have any large installment debts. When the firm's business picks up, their income will probably rise again.

Although these examples are fictitious, they are based on real life and give some idea of the varied financial situations and priorities of different people.

From time to time, the government calculates how the "average" American spends his or her money. Such figures are primarily of interest to statisticians and economists; they are not designed as a guide to how one should spend money. In 1975, for instance, such a breakdown revealed the following:

Expenditure	Percentage
Food, alcohol, tobacco	23.0
Housing	15.4
Household operation	14.7
Transportation	12.9
Clothing	8.4
Medical care	8.9
Recreation	6.8
Personal business	5.2
Personal care	1.5

Source: U.S. Bureau of Economic Analysis.

While these figures provide an interesting comparison, each personal or family budget will vary significantly by income, expenses, and aspirations of the individuals involved.

Putting together a budget that works for you requires a great deal of insight: You must determine your priorities and have a realistic view of your financial position. There is no room for fuzzy or wishful thinking. Most people want more than they can possibly afford. As one's income increases, so do one's aspirations. Thus difficult trade-offs must continually be made. Yet money is printed to be spent. How you decide to spend your money will either bring you closer to your goals or carry you farther from them. This happens whether a person makes these decisions off-the-cuff, with no overall planning, or whether he or she approaches each decision one at a time, with the aid of a planning tool such as a budget. The person who takes the orderly approach is more likely to progress in the desired direction.

Let us go over some general guidelines for setting up a budget. There are some general, underlying similarities that virtually everyone shares, even though each person's financial situation is unique. It is on these similarities that almost all budgets are structured. First, there is the obvious distinction between income and expenses. The natural place to start in drawing up a budget is with how much money one has to spend. Many people, however, begin by putting the cart before the horse, with expenditures before the income. There are 2 basic types of expenses. One type is commonly called *fixed expenses*. These are expenses that must be paid regularly; they include rent, utilities, installment loan payments, and so forth. The other type is called *variable* (or *daily*) *expenses*; they include food, clothing, laundry, and so forth. Second, there are your aspirations. Do you need or want a new car? Does the house need new siding? Do you want the financial security of knowing that you have the equivalent of 6 months' salary tucked away in a savings account? Do you want to take a trip to a foreign country? And so forth. These are the bare bones on which a budget is hung. Let us flesh them out a little.

The basic unit of a budget can be anything you prefer. However budgeting on a monthly basis seems to work best for most people because it fits in nicely with the general billing schedule followed by most businesses. Still some people prefer weekly or quarterly budgets. A good place to start is by drawing up a form on which to record your total income. You can keep this either on a yearly basis or on a monthly basis.

Annual Income Record

Husband's job	_____
Wife's job	_____
Interest	_____
Dividends	_____
Rent (if landlord)	_____
Bonuses	_____
Tax refunds	_____
Gifts	_____
Second job	_____
Sales profits	_____
Business profits	_____
Retirement payments	_____
Social Security	_____
Welfare payments	_____
Alimony	_____
_____	_____
_____	_____
_____	_____
Total	_____
Monthly average	_____

Although this is a quick way to compute your total income at a given time, it must be reworked whenever there is a change. Therefore many people prefer to keep track of their income on a monthly basis as incorporated in Form 1 presented on page 49. The items listed on this and the other budgeting forms in this chapter are suggestions based on common practice. (You may have other types of income and expenses, or you may want to break down the various items in different ways.) Such an annual-income record helps you determine how much money you have to spend or save every month. From this amount you must routinely pay your various fixed expenses.

A recommended minimum for savings is the equivalent of 2 month's income. Keeping such an amount readily accessible acts as a financial "flywheel" as well as a cushion to absorb unexpected or emergency expenses. It also allows you to take advantage of sales without running up large credit-card balances, which you must pay off gradually at high interest rates.

If you are not saving as much money as you should or as you would like, it may help you to treat savings as a fixed expense, just like rent or electricity. Note how it is entered on Form 2. You can either transfer the fixed amount into a savings account each month or, get the bank to do it for you. A small percentage of your monthly income, say 5%, is a good place to begin if you are not currently putting any money away. You will be amazed how fast these small amounts add up.

ANNUAL INCOME RECORD (FORM 1)

FOR THE YEAR OF _____

INCOME*	JAN	FEB	MAR	APR	MAY	JUN	JUL	AUG	SEP	OCT	NOV	DEC	TOTAL
Husband's Job													
Wife's Job													
Interest													
Dividends													
Rent (If Landlord)													
Bonuses													
Tax Refunds													
Gifts													
Second Job													
Sales Profits													
Business Profits													
Retirement Pay													
Social Security													
Welfare Payments													
Other													
TOTAL													

* For paychecks, enter gross rather than take-home amount

FIXED EXPENSE RECORD (FORM 2)
FOR THE YEAR OF _____

EXPENSE*	JAN	FEB	MAR	APR	MAY	JUN	JUL	AUG	SEP	OCT	NOV	DEC	TOTAL
Income Taxes, Social Security, FICA*													
Rent, Mortgage													
Home Heating													
Electricity													
Natural Gas													
Water													
Garbage Collection													
Telephone													
Installment Payments													
Tuition Payments													
Property Taxes													
Auto Insurance													
Life Insurance													
Medical, Dental													
Savings**													
MONTHLY TOTAL													

*Include paycheck deductions if gross salary was used on Form 1.
**You may prefer to handle savings on Form 6.

DAILY EXPENSE RECORD (FORM 3)
FOR THE YEAR OF _____

EXPENSE	JAN	FEB	MAR	APR	MAY	JUN	JUL	AUG	SEP	OCT	NOV	DEC	TOTAL
TOTAL AVAILABLE													
Food, Alcohol, Tobacco													
Household Maintenance													
Furnishings, Equipment													
Clothes													
Transportation													
Medicine, Medical Care													
Personal Care, Grooming													
Education													
Recreation													
Contributions, Donations													
Gifts													
Laundry, Dry Cleaning													
TOTAL EXPENSES													
MONTHLY DEBIT (–) OR CREDIT (+)													
CUMULATIVE DEBIT (–) OR CREDIT (+)													

DAILY EXPENSE RECORD
(FORM 4)

FOR THE MONTH OF _____, 19___.

EXPENSE	AMOUNT ALLOTTED	AMOUNT SPENT
Food, Alcohol, Tobacco		
Household Maintenance		
Furnishings, Equipment		
Clothes		
Transportation		
Medicine, Medical Care		
Personal Care, Grooming		
Education		
Recreation		
Contributions, Donations		
Gifts		
Laundry, Dry Cleaning		
TOTAL		

MONTHLY DEIBT (–) OR CREDIT (+): _____

DAILY EXPENSE RECORD
(FORM 5)

FOR THE WEEK OF_____ , 19____.

EXPENSE	AMOUNT ALLOTTED	AMOUNT SPENT
Food, Alcohol, Tobacco		
Household Maintenance		
Furnishings		
Shop Equipment		
Clothes		
Transportation		
Medicine, Medical Care		
Personal Care, Grooming		
Education		
Recreation, Entertainment		
Contributions, Donations		
Gifts		
Laundry, Dry Cleaning		
Other		
TOTAL		

WEEKLY DEBIT (–) OR CREDIT (+): _____

FINANCIAL GOALS ACHIEVEMENT RECORD
(FORM 6)
FOR THE YEAR OF _____

FINANCIAL GOAL	TOTAL AMT. TO BE SAVED	JAN	FEB	MAR	APR	MAY	JUN	JUL	AUG	SEP	OCT	NOV	DEC	TOTAL
House Downpayment														
New Car														
Emergency Fund														
Stereo System														
New Silver & Dishes														
Vacation Property														
Recreational Vehicle														
Vacation														
Christmas Gifts														
New Television Set														
Retirement Fund														
Others														
TOTAL YEARLY SAVINGS														

If treating savings as a fixed expense does not appeal to you, you may prefer to follow Form 6. This system works best when you have a surplus each month and want to bank it for various short, medium, and long-term goals.

Once you decide whether or not to budget savings as a fixed expense, it is time to work out your daily expenses. By subtracting the monthly totals on the Fixed Expense Record (Form 2) from the respective totals on the Annual Income Record (Form 1), you get the money available for daily expenses. Enter this in the Total Available row that heads up each of the Daily Expense Record forms (annual, Form 3; monthly, Form 4; weekly, Form 5). Now decide what your daily expenses are and how you wish to categorize them. If you have business expenses that are tax-deductible, you will definitely want to separate them. If there are specific areas in which you want to economize, the amount you spend on alcohol, for instance, then you will want to list this separately. The art of budgeting is most profitable in the area of daily expenses. A person has more control over these expenses. Numerous, apparently innocuous expenses, which nibble away at a paycheck with remarkable rapidity, lurk in the daily, out-of-pocket expense category. Economizing in this area can often swing the family budget from red to black.

The key to budgeting is setting realistic, economy-minded limits on each category of spending. You must know how you are currently spending your money, otherwise setting up a budget becomes a trial-and-error process.

Behaviorists claim that the one essential in changing human behavior (either one's own or another's) is to have some sort of a "yardstick" to measure progress. Therefore, it is important to compare what you actually spend with how much you have allotted. Forms 4 and 5 provide a column for actual expenditures next to the column for the amount budgeted. Similarly in the Daily Expense Record (Annual, Form 3), there are two rows: monthly and cumulative (annual) debits or credits. In the monthly row goes the difference between the budgeted expenses and the actual expenditures. If this figure is plus, you are ahead of the game. If it is negative, you have fallen behind. Summing these up month by month in the cumulative column will give a yearly perspective on your money management efforts.

If you consistently have a surplus, you will want to pidgeon-hole this for various goals. Form 6 is provided for this purpose. You may want to use this form to save only for short-term goals and to put savings for longer-term goals, such as buying a house or retirement, under fixed expenses.

You might want to photocopy these forms and adapt them to your own budget. They will save you some tedious line drawing.

PROBLEMS

1 Make a list of the categories of expenses you would use to set up a personal budget.

2 Using the list from problem 1, go through your financial records for the last three months. Determine as best you can how you have spent your money. What are the categories for which you have fairly complete records? Where are they sketchy? Total your expenses and compare this with the total amount of money you spent during this period. How do they compare?

3 Draw up a budget for a week or a month. Keep track of how you spend your money during this time. How well did you stay within your budgetary limits? Would you increase the amounts of some categories of spending and decrease the amounts of others for a permanent budget?

6

Numbers to Powers:
Using the Simplest Calculator
to Solve Complicated Formulas

THE LOGARITHM APPROACH

There are some ideas that seem difficult simply because of their names. This is true of *logarithm:* a simple idea with a peculiar name, which comes from the prefix *log,* meaning speech or discourse, and the Greek word *arithmos,* meaning number. Thus the logarithm received its name because it is a special numerical language—one that can greatly expand the capabilities of your 4-function calculator.

In 1614 Scottish mathematician John Napier came up with the concept of logarithms to simplify calculations required for celestial navigation and other astronomical problems. This system cleverly converts multiplication into addition, and it converts taking numbers to a power—squaring, cubing, and so forth—into multiplication. Since taking a number to a power is necessary to figure mortgages, compound interest, and other important financial quantities, you can see how this will come in handy.

The common abbreviation for logarithm is log. If your calculator has a *log* key, then you don't need to go through this section. If you have an electronic slide rule or a business analyst model, you also have a $\boxed{y^x}$ key that allows you to take a number to a power more simply than using logs. Taking numbers to a power on a 4-function calculator without such a key and without using logarithms, however, is quite tedious and error-prone (when it is possible at all).

Just what, then, are these handy things called logarithms? To understand them, we begin with the number 100. This can also be written as 10^2; any number can be written as 10 to some power.[1] For instance, $1,000 = 10^3$ and $25 = 10^{1.4}$. (You may feel at home with integer exponents but a

57   [1] At least all rational numbers (those used in monetary transactions).

58

NUMBERS TO
POWERS: USING
THE SIMPLEST
CALCULATOR
TO SOLVE
COMPLICATED
PROBLEMS

little uncomfortable with raising numbers to a power such as 1.4. Don't worry, because exponents with decimals behave just like integer powers.) To carry this further, we get,

$$
\begin{aligned}
5 &= 10^{0.7} \\
10 &= 10^{1} \\
15 &= 10^{1.18} \\
50 &= 10^{1.7} \\
100 &= 10^{2} \\
123 &= 10^{2.09} \\
150 &= 10^{2.18} \\
500 &= 10^{2.7} \\
1,000 &= 10^{3}
\end{aligned}
$$

Notice a pattern in the sequence above. The exponent for 50 is 1 greater than that for 5, and the exponent for 150 is 1 greater than that for 15. In other words, multiplying a number by 10 increases the exponent by 1. Dividing a number by 10 decreases the exponent by 1. Napier, in the course of his mathematical research, noticed this characteristic of exponents and realized it could be a real time saver. (Even in those days people were looking for ways to cut down on the drudgery of arithmetic.) The seventeenth-century mathematician decided to write these exponents in a *notation*, or mathematical language. For instance, instead of 100, or 10^{2}, Napier wrote 2 = log 100, or 100 = antilog 2.

In this language, the power of 10 which is equivalent to an ordinary number becomes its logarithm. Conversely, the antilog of a logarithm is the regular number with the same value as the logarithm. In essence, this is mathematical shorthand: Instead of writing 10^{2} or 10^{346} or $10^{.078}$, in logarithm shorthand, you can write *2, 346,* and *.078* and mean exactly the same thing.

Logarithm "grammar" turns out to be substantially different from that of ordinary mathematics. Its basic rules are

$$\log (a \times b) = \log a + \log b$$

$$\log (a \div b) = \log a - \log b$$

$$\log a^{n} = n \times \log a$$

In other words, the logarithm of 2 numbers multiplied by each other is the sum of the logarithms of the 2 numbers; the logarithm of a number divided by another is the same as the logarithm of the second subtracted from that of the first; the logarithm of a number raised to a power is simply the power multiplied by the logarithm of the number. It is this last aspect of log grammar that we will use extensively in future chapters.

Logarithms reduce the process of taking numbers to powers to simple multiplication. But there is a penalty to pay for this advantage: The process of translating ordinary numbers into logarithms and logarithms back into ordinary numbers—one very much like translating from one language into another. Each ordinary number has a logarithm equivalent and each loga-

59

NUMBERS TO
POWERS: USING
THE SIMPLEST
CALCULATOR
TO SOLVE
COMPLICATED
PROBLEMS

rithm has an ordinary number with the same value. The "dictionary" for translating ordinary numbers into logarithms is a set of tables called log tables. The dictionary for translating logarithms back into ordinary numbers is a set of tables called antilog tables. Unless your calculator has a *log* key to translate from ordinary numbers to logs, you must use the log tables in Appendix 2. A section of the 4-place log table is reproduced here:

FOUR-PLACE

N	0	1	2	3	4	5	6	7	8	9	Proportional Parts								
											1	2	3	4	5	6	7	8	9
10	0000	0043	0086	0128	0170	0212	0253	0294	0334	0374	*4	8	12	17	21	25	29	33	37
11	0414	0453	0492	0531	0569	0607	0645	0682	0719	0755	4	8	11	15	19	23	26	30	34
12	0792	0828	0864	0899	0934	0969	1004	1038	1072	1106	3	7	10	14	17	21	24	28	31
13	1139	1173	1206	1239	1271	1303	1335	1367	1399	1430	3	6	10	13	16	19	23	26	29
14	1461	1492	1523	1553	1584	1614	1644	1673	1703	1732	3	6	9	12	15	18	21	24	27

To look up the log of 1.21 in this log table, we find where the first 2 digits of the number are listed in the left-hand column. The third digit of the number is in the upper-most row. Thus, to translate 1.21 into a log, we find the row defined by *12* and the column defined by *1*. At the intersection of the row and column we find the number 0828. This is the *decimal part* of the log, which determines the sequence of digits in the ordinary number. Mathematicians call this the *mantissa*. [3]

The *integer part* of the log is related to the position of the decimal point in the original number in the following fashion:

ORIGINAL NUMBER	INTEGER PART OF LOG
9,999.9999 − 1,000	3
999.99999 − 100	2
99.999999 − 10	1
9.9999999 − 0	0
.99999999 − .1	−1
.09999999 − .01	−2
.00999999 − .001	−3

The integer part of the logarithm can be determined by a simple place-counting rule. First, we must define the *zeroth* position. This is the position between the first and second digits of a number. In the following numbers the zeroth position is indicated by an asterisk:

1*21.075
1*022,000.5
0.005*764
1*755623
0.1*

---

[3]*Mantissa* is an old Etruscan word meaning a small or insignificant addition. In logs, the mantissa may be small, but it is extremely important.

60

NUMBERS TO
POWERS: USING
THE SIMPLEST
CALCULATOR
TO SOLVE
COMPLICATED
PROBLEMS

When the decimal point and the zeroth position coincide, the integer part of the log is zero. If the decimal point is to the right of the zeroth position, then the integer part is positive; if to the left, it is negative. The number of places to the right or left determines the size of the integer. Thus:

ORIGINAL NUMBER	INTEGER PART OF LOG
1 *21,075	2
1 *022,000,5	6
0,005 *764	−3
1 *755623	0
0,1 *	−1

In the case of 1.21, the decimal point is in the zeroth position, so the integer part of the log is 0. The log of 1.21 is 0.0828.

If the number we were looking up was 12.1, however, the integer part of the log would be 1. Consequently, log 12.1 = 1.0828. Similarly, if the number was .121, the integer part of the log would be −1. This means that the log of .121 = −1 + .0828. Since the values listed in the log tables are always positive, you must add negative integer parts to positive mantissas to get negative logs. Therefore, log .121 = −1 + .0828 = −0.9172. For this reason the logs of numbers less than 1 may appear to have decimal parts different from numbers with identical digits that are greater than 1. (One of the most common mistakes made in using logarithms is forgetting to convert negative logs into a positive mantissa when using the antilog tables.)

To the right of the 4-place log tables, you will find a section entitled *proportional parts*. The purpose of this section is to allow you to determine the log of a 4-digit number. If, for instance, we were looking for the log of 1.217, we first find the log of 121, which is 0828. Then we look down the column in the Proportional Parts section under 7 until we come to the row defined by 12. There we find the number 24. Adding this to 0828 gives the correct mantissa for 1217: 0828 + 24 = 0852. The log of 1.217 = 0.0852.

Translating from logarithms back to regular numbers is a reverse, but almost identical process. Reproduced here is a section of the antilog tables from Appendix 2.

ANTILOGARITHMS

	0	1	2	3	4	5	6	7	8	9	Proportional Parts								
											1	2	3	4	5	6	7	8	9
.30	1995	2000	2004	2009	2014	2018	2023	2028	2032	2037	0	1	1	2	2	3	3	4	4
.31	2042	2046	2051	2056	2061	2065	2070	2075	2080	2084	0	1	1	2	2	3	3	4	4
.32	2089	2094	2099	2104	2109	2113	2118	2123	2128	2133	0	1	1	2	2	3	3	4	4
.33	2138	2143	2148	2153	2158	2163	2168	2173	2178	2183	0	1	1	2	2	3	3	4	4
.34	2188	2193	2198	2203	2208	2213	2218	2223	2228	2234	1	1	2	2	3	3	4	4	5

In the antilog tables, the first 2 digits of the mantissa are listed in the left-hand column, and the third digit in the top row. We are looking up the

61

NUMBERS TO
POWERS: USING
THE SIMPLEST
CALCULATOR
TO SOLVE
COMPLICATED
PROBLEMS

antilog of 3.348. First, we separate the integer and the fractional parts: 3 + .348. Because the fractional part is positive, we can use it directly in the antilog table. The number at the intersection of the row defined by .34 and the column defined by 8 is 2228. Now that we have the number, we must determine the placement of the decimal point. Since the integer portion of the log is 3, the decimal point is shifted 3 places to the right of the zeroth position:

$$\text{antilog } 3.348 = 2.228 = 2,228$$

Now let us find the antilog of a negative logarithm, for instance, −2.652. First, we separate the integer and the fractional parts: −2 − .652. Next, we make the decimal part positive by adding zero in a special form: −1 + 1. Thus,

$$-2 - .652$$
plus
$$-1 + 1.000$$
equals
$$-3 + .348$$

Now that we have a positive mantissa, we can look up the corresponding regular number in the antilog table. Note that the mantissa is the same as that of 3.348. So the corresponding number is also 2228: Only the decimal point is in a different position. In this case, the integer of the logarithm is −3, so the decimal point is shifted to the left 3 places from the zeroth position:

$$\text{antilog } -2.652 = \text{antilog } (-3 + .348)$$

$$= 2.228 \times 0.001$$

$$= 0.002228$$

The Proportional Parts section of the antilog table is used in the same way as that of the Four-place Log Table. If, for instance, we wanted the antilog of 3.3483 instead of 3.348, we would first find the antilog of the mantissa .348 = 2228 and add it to the value listed in the .34 row and the column headed by 3 in the Proportional Parts section. Since this is 2, the number corresponding to .3483 is 2228 + 2 = 2230. The antilog of 3.3483 is 2,230.

Following is a summary of the procedure for converting normal numbers to logs and logs to normal numbers:

Regular Numbers to Logs

Step 1. Turn to the 4-place Log Tables.

Step 2. Locate the first 2 digits of the number in the left-hand column of the table. Find the third digit in the top row.

Step 3. In the intersection of the row defined by the first 2 digits and the column defined by the third is the mantissa of the log.

62

NUMBERS TO
POWERS: USING
THE SIMPLEST
CALCULATOR
TO SOLVE
COMPLICATED
PROBLEMS

Step 4. If you wish 4-place accuracy, find the number determined by the row of the first 2 digits and the column headed by the fourth digit in the Proportional Parts section. Add this number to the mantissa from Step 3.

Step 5. Is the original number greater than or equal to 1? If so, go to Step 6. If the original number is less than 1, go to Step 7.

Step 6. Count left from the decimal point of the regular number to the position just behind the first digit. The number of places is the integer part of the logarithm and is added to the mantissa.

Step 7. Count right from the decimal point of the regular number to the position just behind the first digit. The number of places is the negative integer part of the logarithm and should be subtracted from the positive mantissa.

Logs to Regular Numbers

Step 1. If the logarithm is positive, go to Step 3.

Step 2. If the logarithm is negative, separate the integer and decimal parts. Add −1 to the integer part and +1 to the decimal part.

Step 3. Turn to the antilog table.

Step 4. Look up the first 2 digits of the mantissa in the left-hand column. Find the third digit in the top row.

Step 5. Where the row defined by the first 2 digits and the column headed by the third digit intersect are the digits of the corresponding regular number.

Step 6. If 4-place accuracy is desired, find the fourth digit in the Proportional Parts section where the column it defines intersects with the row defined by the first 2 digits. Add this to the value determined in Step 5.

Step 7. To locate the position of the decimal point look at the integer part of the log. If it is negative, go to Step 9.

Step 8. If the integer part is positive, shift the decimal point right by a corresponding number of places from the position directly behind the first digit.

Step 9. If the integer part is negative, be sure to use the value determined in Step 2. Shift the decimal point left a corresponding number of places from the position directly behind the first digit.

TAKING NUMBERS TO POWERS
WITH LOGS

In the following chapters the predominant way in which we will use logarithms is to take numbers to powers. If you have ever tried to do more than squaring or cubing a number with a 4-function calculator, you know it is a laborious process. It is much easier to do with logs. The basic process to find the value of y^x is outlined below:

63

NUMBERS TO
POWERS: USING
THE SIMPLEST
CALCULATOR
TO SOLVE
COMPLICATED
PROBLEMS

Step 1. Find the log of y.

Step 2. Multiply it by x.

Step 3. Find the antilog of the product.

EXAMPLE: Use logs to evaluate 2^2.

Step 1. Turning to the log tables, we find the mantissa defined by 200. This proves to be 3010. Since the decimal point is in the zeroth position, log 2 = 0.3010.

Step 2. Multiplying log 2 by 2 gives

$$0.3010 \times 2 = 0.6020$$

Step 3. Turning to the antilog table, we find the number defined by 602. This is 3999. Because the integer part of the log is 0, the antilog 0.6020 = 3.999.

As you can see, using the log and antilog tables introduces a small amount of error into our calculations: in this case, 0.001.

EXAMPLE: Use logs to evaluate 1.5700^{60}.

Step 1. From the log table we find that the mantissa for 1570 is 0.1959. Because the decimal point is immediately following the first digit, log 1.5700 = 0.1959.

Step 2. Multiplying the log of 1.5700 by 60 gives

$$0.1959 \times 60 = 11.754$$

Step 3. Turning to the antilog table, we find the value defined by the mantissa 0.754. This is 5675. The integer part of the log is 11 and positive. Therefore,

$$1.5700^{60} = 567,500,000,000$$

EXAMPLE: What is $.7770^{12}$?

Step 1. From the log table we find that the mantissa for 777 is 8904. Since the decimal point is 1 place to the left of the position following the first digit, the integer part of the log is −1.

$$\log 0.7770 = -1 + .8904 = -0.1096$$

Step 2. Multiplying this by the power of 12 gives

$$-0.1096 \times 12 = -1.3152$$

Step 3. Because this is negative, we must subtract 1 from the integer part and add 1 to the decimal part to get a positive mantissa:

64

NUMBERS TO
POWERS: USING
THE SIMPLEST
CALCULATOR
TO SOLVE
COMPLICATED
PROBLEMS

$$-1.3152 \ = \ -2 + (1 \ -0.3152)$$

$$= \ -2 + 0.6848$$

We look up 0.6848 in the antilog table. The number defined by 0.684 is 4831. The 0.68 row and the 8 column in the Proportional Parts section gives a value of 9, which we must add to 4831: $4831 + 9 = 4840$.

All that remains is to determine the position of the decimal point. The integer part of the log is -2. Therefore, we must start at the position to the right of the first digit and shift the decimal 2 places to the left. This gives .0484. Thus

$$.7770^{12} \ = \ .0484$$

One situation that we encounter later is the necessity for evaluating numbers to a negative power. Putting a minus sign in front of an exponent is shorthand for a reciprocal, a number divided into 1:

$$y^{-x} \ = \ \frac{1}{y^x}$$

You can handle such a situation in one of two ways. You can follow the steps for using logs to evaluate a number to a power given previously. In Step 2, when you multiply the log of the number by the exponent, you must handle the negative sign on the exponent properly. If the log of the number is positive, then the product of the log and a negative exponent will be negative. If the log of the number is negative, however, then the product of the 2 will be positive. Alternatively, you may prefer to use logs to evaluate y^x and then divide this into 1 to get the value of y^{-x}. The 2 procedures will give you slightly different answers, but only by a few hundredths of a percent.

EXAMPLE: Evaluate 1.459^{-13} by both methods described previously. First, we use the straight log method.

Step 1. Use the log table to find log 1.459. The mantissa of 145 is 1614. The proportional part in the 9 column is 27, and the mantissa for 1459 is $1614 + 27 = 1641$. Because the decimal point in 1.459 is in the zeroth position:

$$\log 1.459 \ = \ 0.1641$$

Step 2. Now the exponent is -13, so

$$0.1641 \ \times \ (-13) \ = \ -2.1333$$

Step 3. At this point we must find the antilog of -2.1333. Since it is a negative number, we must first separate the integer and fractional

65

NUMBERS TO
POWERS: USING
THE SIMPLEST
CALCULATOR
TO SOLVE
COMPLICATED
PROBLEMS

parts and subtract 1 from the integer part and add 1 to the fractional part:

$$-2.1333 = -2 - .1333 = -3 + (1 - .1333)$$

$$= -3 + .8667$$

Looking up 0.8667 in the antilog table, we find that the number corresponding to .866 is 7345. The value from the Proportional Parts section under 7 is 12. Thus the equivalent of 0.8667 is 7345 + 12 = 7357. Since the integer part of the log is −3, the decimal point goes 3 places to the left of the zeroth position: 0.007357. Therefore,

$$1.459^{-13} = .007357$$

Now we can try the alternative approach. In this case, we begin by evaluating 1.459^{13}.

Step 1. We have already determined the log of 1.459. It is 0.1641.

Step 2. The exponent is +13, thus

$$0.1641 \times 13 = 2.1333$$

Step 3. Because 2.1333 is positive, we look up 0.1333 in the antilog table. The first 3 digits give a value of 1358. The proportional part under 3 is 1. So the digits corresponding to 0.1333 are 1359. Since the integer part of the log is 2, we must locate the decimal point 2 places to the right of the position immediately following the first digit.

$$1.459^{13} = 135.9$$

Finally, to get $1,459^{-13}$, we must divide 135.9 into 1:

$$\frac{1}{135.9} = 0.00735835$$

As you can see, there is a slight difference between the 2 values.

SEVEN-PLACE LOG TABLES

In most cases the errors introduced by using the four-place log tables are insignificant. However, in a number of calculations involving compound interest and installment buying, we must take a number, such as 1.005, to a large power and then multiply the result by a large number. In such cases the errors introduced by the four-place table can be significant. For this reason, Appendix 2 also contains a portion of a seven-place log table, which runs from 10000 to 12009. Using this table for numbers a few hundredths or thousandths greater than 1 will reduce the errors to a tolerable level.

66

NUMBERS TO
POWERS: USING
THE SIMPLEST
CALCULATOR
TO SOLVE
COMPLICATED
PROBLEMS

A section of the seven-place log table is reproduced here:

LOGARITHMS

N.	0	1	2	3	4	5	6	7	8	9	d.
1000	000 0000	0434	0869	1303	1737	2171	2605	3039	3473	3907	434
1001	4341	4775	5208	5642	6076	6510	6943	7377	7810	8244	434
1002	8677	9111	9544	9977	*0411	*0844	*1277	*1710	*2143	*2576	433
1003	001 3009	3442	3875	4308	4741	5174	5607	6039	6472	6905	433
1004	7337	7770	8202	8635	9067	9499	9932	*0364	*0796	*1228	432
1005	002 1661	2093	2525	2957	3389	3821	4253	4685	5116	5548	432
1006	5980	6411	6843	7275	7706	8138	8569	9001	9432	9863	431
1007	003 0295	0726	1157	1588	2019	2451	2882	3313	3744	4174	431
1008	4605	5036	5467	5898	6328	6759	7190	7620	8051	8481	431
1009	8912	9342	9772	*0203	*0633	*1063	*1493	*1924	*2354	*2784	430

The seven-place table is used in basically the same way as the four-place table, except for the handling of proportional parts. Here are the steps to follow when using the seven-place log table:

Step 1. Locate the first 4 digits of the number in the left-hand column of the table. Find the fifth digit in the row at the top.

Step 2. At the intersection of the row defined by the first 4 digits and the column headed by the fifth digit is the mantissa of the log.

Step 3. If you wish 6-place accuracy, find the value in the column headed d and the row defined by the first 4 digits of the number. The values listed under column d are the differences between successive log values in each row. If the sixth digit of the regular number is g and the appropriate value under column d is d, the amount you must add to the mantissa to account for g is

$$\frac{g \times d}{10}$$

Step 4. If the regular number is greater than or equal to 1, go to Step 5. If the regular number is less than 1, go to Step 6.

Step 5. Count left from the decimal point of the regular number to the position just behind the first digit. The number of places is the integer part of the logarithm and is added to the mantissa.

Step 6. Count right from the decimal point of the regular number to the position just behind the first digit. The number of places is the negative integer part of the logarithm, and it should be subtracted from the positive mantissa.

EXAMPLE: Find the seven-place log for 1.00153.
In the left-hand column of the seven-place table we find 1001. In the uppermost row we locate the fifth digit, 5. At the intersection of this row and column is the 4-digit number 6510. You will see to the left

67

NUMBERS TO
POWERS: USING
THE SIMPLEST
CALCULATOR
TO SOLVE
COMPLICATED
PROBLEMS

of the zero column a series of 3-digit numbers. These are the first 3 digits of the mantissa. The mantissa defined by 10015 is 0.0006510. Note that some of the 4-digit numbers in the table are preceded by asterisks. This means that the value of the third digit of the mantissa must be increased by 1. Next, we must correct the mantissa for the sixth digit of the original number, in this case 3. The correct value from the *d* column is 434, thus

$$\frac{3 \times 434}{10} = 130.2$$

The mantissa for 100153, then, is

$$.0006510 + .0000130 = .0006640$$

Because the decimal point in the original number, 1.00153, is in the zeroth position,

$$\log 1.00153 = 0.0006640$$

EXAMPLE: Use 7-place logs to calculate 1.00153^{360}. We have already determined the log of 1.00153 to be 0.0006640. Multiplying this by 360 gives

$$0.0006640 \times 360 = 0.2390266$$

Using the antilog tables, we find the antilog for 0.2390 is 1734. Since the integer part of the log is 0,

$$1.00153^{360} = 1.734$$

If we had used the 4-place log table, what would we have gotten?
First, we would have been forced to round off 1.00153 to 4 places in order to use the table. Thus, we would have looked up the log of 1.002. The mantissa of 100 is 0000. Under 2 in the Proportional Parts section is a value of 0. Therefore, the log of 1.002 is 0.0008. Multiplying this by 360 gives

$$0.0008 \times 360 = 0.28800000$$

Looking up the antilog of .288 we find 1941. Therefore,

$$1.002^{360} = 1.941$$

As you can see, there is a 12% difference in these 2 numbers. The value of this number to calculator, 8-place accuracy is 1.7339102. Thus, using the 4-place tables in these circumstances leads to unacceptably high errors.

SERIES APPROXIMATION

Perhaps after all has been said and done, you still find logarithms confusing, or perhaps you simply dislike repeatedly referring to log tables. There is, however, an alternative.

The bulk of exponential expressions used in financial matters has a standard, convenient form. This is:

$$(1 + X)^N$$

which can be approximated by the following mathematical series:

$$(1 + X)^N = 1 + NX \left(1 + \frac{X(N-1)}{2} \left(1 + \frac{X(N-2)}{3}\right.\right.$$

$$\left.\left.\left(1 + \ldots \left(1 + \frac{X(N-k)}{k} (1 + \ldots)\right)\right)\right)\right) \qquad \textbf{(Equation 6-1)}$$

This series has N terms. It is called the *Binomial Expansion* and is valid where X^2 is less than 1. For our purposes, we must further limit it to cases where $-1 \leqslant NX \leqslant 1$. This allows us to get a good approximation with only a few terms: each succeeding term is smaller than the previous one.

Obviously, computing such a series with a large number of terms is tedious and error-prone. Therefore, we need an idea of the accuracy involved in carrying out the series to various lengths. Table 6-1 will help us do this. The errors listed in the table are maximum ones. In general, for a given value of NX, the closer NX is to 0, the smaller the error in the approximation, and the greater the value of N, the larger the error.

Suppose you wish to evaluate the following expression:

$$\$15,000 \; (1 + .09)^{10}$$

Table 6-1 Accuracy of Binomial Expansion $(-1 \leqslant NX \leqslant 1)$

EXPANSION	ERROR
$1 + NX$	< 0.7
$1 + NX \left(1 + \frac{X(N-1)}{2}\right)$	< 0.2
$1 + NX \left(1 + \frac{X(N-1)}{2} \left(1 + \frac{X(N-2)}{3}\right)\right)$	< 0.07
$1 + NX \left(1 + \frac{X(N-1)}{2} \left(1 + \frac{X(N-2)}{3} \left(1 + \frac{X(N-3)}{4}\right)\right)\right)$	< 0.01
$1 + NX \left(1 + \frac{X(N-1)}{2} \left(1 + \frac{X(N-2)}{3} \left(1 + \frac{X(N-3)}{4} \left(1 + \frac{X(N-4)}{5}\right)\right)\right)\right)$	< 0.002
$1 + NX \left(1 + \frac{X(N-1)}{2} \left(1 + \frac{X(N-2)}{3} \left(1 + \frac{X(N-3)}{4} \left(1 + \frac{X(N-4)}{5} \left(1 + \frac{X(N-5)}{6}\right)\right)\right)\right)\right)$	< 0.0004

69

NUMBERS TO
POWERS: USING
THE SIMPLEST
CALCULATOR
TO SOLVE
COMPLICATED
PROBLEMS

The number of terms in the binomial expansion you would use depends on the accuracy desired. To determine the amount of error in any given answer, you must multiply the error in the expansion (as listed in Table 6-1) times $15,000. Thus, $1 + NX$ will give an answer to within $0.7 \times \$15,000 = \$10,500$. Adding another term will slightly increase the accuracy to within $0.2 \times \$15,000 = \$3,000$. An error of 0.07 in the expansion becomes $0.07 \times \$15,000 = \$1,050$ in the answer. And so on. If an answer to within $1,050 is adequate, then

$$(1.09)^{10} = 1 + (10 \times .09) \left(1 + \frac{.09 \times 9}{2} \left(1 + \frac{.09 \times 8}{3}\right)\right)$$

$$= 1 + .9 \left(1 + 0.405 \left(1 + .24\right)\right)$$

$$= 2.35198$$

and

$$\$15,000 \ (1.09)^{10} = \$15,000 \times 2.35198 = \$35,279.70$$

If greater precision is needed, then more terms must be added to the approximation.

As suggested by the illustration above, the series is best calculated by starting within the innermost parentheses and working outward. If your calculator has an accessible memory, then storing X and recalling it when needed reduces the work somewhat.

In the case where N is negative, calculate the series as if it were positive and then divide the sum into 1. In this case, you should also divide the error values into 1 as well to determine the amount of error in the estimation.

The binomial expansion can be used in cases where NX is greater than 1. In this case, however, successive terms in the series get larger and larger. For that reason, the first few terms are considerably smaller than the correct answer. Therefore, when NX is greater than 1, it is essential to carry out the series to the bitter end.

In the case where NX is greater than 1 and a large exponent is involved —12, 24, 360, and so forth—going the logarithm route is invariably faster and simpler.

PROBLEMS

1   Find the four-place logs of the following numbers:

    a.   1776

    b.   .0022

    c.   158,200

    d.   27.656234

    e.   19.9

    f.   1,224,000,000

NUMBERS TO
POWERS: USING
THE SIMPLEST
CALCULATOR
TO SOLVE
COMPLICATED
PROBLEMS

2   Find the antilogs of the following numbers:

    a.   2.0784

    b.   −.7622

    c.   5.9455

    d. −3.007

    e.   1.0044321

    f.   .0022

3   Multiply 14,320 times 0.12 with regular numbers and using logs. Remember that the $\log (a \times b) = \log a + \log b$.

4   Use four-place logs to calculate 7.47^5.

5   Use four-place logs to calculate 7.47^{-8}

6   What is 2.0076^{15}?

7   Use seven-place logs to determine 1.0083333^{12}.

8   Calculate 1.0005^{-240}.

9   Using 3- and 6-term binomial expansions, compute the value of 1.0083333^{12}. (For this purpose, the initial 1 in the series is considered the zeroth term.)

10   Using a 4-term binomial expansion, compute the value of 1.0005^{-60}.

11   Using a 2-term expansion, compute the value of 1.033333^6.

12   You wish to solve the equation,

$$PMT = \frac{5000 \times .05}{1 + (1.05)^{-12}}$$

and you want the answer to be accurate to within 1 dollar. How many terms in the binomial expansion must you use for 1.05^{-12} in order to get this accuracy? Using this expansion, what is the value of PMT?

7

Inflation

These days the subject of inflation is strikingly like that of the weather: It is something everybody talks about and something no one seems to be able to do anything about. Of course, there is one important way in which inflation differs from the weather. No one can consider it an act of God or nature: it is clearly the aggregate result of our own actions and those of our fellow citizens. This makes it, in many ways, even more frustrating.

Unfortunately, the net result of the economic decisions of a few hundred million people seems even more difficult to understand and predict than the interactions between the billions of molecules of water vapor that make up a typical cloud.

Looking into the future with the distant gaze of a scholar-economist, John Kenneth Galbraith reassures us that, "Nothing . . . lasts forever. That is true of inflation. It is true of recession. Each stirs the attitudes, engenders the action which seeks to bring itself to an end—and eventually does."[1] Even with such an historical basis for optimism, the noted economist does admit that which is well established is likely to last for a time.

A number of economic planners now feel that inflation has become so entrenched in the U.S. economy that we should expect an annual rate of at least 6% between now and the end of the century. Thus we had all better learn how to cope with its insidious effects until history takes its inevitable course.

Undoubtedly, you already have a descriptive idea of what inflation is and what its general effects are. But a quantitative understanding of this economic fact of life and how it directly affects your personal finances can help you avoid its worst side effects and possibly even help you profit by the current situation.

[1]John Kenneth Galbraith, *Money*, Boston, Massachusetts: Houghton Mifflin, 1975, pp. 376-77.

According to the dictionary, inflation is an increase in the volume of money and credit relative to available goods, resulting in a substantial and continuing rise in the general price level.

CONSUMER PRICE INDEX

The yardstick by which inflation is commonly measured is called the *Consumer Price Index* (CPI). This is compiled monthly by the U.S. Bureau of Labor Statistics. The CPI is a somewhat arbitrary, though useful, measure of inflation. Up until 1978, the basis of the index was the pattern of purchases typical of an urban worker's family. The Bureau of Labor Statistics had a shopping list of goods and services that it felt was representative. Each month the Bureau priced these items in 56 different cities—some small in population, some medium, and some large. Then, with a little statistical magic, these numbers were transformed into a single figure—the Consumer Price Index. Since 1978, however, the basis for the index is slightly different. The government statisticians now compile it from the consumption patterns of all urban consumers, rather than just from that of the wage earner. The base year for this index is 1967. It is given a value of 100. In January 1978, the CPI was 187.2. This means that the average retail prices of all the items on the Bureau of Labor's shopping list were 87.2% higher in 1978 than they were in 1967.

The index is calculated as an overall figure, as well as for specific categories—types of food, housing costs, rent, gas and electricity, fuel and utilities, clothing, transportation, medical care, recreation, and so forth. Each category has its own index, with the prices for 1967 given as 100.[2] As with the overall index, the specific consumer price indexes give the percentage change from the base year. The Consumer Price Index is carried monthly in many newspapers. These often list values for your specific locality as well as the national average. The indexes for years past can be found in most almanacs. Many public libraries have reports with a detailed breakdown of the CPI.

DECLINING VALUE
OF THE DOLLAR

There is a direct relationship between the Consumer Price Index and the value of the dollar. The dollar's value is its purchasing power. In a given year a dollar will buy a certain amount of goods and services. In another year it will buy a greater or lesser amount.

The Consumer Price Index measures the price of goods and services that urban consumers purchase relative to 1967. Therefore, it is the reciprocal of the dollar's value relative to 1967.

$$Dollar\ Value\ =\ \frac{100}{CPI}$$

(Equation 7-1)

(Division by 100 is necessary to convert the CPI from a percentage to a decimal.)

---

[2]There are some exceptions to this, for instance, hospital daily services. The Bureau did not include this until 1972, so that year is considered the baseline and and given the value of 100.

In their reports on inflation early in the year, newscasters will often tell you what the annual inflation rate—let's call it R—will be for the year if prices continue to rise at the same rate. It is possible to estimate R from changes in the Consumer Price Index for any part of a year. If CPI_i is the Consumer Price Index for month i and CPI_j is the Consumer Price Index for month j where i and j are less than a year apart, then

$$R = \frac{(CPI_j - CPI_i)}{CPI_i (j - i)} \times 1,200 \qquad \text{(Equation 7-2)}$$

EXAMPLE: The CPI for December 1977 is 186.1. The CPI for March 1978 is 189.8. What is the projection for R during 1978? Let December be month 1. Then March is month 4. So,

$$R = \frac{(189.8 - 186.1) \times 1,200}{186.1 \times (4 - 1)}$$

$$= \frac{3.7 \times 1,200}{186.1 \times 3}$$

$$= \frac{4,400}{558.3}$$

$$= 7.95\%$$

THE WAGE-PRICE SPIRAL

As inflation diminishes the value of the dollar, your income must increase to keep pace. If your salary does not increase fast enough, you will be losing purchasing power. It is easy (although not always encouraging) to figure out whether you are gaining or losing ground to inflation. Given your current income, S, and the annual inflation rate, r, expressed as a decimal, the following formula calculates how much you must make next year (S') to maintain your purchasing power:

$$S' = S \times (1 + r) \qquad \text{(Equation 7-3)}$$

EXAMPLE: Janice's take-home pay in December 1977 was $196.20. If the annual inflation rate for 1978 is estimated to be 7.95%, how much must she take home in December 1978 to have the same purchasing power?

$$S' = \$196.20 \times (1 + 0.0795)$$

$$= \$211.80$$

You can use your gross income with this formula as well as your take-home pay. However, it is better to use your income after taxes. It is this portion of your income that goes toward buying consumer goods and that is tied to the inflation rate. A secondary effect of inflation is to disproportionately increase the amount of income taxes you pay because tax rates rise with income.

There are 3 approaches that you can use to estimate how your income should grow over a number of years to keep up with inflation.

Approach A—Consumer Price Index

If you have a listing of the Consumer Price Index handy (it is in most almanacs), you can estimate the percentage increase in prices for a certain period, and use this to compare your purchasing power. First, look up the CPI for the period in question.[3] Then figure the percentage difference from the beginning of the period to the end using Equation 3-5. Express this difference, d, as a decimal. Add 1 and multiply it times your initial salary. The product will be the amount your ending salary should be to have the same purchasing power. Mathematically, this is

$$S' = S \times (1 + d) \qquad \text{(Equation 7-4)}$$

EXAMPLE: George's after-tax income in 1970 was $11,220, and the CPI for 1970 was 116.3. By 1976 George was netting $16,500, and the CPI had risen to 170.5. Has George gained or lost ground to inflation?

First, we must determine d. Because d is a decimal and Equation 3-5 gives the answer in percent, eliminating the 100 will give us d directly:

$$d = \frac{CPI_2 - CPI_1}{CPI_1}$$

$$= \frac{170.5 - 116.3}{116.3}$$

$$= 0.46603611$$

Now we can calculate what George's salary should be in 1976 to equal his purchasing power in 1970.

$$S' = \$11,200 \times (1 + 0.46603611)$$

$$= \$16,419.60$$

---

[3] In sources such as an almanac, you will find yearly averages rather than values for a specific month. You can use these in the formula. They will, however, give you slightly different values than if you use the monthly index figures.

Although his take-home pay has increased by 47% during the 6 years, George's purchasing power is about the same as it was in 1970; he is running in place, economically speaking.

Approach B—Annual Inflation Rate

The second way to approach this problem uses annual inflation rates rather than the Consumer Price Index. As you recall, for 1 year $S' = S (1 + r)$. You cannot simply add together the annual inflation rates for several years, even though some sources do recommend it. Five years of 5% annual inflation does not equal 25% inflation. For a period of n years, with annual inflation rates of $r_1, r_2, \ldots r_n$

$$S' = S (1 + r_1) (1 + r_2) \ldots (1 + r_n) \qquad \textbf{(Equation 7-5)}$$

EXAMPLE: From 1970 to 1976 the annual inflation rates were 4.30%, 3.30%, 6.23%, 10.97%, 9.14%, and 5.77%, respectively. For George's case from the previous example, compute S'.

$S' = \$11,200 \, (1.0430) \, (1.0330) \, (1.0623) \, (1.1097) \, (1.0914) \, (1.0577)$

$ = \$16,421.09$

(The difference between this value and the one arrived at previously is due to the error introduced by rounding off the annual inflation rates to 3 places.)

Approach C—Average Annual Inflation

The second method for figuring inflation is complicated, particularly when applied to long periods of time. One simplification is first to determine the average annual inflation rate and use this instead.

Let the average annual inflation rate be r_{av}. Then, for T years,

$$r_{av} = \frac{r_1 + r_2 + \ldots + r_T}{T} \qquad \textbf{(Equation 7-6)}$$

Substituting r_{av} into Equation 7-5 gives it a slightly different form:

$$S' = S (1 + r_{av})^T \qquad \textbf{(Equation 7-7)}$$

EXAMPLE: From the values in the previous example, calculate the average annual inflation rate from 1970 to 1976. Use this to calculate S' from George's 1970 salary.

$$r_{av} = \frac{0.0430 + 0.0330 + 0.0623 + 0.1097 + 0.0914 + 0.0577}{6}$$

$$= \frac{0.3971}{6}$$

$$= 0.0662$$

and

$$S' = \$11,200 \, (1 + 0.0662)^6$$

$$= \$16,451.64$$

As you can see by comparing this value with those computed previously, the process of averaging introduces an even greater error into the answer. You should not let this worry you, because inflation is by nature an imprecise quantity. Differences of even several tenths of a percent in the inflation rate are of questionable relevance.

Equation 7-7 allows us to take inflationary effects into account in financial planning. To do so, we must assume a certain average annual inflation rate for future years, and use this to set financial goals.

EXAMPLE: In 1977 the members of the local mass-transit employees' union were making an average of $278.29 per week. When it was time to negotiate a new, 5-year contract, union officials felt it reasonable to demand a 2% annual salary increase on top of inflation. Management refused to consider an annual inflation adjustment. So what should the union's minimum salary demands have been? What would this have meant in terms of the average weekly salary for their members?

It was generally felt at that time that 6% was the minimum inflation rate that the U.S. economy would experience. The average inflation rate for the previous 5 years had been 7.7%. The union leaders, being sensitive to federal efforts to fight inflation, decided to assume only a 7% inflation rate for the next 5 years. Then, to achieve a 2% annual increase in purchasing power, the union had to demand a 9% annual salary increase. This meant that in 1982 the average salary of members would be

$$S' = \$278.29 \, (1 + 0.09)^5$$

$$= \$428.18$$

which is a 54% increase.

CONSTANT-VALUE DOLLARS

Another valuable way to account for inflationary effects is using the constant-value dollar, which keeps the same purchasing power over the period in question. For instance, if you inherited a sum of $10,000 in 1967, and if you kept this in a safe or stuffed in a mattress, inflation would continually be diminishing the value of this money. By 1970 it would only purchase as much as $8,600 would have purchased in 1967, by 1973, $7,520, and by 1976, the financial clout of the mattress full of money would have shrunk to $5,870. In constant 1967-dollars, then, the value of $10,000 in 1976 is only $5,870 by 1978. It is almost as if inflation were an invisible thief who every day steals a few dollars from your money mattress—a thief whom you have no way to catch.

If $PV(A)$ is the value in year-A dollars, $FV(B)$ is the amount of money in year-B dollars, r_{av} is the average inflation rate, and T is the number of years between A and B, then

$$PV(A) = FV(B)(1 + r_{av})^{-T} \qquad \text{(Equation 7-8)}$$

EXAMPLE: Four years ago Charlotte deposited $5,000 in a savings certificate with an annual percentage rate of 6%. She now has $6,312.38. It is time to renew the certificate. If the average inflation rate for this period was 7.7%, has her money increased or decreased in value and by how much?

To answer this question we can use Equation 9-9 to determine how much the final value of Charlotte's account is worth in the dollars of the year in which the principal was deposited.

$$PV = \$6,312.38 (1 + 0.077)^{-4}$$

$$= \$6,312.38 (0.74325388)$$

$$= \$4,691.70$$

The purchasing power of Charlotte's investment has shrunk by 6.2%. However, if she had kept it in a checking account that did not earn any interest, its buying power would have shrunk considerably more.

$$PV = \$5,000 (1.077)^{-4}$$

$$= \$5,000 (0.74325388)$$

$$= \$3,716.27$$

In following chapters we use constant-value dollars to investigate the effects of inflation on savings and installment buying.

INFLATION
WITH A BUSINESS-ANALYST CALCULATOR

Business-analyst calculators do not deal with inflation directly. However, their built-in functions can be used for this purpose. Using Equation 9-8, which calculates the number of dollars, S', required to maintain a given amount of purchasing power over T years with an average annual inflation rate of r_{av},

$$S' = S(1 + r_{av})^T$$

On the calculator you will find the following keys: $\boxed{n}$, $\boxed{i}$, $\boxed{PV}$, and $\boxed{FV}$. The purpose of these keys is ordinarily for compound interest and installment buying. $\boxed{n}$ is the number of compounding periods, $\boxed{i}$ is the periodic interest rate as a percentage, $\boxed{PV}$ is the present value of the account, and $\boxed{FV}$ is its future value.

By a simple substitution we can use these functions to calculate inflation. The annual inflation rate as a percentage, R_{av}, is entered in $\boxed{i}$. The number of years, T, is entered in $\boxed{n}$. S, the amount in present-day dollars, is entered in $\boxed{PV}$. Then pushing $\boxed{FV}$ gives S'.

EXAMPLE: Members of the local union are making $278.29 per week. If inflation averages 9% per year, what must their salaries be 5 years from now in order for them to maintain the same buying power?
Enter $\boxed{9}$ in $\boxed{i}$, $278.29 in $\boxed{PV}$, and 5 in $\boxed{n}$. To determine S', key $\boxed{FV}$. You should get $428.18.

In the case of constant-value dollars,

$$CV = FV(1 + r_{av})^{-T}$$

the same keys are employed. Only in this case enter $-T$ in $\boxed{n}$, r_{av} in $\boxed{i}$, and FV in $\boxed{PV}$. Then CV is computed by keying $\boxed{FV}$.

EXAMPLE: Five years ago Bick Bronson invested $12,000 in a savings account. The balance of the account now stands at $16,565.04. If inflation has averaged 8.7% a year over this period, has he gained or lost purchasing power?
In this case $FV = \$16,565.04$, $R = 8.7\%$, and $T = 5$. Enter $16,565.04 in $\boxed{PV}$, -5 in $\boxed{n}$, and 8.7 in $\boxed{i}$. Then keying $\boxed{FV}$ yields $10,915.53. Thus, in constant-value dollars, Bick has lost $1,048.47.

PROBLEMS

1   When the Consumer Price Index reaches 207.9, what will be the value of the dollar relative to 1967?

2   If in the year 1990 the value of the dollar has shrunk to 1/3 the value of the dollar in 1967, what will the Consumer Price Index be?

3   What would be the annual inflation rate for the year 2000 if the Consumer Price Index for December 1999 is 1011.7 and for December 2000 is 1092.7?

4   The Consumer Price Index for transportation for March 1977 was 174.7. By March 1978, the Index had risen to 179.9. What was the inflation rate for transportation for this 12-month period?

5   The Consumer Price Index for food was 197.3 in February 1978. If the Index was 191.9 in December of 1977, what was the projected annual inflation rate for food for 1978?

6   Ward's present salary is $16,350 per year. What must his salary be a year from now to have the same purchasing power if the inflation rate is 6%? 8%? 10%?

7   The Consumer Price Index for December 1977 was 186.1. If by December 1987 the Index has risen to 383.6, what salary would have an equivalent purchasing power to $20,000 at the end of 1977?

8   If the average annual inflation rate runs at 8¼% from 1980 to the year 2000, how must an income of $6,000 per year increase to keep pace with inflation?

9   In 1978 a certain refrigerator cost $450. If inflation averages 6% per year for the next 12 years, what will the equivalent price of the refrigerator be in 1990?

10   What is the value of $25,000 in 1985 in 1978-dollars if the annual inflation rate is 7.5%?

8

Savings

Almost 200 years ago Benjamin Franklin gave $5 to the city of Boston on the condition that the money be put in a savings account and be left on deposit for 2 centuries. As a result, the city will soon receive almost $14 million from the behest.

In 1626 Peter Minuit, the first Director General of New Netherland province is said to have purchased Manhattan Island from the Canarsee Indians with $24 worth of trade goods. If the Canarsee Indians had happened to have a Benjamin Franklin among them, had insisted on the sum in guilders, and had deposited the money in European (and then American) banks, they would have by now amassed a fortune almost big enough to buy the island back.

Welcome to the strange world of compound interest where a penny saved is actually *more* than a penny earned: It's a penny *plus interest*, as Benjamin Franklin demonstrated.

An understanding of the compounding process is essential if you wish to plan for the future. This is even true if you are not stashing away a little money each month. It is the monetary form of *exponential growth* that is at the center of the current debate concerning the necessity and wisdom of limiting all types of growth: economic, industrial, and population.

Compounding is a mathematical process with an ancient history. There is an old Persian legend about a clever courtier who presented his king with a beautiful chessboard. In return he asked that the king grant him 1 grain of rice for the first square, 2 grains for the second square, 4 grains for the third, and so on. The king readily agreed until he realized that this would require more rice than he had in his kingdom: The final square alone would be 9 quintillion grains.

Just as the Persian king was confounded by the results of compounding the grains of rice on the chessboard, so the implications of various forms of compounding on our individual financial lives can be surprising. Although the calculations are fairly ambitious, with a 4-function calculator and log tables[1], (or an advanced model), they represent only a minor difficulty. I am sure the Persian mathematicians who had to work out the rice grain problem would have welcomed such an aid.

COMPOUNDING

First, let us examine the compounding process in the abstract to determine its basic nature, and then we will plunge into the various twists and turns that financial institutions have added to this process for their own purpose: making a profit. The basic idea behind interest is one of simplicity itself. You can invest a given amount of money, and that money will "work" for you. Essentially, the money earns a wage; that wage is a percentage of the amount of money invested. Suppose $1,000 were placed in a savings account which earned 6.5% annual interest. This means that every year the $1,000 earns $1,000 × .065 = $65. If the $65 were withdrawn each year, the $1,000 would continue to earn $65 per year for as long as it is kept in the account. This is called simple interest. It is calculated by the following formula:

$$INT = P \times i \times n \qquad \text{(Equation 8-1)}$$

where INT is the interest, P is the principal, i is the periodic interest rate (a decimal), and N is the number of periods the principal is invested.

EXAMPLE: If $10,000 is invested at 8% annual interest, how much simple interest will be earned after 2 years? After 5 years?

Here P is $10,000 and i is the decimal equivalent of 8%, .08. Because this is an annual interest rate, the period for the account is 1 year.

Therefore, after 2 years N = 2, and after 5 years N = 5.

After 2 years the simple interest is

$$INT = \$10,000 \times .08 \times 2 = \$1,600$$

After 5 years

$$INT = \$10,000 \times .08 \times 5 = \$4,000$$

The picture gets more complicated—and interesting—when the interest is continually added to the principal. It is in this fashion that one gets the ever-increasing growth that is enabling Franklin's $5 to grow to $14 million, a 28,000% increase. Such increases are possible, because as the principal grows, so does the percentage that is being added to it. This results in an ever-increasing rate of growth.

The curve that you see on Graph 8-1 is known as an *exponential growth curve*. Looking at the balance of our $1,000 account, you will see that it

[1] See Chapter 6.

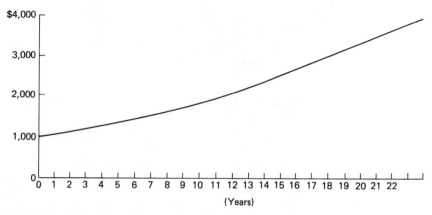

Graph 8-1 Balance in an Account where $1,000 is Invested at 6.5%

takes about 11 years to reach $2,000. In another 11 years, the balance is about $4,000. This process is analogous to that of the grains of rice and the chessboard. In this case, you begin with $1,000 instead of with 1 grain of rice, and there are 11-year periods instead of squares on the chessboard. Each 11 years the amount in the savings account doubles. In 33 years, the balance is $7,990, and in 44 years, $15,973. If this process is continued for long periods, the results can be staggering. Leaving our $1,000 in the account for 704 years is the equivalent of adding all the grains on the chessboard. This works out to a balance of $18 sextillion ($18 followed by 21 zeros).

Of course, calculations of this sort are a financial fantasy for most of us. Yet they illustrate the basic process involved—a process called *exponential growth* because the equation which describes it involves raising a number to a power. The equation is

$$FV = P \times (1 + i)^N \qquad \text{(Equation 8-2)}$$

where FV is the final value (balance in the account), P is the principal, i is the periodic interest rate, and N is the total number of compoundings.

In this context, both i and N require further explanation. In the example used previously of the $1,000 account at 6.5% interest, it was assumed that the interest was calculated once per year and added to the balance at that time. Thus, one year is the *compounding period*, the time between interest computations. Let n be the number of compounding periods per year. For monthly compounding, for example, $n = 12$. If we define T as time in years, then

$$N = n \times T \qquad \text{(Equation 8-3)}$$

Thus, if you want to know the number of periods (N) for an account compounded monthly after 5 years, $N = 12 \times 5 = 60$. N is always an integer. It cannot have a decimal part. So if $n = 1$ and T is 5 1/12 or 5 1/2 or 5 11/12 years, N would be just 5. This is expressed mathematically by

82

$$N = Integer (n \times T) \qquad \text{(Equation 8-4)}$$

where *Integer* means to take only the part of any given number to the left of the decimal point.

EXAMPLE: If T is 6 years 2 months, and there are 2 compoundings per year, then

$$N = Integer\left(6\frac{2}{12} \times 2\right)$$

$$= Integer\,(12.333333)$$

$$= 12$$

In savings accounts the interest is usually quoted as an annual percentage rate (*APR*). This is not the same as i in the compounding formula. If the compounding period is 1 year, then i is 1/100 of the *APR*; if interest is compounded twice a year, then i is 1/200 of the *APR*; and if monthly, then i is 1/1200 of the *APR*. In general then,

$$i = \frac{APR}{100 \times n} \qquad \text{(Equation 8-5)}$$

where n is the number of compounding periods per year.

EXAMPLE: How do different methods of compounding affect the amount of interest paid on a savings account?

To investigate this, let's examine several common compounding schemes and determine their effect on $1,000 put in an account with a 6.5% annual interest rate. In the case of semi-annual compounding

$$i = \frac{6.5}{100 \times 2} = 0.0325$$

Thus 0.0325 is the proportion of the balance that is added every 6 months.

For 1 year, $N = 2$; for 2 years, $N = 4$; for 3 years, $N = 6$; and so on. The final value in the account after 1 year is

$$FV = \$1,000 \times (1 + 0.0325)^2$$

As explained in Chapter 8,

$$\log(1.0325)^2 = 2 \times \log(1.0325)$$

Using the 7-place log tables, we find

$$\log(1.0325) = 0.0138901$$

Multiplying by 2 and finding the antilog gives

$$0.0138901 \times 2 = 0.0277202$$

$$\text{antilog } 0.0277 = 1.0661$$

thus,

$$(1.0325)^2 = 1.0661$$

and, finally,

$$FV = \$1{,}000 \times 1.0661 = \$1{,}066.10$$

This is $1 more interest in the first year, than when the interest is compounded annually. If you leave the account untouched for 11 years, you will garner an extra $22 with semi-annual compounding.

Many banks compound interest every month. On our illustrative account, the amount of interest added each month is

$$i = \frac{6.5}{100 \times 12} = 0.0054167$$

where N is the number of years times 12. The formula for the final value after one year becomes

$$FV = \$1{,}000 \times (1 + 0.0054167)^{12}$$

To solve this, we again resort to logs to evaluate the number to the power. First, we must round off 1.0054167 to 6 digits. It becomes 1.00542. Turning to the 7-place log table, we determine its logarithm

$$\log 1.00542 = 0.0023475$$

and knowing that

$$\log (1.00542)^{12} = 12 \times \log 1.00542$$

$$= 12 \times 0.0024375$$

$$= 0.0281702$$

allows us to look up the value of $(1.00542)^{12}$ by finding the antilog of 0.0281702 (first rounding it off to 0.0282). This is 1.067.

Plugging this into our original equation gives

$$FV = \$1{,}000 \times (1.067) = \$1{,}067.$$

Thus, you can see that monthly compounding gives $1 more interest in the first year than does semi-annual compounding and $2 more interest than does annual compounding. After 11 years, you would have an extra $41 in the bank and in 22 years, an extra $166.

In the scramble for your savings dollars, more and more banks are offering daily and "continuous" compounding. Although it sounds alluring, continuous compounding is essentially a mathematical exercise producing the same result as daily compounding. And, as you will see, the difference between daily and monthly compounding is not all that great. It sounds better than it really is. For instance, banks put some clever twists on daily compounding in order to boost the annual yield figures for their accounts. The annual yield is the yearly percentage increase of an account if you leave principal and interest intact. These are the figures they like to stress because they are higher. Bankers may decide to use either a 360- or 365-day year. The 365-day year is less tidy, with quarters of 90, 91, 92, and 93 days, respectively. Another thing they do is use a 360-day year to determine i (the compounding interest rate), and a 365-day year for n (the number of compounding periods). This slightly increases the annual yield.

Starting with a 360-day-per-year compounding, a $1,000 principal, and an annual percentage rate of 6.5,

$$i = \frac{6.5}{100 \times 360} = 0.0001806$$

$$n = 360 \text{ days per year}$$

and the amount in the account after the first year is computed as,

$$FV = \$1,000 \times (1 + 0.0001806)^{360}$$

In the 7-place log tables, we find

$$\log(1.0001806) \cong 0.0000784$$

Now we must multiply this by 360,

$$0.0000784 \times 360 = 0.0282169$$

To look this up in the antilog table, we must round it off to 0.0282. This is the same log that we came up with for the monthly compounding case. Thus, to the nearest dollar, daily compounding would also yield $1,067 after the first year. Actually there are a few pennies difference: daily compounding gives you an added 18 cents, to be exact. After 11 years this amounts to an extra $3.81. Obviously, the emphasis that some banks and savings institutions put on daily or continuous compounding has little substance.

TOTAL EARNINGS

Equation 8-2 gives you the final value in a savings account. Often you will be interested in the amount of interest your money will earn for a given period. In an account with a single deposit at the beginning, the interest is the final value minus the principal, or

$$INT = P(1 + i)^N - P \qquad \text{(Equation 8-6)}$$

EXAMPLE: Joan Appleby has a trust fund of $57,000 that earns 8.25% annual interest. If she uses only the interest, how much annual income does she have?

In this case, P = $57,000 and N = 1. Because this account is compounded yearly, i = 0.0825.

$$INT = \$57{,}000 \ (1.0825)^1 - \$57{,}000$$

$$= \$57{,}000 \times 1.0825 - \$57{,}000$$

$$= \$61{,}702.50 - \$57{,}000$$

$$= \$4{,}702.50$$

EXAMPLE: George Johnson has $10,000 that he is thinking about investing in an 8% annual interest account compounded quarterly. He intends to use the $10,000 in 2 years, and wants to know how much interest it will earn in the interim.

Here P = $10,000. There are 4 compounding periods per year, so i = 8/400 = 0.02 and, for 2 years, N = 8. Therefore,[2]

$$INT = \$10{,}000 \ (1.02)^8 - \$10{,}000$$

$$= \$10{,}000 \times 1.1717 - \$10{,}000$$

$$= \$11{,}717 - \$10{,}000$$

$$= \$1{,}717$$

The calculations up to now all involved money that is deposited in a savings account and just left there. This is true of some kinds of accounts, namely, time deposits, but it is not the case for the most common type of savings account, the passbook account, which usually earns 5.25% annual interest. Most people regularly deposit and withdraw money from such an account.

With a passbook account, other aspects of bank procedure can make a far greater difference on the actual interest your money earns than do the variations in compounding.

CREDITING PERIODS

An extremely important aspect of a savings account that few people realize is the crediting period. This is the frequency with which interest is actually credited, or paid, into the account. Interest compounded daily does not

[2] From this point on, the steps involved in taking a number to a power will not be shown.

necessarily mean that each day a certain amount of interest is added to a savings account balance. Instead, the interest may be added once a quarter, semi-annually, or annually. This has no effect on an inactive account or on a time certificate that you leave untouched for the maturity of the account. But for a passbook account, it can make a tremendous difference.

Suppose you had $1,000 in a 5.25% passbook account. The bank credits interest to your account quarterly, but you do not know this, and withdraw $500 for a new stereo the day before the interest is to be credited. Thus for that quarter the bank will only pay you interest on $500 even though you had $1,000 in the account for all but one day.

Some savings institutions give you a grace period. Usually these periods are for deposits and are promoted with slogans such as "deposit on the 10th, earn interest from the 1st." Similar to other benefits that lenders tout, grace days for deposits confer only a modest financial benefit. Few institutions offer grace periods for withdrawals, which could make a greater difference.

COMPUTING THE BALANCE
OF AN ACTIVE ACCOUNT

In the illustration concerning an early withdrawal, the amount of interest that would be lost can vary greatly depending on how the lender computes the balance of the account. According to Professor Richard L. D. Morse of Kansas State University, who has been studying savings institutions for over twenty years, it is possible for the actual interest paid on active accounts having identical Annual Percentage Rates and compounding periods, to vary by as much as 171% over a 6-month period. The variation is due to differences in crediting and computing practices. Professor Morse believes that Truth in Savings legislation is required similar in intent to the Truth in Lending Act passed in the 1960s, because today savers are not given enough information to compare different savings accounts or to check the accuracy of the bank's calculations.

Following is a brief description of the five basic computing methods used by a majority of banks.

1. *Day-in-day-out (DIDO):* Interest is calculated on funds in the account from the day they are deposited to the day they are withdrawn.
2. *Low balance:* Interest is calculated only on the lowest balance in the account during the crediting period.
3. *Day of deposit to crediting date:* Interest is calculated only on funds left until the end of the period.
4. *First-in-first-out (FIFO):* For a crediting period withdrawals are subtracted from funds in the account for the longest time before interest is calculated.
5. *Last-in-first-out (LIFO):* Withdrawals are deducted from the most recent deposits and the interest is calculated on the remainder.

Of these, the most favorable to the consumer is the Day-in-day-out method. Particularly for savings accounts where you will be depositing and withdrawing money regularly, it is to your advantage to find a bank that uses DIDO.

This should not be too hard to do since over 46% of the members of the American Bankers' Association report that they employ this method.

For savings accounts in which the lender uses DIDO and daily compounding, Professor Morse has developed a method for figuring earnings for any calendar quarter. Savers can use this method to check the interest paid and to predict how much money their savings accounts will earn or lose if they deposit or withdraw money at a given time.

QUARTERLY EARNINGS
FROM A PASSBOOK SAVINGS ACCOUNT

Before we begin, there is some specific information about your savings account that is essential:

1. What is the periodic interest rate? The lender may quote you a periodic percentage rate. If so, divide it by 100 to get i. This is the actual number they use to determine the amount of interest your money earns.

2. On what dates is the interest credited to your account? Chances are good that it will be once per quarter.

Step A: Dates and Activities

With the calendar in Appendix 3, determine the beginning and closing dates for the quarter you wish to check. On the calendar in the upper left-hand corner of each day you will see a small number. These numbers run chronologically from 1 to 365 and are an aid for calculating the number of days between 2 dates. On a piece of scratch paper write down the dates with their respective day numbers.

Now make a list of the beginning balance plus all the transactions during this period, including the day number and amount of the withdrawal or deposit. You should have a list similar to the following:

TRANSACTION	CALENDAR DATE	DAY NUMBER
qtr beginning	Jul 1	182
qtr closing	Sep 30	273
beginning bal: $2,125.54	Jul 1	182
+$250	Jul 18	199
+$250	Aug 1	213
+$250	Aug 19	231
−$425	Aug 29	241
+$275	Sep 15	258

Step B: Earnings on Beginning Balance

Subtract the day number of the beginning date from that of the closing date. Substitute the difference between the 2 for N and the beginning balance for P in Equation 8-7 to determine the earnings on the beginning balance.

$$INT(Bal) = P(1 + i)^N - P \qquad \text{(Equation 8-7)}$$

EXAMPLE: For the quarter from July 1 to September 30, what are the earnings on the beginning balance of $2,125.54 in an account with a daily interest rate of 0.0001438?

The day number of September 30 is 273, while that of July 1 is 182. Therefore,

$$N = 273 - 182 = 91$$

And the interest earned is

$$INT(Bal) = \$2,125.54 \, (1 + 0.0001438)^{91} - \$2,125.54$$

$$= \$28.06$$

Step C: Earnings on Deposits

For each deposit, determine the number of days of interest earned by subtracting the day number of the deposit date from the day number of the last day of the quarter. Use the amount of the deposit as P and the number of days as N in Equation 8-7 to determine its earnings for the period.

EXAMPLE: Figure the interest earned by three $250 deposits on July 18, August 1, and August 19, respectively, plus that of a $275 deposit on September 15.

If the end of the quarter is September 30, then

$$Days\ First\ Deposit = 273 - 199 = 74$$

$$Days\ Second\ Deposit = 273 - 213 = 60$$

$$Days\ Third\ Deposit = 273 - 231 = 42$$

$$Days\ Fourth\ Deposit = 273 - 258 = 15$$

The interest each earns is

$$INT_1 = \$250 \cdot (1.0001438)^{74} - \$250$$

$$= \$2.68$$

$$INT_2 = \$250 \cdot (1.0001438)^{60} - \$250$$

$$= \$2.18$$

$$INT_3 = \$250 \cdot (1.0001438)^{42} - \$250$$

$$= \$1.53$$

$$INT_4 = \$275 \cdot (1.0001438)^{15} - \$275$$

$$= \$0.61$$

So the total interest the deposits should have earned is

Interest on Deposits = $\$2.68 + \$2.18 + \$1.53 + \$0.61 = \$7.00$

Step D: Earnings Lost on Withdrawals

For each withdrawal determine the number of days from the date of the transaction to the last day of the period. Use the amount of each withdrawal as P and the number of days as N in Equation 8-7 to determine how much interest has been lost as a result of the withdrawal.

EXAMPLE: If $425 is withdrawn on August 29, how much interest is lost through September 30?

The day number for the withdrawal is 241, while that for September 30 is 273. Then,

$$Days\ Withdrawal = 273 - 241 = 32$$

If N is 32, then

$$INT(Withdrawal) = \$425\,(1.0001438)^{32} - \$425$$

$$= \$425 \times 1.0046 - \$425$$

$$= \$1.96\,.$$

Step E: Total Earnings

Total earnings are simply the sum of the interest on the beginning balance and deposits less the earnings lost on withdrawals.

$ _____   Interest on beginning balance

_____ + Interest on deposits

_____ − Interest lost on withdrawals

$ _____ = Total earnings for the period

EXAMPLE: If the interest on the beginning balance is $28.06, that on the deposits—$7.00, and that lost on withdrawals—$1.96, what is the total earnings?

$$Total\ Earnings = \$28.06 + \$7.00 - \$1.96$$

$$= \$33.10$$

TIME CERTIFICATES

While the methods banks use for crediting and computing interest on pass-book accounts are seldom specified, these details are usually stated more clearly for time deposits. By agreeing to keep the money in the account for a specified period of time (maturity), ranging from 90 days to over 6 years, it is possible to get a higher interest rate. The problem with these types of accounts is that the bank can refuse to allow you to withdraw any money before the time specified or, if they do allow it, there may be a substantial interest penalty. Most banks or savings institutions, however, will allow you to withdraw portions of a time deposit if you request it. While they emphasize the penalty because they do not want you to take the money out of their hands, you are often better off putting much of your savings in these higher yield accounts even if you may be forced to withdraw some portion of it before maturity.

You should check your own bank for their policy on withdrawals and interest penalties.

EXAMPLE: To illustrate the advantages of time accounts, suppose you put $2,000 in a 4-year, 7.5% account, but after 2 years you are forced to withdraw $750.

Typically, you would lose the higher interest rate on the $750. However, you may be credited with the passbook interest rate on the sum for the period it was in the account. You would still be getting 7.5% on the remaining $1,250 unless the account specifies a minimum balance above this sum. Then you lose the higher interest rate on the balance as well.

Assuming this is not the case, the interest your money would have earned in 2 years is:[3]

$$INT(7.5\%) = \$1,250 \times (1 + 0.075)^2 - \$1,250$$

plus

$$INT(5.25\%) = \$750 \times (1 + 0.004375)^{24} - \$750$$

Doing the arithmetic,

$$INT(7.5\%) = (\$1,250 \times 1.1556) - \$1,250$$

$$= 1,444.50 - 1250 = \$194.53$$

$$INT(5.25\%) = (\$750 \times 1.1105) - \$750$$

$$= \$832.88 - \$750 = \$82.88$$

[3]The first two equations here express interest compounded yearly and monthly, respectively.

So, the total interest your money has earned is

$$INT(Total) = \$194.53 + \$82.84 = \$277.37$$

How does this compare with the interest you would have earned if you had simply put the money into a 5.25% passbook account? In this case, the interest (compounded monthly) would be

$$INT(Passbook) = \$2,000 \times (1.004375)^{24} - \$2,000$$

$$= (\$2,000 \times 1.1105) - \$2,000$$

$$= \$2,221.00 - \$2,000$$

$$= \$221.00$$

Therefore you gained $56.46 by putting the money in the time deposit, even with the penalty.

This is an example of the effect that different interest rates can have on savings. Exploring this further, we will find that the bigger the savings account balance, the more important it is to maximize the interest rate.

In Graph 8-2, the final values of $1,000 invested at annual percentage rates ranging from 5.25% to 7.75% are plotted for different maturities. This clearly illustrates the effect that higher interest rates have on savings over time. While a 2½%-point spread makes only a few dollars difference in the balance in the first year; by 5 years the difference is over $100; by 15 years it is in the thousands; the divergence between them widens at an ever-increasing rate from then on.

In Graph 8-3, a different but related point is illustrated: Instead of measuring a single amount of principal with various annual percentage rates over time, it measures the net results of varying the *APR* on one year's interest on different size balances. The bottom set of solid points connected by the solid line is the interest earned by $1,000. As you can see, there is not much difference between the 5.25% and the 7.75% accounts: $54 as opposed to $80. This is quite a contrast from the principal of $30,000, illustrated in the series of circled points connected by the dotted line. In the case of this large balance, the difference in interest between a 5.25% and a 7.75% interest rate is $796.

Another way to look at this graph is in terms of the relationship between the size of the principal and the interest rate. You can see, for instance, that $20,000 will yield as much interest at 7.75% as $30,000 does at 5.25%. Similarly, $15,000 deposited at 7.5% has a return slightly greater than $20,000 at 5.25%.

From this it is clear that the greater your savings the more important it is to pay attention to a fraction of a percent difference in interest rates. And, as we also determined, the longer you intend to maintain an account, the more important the interest rates become.

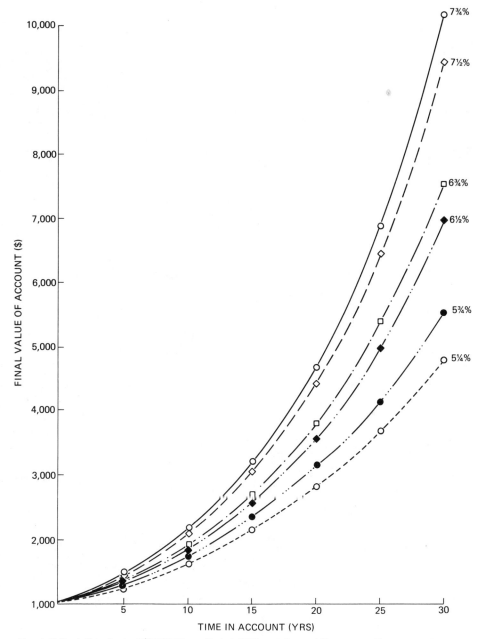

Graph 8-2 A Principal of $1000 Deposited at Different Annual Percentage Rates

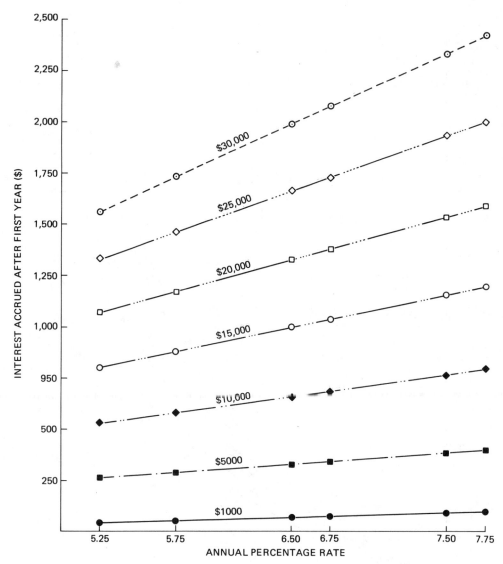

Graph 8-3 Effect of Annual Percentage Rate on Interest Earned by Different Amounts of Principal

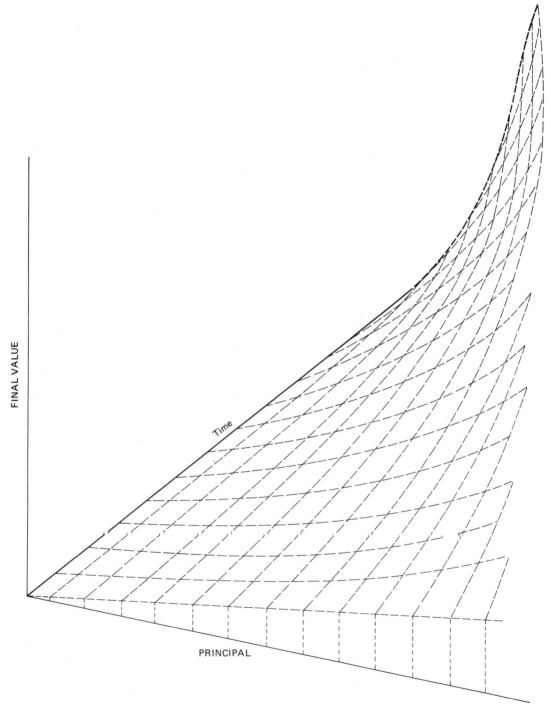

Graph 8-4 Time, Principal, and Final Value of Compounded Savings Account

Graph 8-4 pictures the combined effects of time and principal on the final value of a savings account. The steeper the slope of the 3-dimensional surface, the greater the effect of increasing or decreasing the interest rate. The higher you climb *this* "mountain," the *faster* you go.

This graph illustrates the remarkable financial progress that can be made if even extremely small amounts of money are deposited in a savings account each month and allowed to grow.

TIME REQUIRED FOR A PRINCIPAL TO GROW TO A GIVEN AMOUNT

In certain circumstances, you may want to know how long it will take for an account to grow to a specific value. This can be done with the following formula:

$$N = \frac{\log\left(\dfrac{FV}{P}\right)}{\log (1 + i)} \qquad \text{(Equation 8-8)}$$

EXAMPLE: Janet has $15,000 in a 4-year certificate, with a 7.25% interest rate, compounded annually. She would like to know how long it will take for the account to build up to $30,000.

$P = \$15,000$; $FV = \$30,000$; and $i = 0.0725$; then,

$$N = \frac{\log\left(\dfrac{\$30,000}{\$15,000}\right)}{\log (1 + 0.0725)}$$

$$= \frac{\log 2}{\log 1.0725}$$

Turning to the log tables, we find

$$\log 2 = 0.30103$$

$$\log 1.0725 = 0.030397$$

and

$$N = \frac{0.30103}{0.030397}$$

$$= 9.9032799 \cong 10$$

Since each period is 1 year long, it will take the account 10 years to reach $30,000.

INTEREST RATE, GIVEN PRINCIPAL, COMPOUNDING PERIOD, AND FINAL VALUE

There is another equation that is occasionally handy and that allows you to determine the periodic interest rate when you know the final value, principal, and the number of compounding periods. This is a good way to check the bank's calculation of the balance in your savings account.

$$i = \left(\frac{FV}{P} \right)^{\frac{1}{N}} - 1 \qquad \text{(Equation 8-9)}$$

This equation only applies for periods without withdrawals.

EXAMPLE: Paul put $4,000 into a 5.75%, 3-month-certificate account some time ago. Recently, he got a statement from the savings and loan, indicating that, for the current three-month period, the beginning balance in the account was $4,050.79, that the account had earned $58.66, and that the ending balance was $4,109.45. He wants to check these figures.

For this account, i should be 0.0575/4 = 0.014375 for quarterly compounding of interest. If FV = $4,109.45, P = $4,050.79, and N = 1, then

$$i = \left(\frac{4,109.45}{4,050.79} \right)^{\frac{1}{1}} - 1$$

Since a number taken to the first power equals itself, then

$$i = \frac{4,109.45}{4,050.79} - 1$$

$$= 1.01448113 - 1$$

$$= 0.01448$$

This is a slightly higher interest rate than Paul had expected. Turning to the explanation of the account, he discovers that it is compounded daily instead of quarterly. Redoing the calculation gives

$$i = \left(\frac{4,109.45}{4,050.79} \right)^{\frac{1}{90}} - 1$$

$$= (1.0144811)^{0.01111111} - 1$$

$$= 1.0002 - 1 = 0.0002$$

This is the daily periodic interest rate which, going back to the 5¾% interest rate, should be about

$$i = \frac{0.0575}{360} = 0.00015972 \text{ or } 0.0002$$

Thus, the interest rate agrees within the uncertainties of the calculation.

In Appendix 4 you will find a Savings Account Analysis Form. This is designed to help you compare different lenders. It gives you a single form on which you can compile information such as the *APR*, compounding periods, crediting periods, computing methods, grace days, and penalties, allowing you to compare each lender or type of account.

You will have to ask for much of this information since it is not in any of the banks' and savings institutions' brochures. Take a photocopy of the form with you into the bank, so that you can fill in all the important information explained in the previous pages.

PERIODIC SAVINGS

Periodic savings can be expressed graphically with a time line

where *PMT* stands for the amount of the payment, N is the number of payment periods, and FV is the final value of the account.

In this case, the formula for the final value of such a savings account is

$$FV = \frac{PMT}{i} \left[(1 + i)^{N+1} - (1 + i) \right] \qquad \text{(Equation 8-10)}$$

Here the periodic interest rate, i, is

$$i = \frac{APR}{100 \times n_{pmt}} \qquad \text{(Equation 8-11)}$$

where n_{pmt} is the number of payment periods per annum.[4]

To begin with, let us take a ridiculous, almost trivial case: a person who saves a dime a day. This is $3 per month. Now, let's say he puts this in a passbook savings account at 5.25%. How much does he have in the account after 5 years, 10 years, 15 years, 20 years?

[4]This assumes that the payment periods are as frequent as or less frequent than the compounding periods. If the compounding period is less frequent, you should use the compounding period to determine *PMT* and n_{pmt}. You must also use the total amount of money paid in per compounding period as *PMT*. If you deposit money once a month but the compounding period is quarterly, then using $n_{pmt} = 4$ and *PMT* equal to 3 times your monthly payment will give the most accurate answer.

Using PMT = $3, N = number of months, and $i = 5.25/(100 \times 12)$ = 0.004375:

$$FV \text{ (5 yrs)} = \frac{\$3}{0.004375} [(1 + 0.004375)^{60+1} - (1 + 0.004375)]$$

$$= \$685.71429 \times 0.30073$$

$$= \$206.21$$

Similarly,

$$FV \text{ (10 yrs)} = \$685.71429 [(1.004375)^{120+1} - 1.004375]$$

$$= \$474.19$$

and,

$$FV \text{ (15 yrs)} = \$685.71429 [(1.004375)^{180+1} - 1.004375]$$

$$= \$822.39$$

and finally,

$$FV \text{ (20 yrs)} = \$685.71429 [(1.004375)^{240+1} - 1.004375]$$

$$= \$1,274.90$$

Now, what happens if we increase this a hundredfold to $300 per month and put it in a time deposit earning 7.5% annually? This type of certificate is generally compounded once per year, so we will add $3,600 annually. Thus, PMT = $3,600, N = 1 per year, and $i = 0.075$. Now,

$$FV \text{ (5 yrs)} = \frac{\$3600}{0.075} [(1 + 0.075)^{5+1} - (1 + 0.075)]$$

$$= \$48,000 \times 0.468300000$$

$$= \$22,478.40$$

$$FV \text{ (10 yrs)} = \$48,000 [(1.075)^{10+1} - 1.075]$$

$$= \$48,000 \times 1.14060$$

$$= \$54,748.80$$

$$FV \text{ (15 yrs)} = \$48,000 [(1.075)^{15+1} - 1.075]$$

$$= \$48,000 \times 2.1058$$

$$= \$101,078.40$$

$$FV\ (20\text{ yrs}) = \$48{,}000\ [(1.075)^{20+1} - 1.075]$$

$$= \$48{,}000 \times 3.4915$$

$$= \$167{,}592.00$$

As you can see, a hundredfold increase in the amount saved multiplies into more than a one-hundred-thousandfold increase in the value of the savings after 20 years. True, part of this is because of the higher interest rate assumed for the $300 per month saver. But this is fairly realistic. Most time deposits have minimum balances and, in general, the larger the sum you put into an account, the higher the interest rate you can command.

In many cases you will want to know how much money to put aside monthly or yearly to achieve a specific financial goal: children's education, a new automobile, or an appliance. Although largely passé, saving to buy major purchases rather than buying them on time is the least expensive way to finance.

The following equation allows you to calculate the size of the periodic payments, PMT, required to achieve a given sum, FV, with a specified periodic interest rate, i, in a set number of periods, N:

$$PMT = \frac{FV \times i}{(1 + i)^{N+1} - (1 + i)} \qquad \textbf{(Equation 8-12)}$$

EXAMPLE: Mike Jefferson's old car is on its last legs. He figures it will continue to run another year. He then intends to buy a second-hand replacement for about $2,500. If he puts the money in a 5½% passbook account, how much should he deduct from his weekly paycheck to save up this amount?

In this case $FV = \$2{,}500$. Assuming weekly compounding, $i = 0.055/52 = 0.0010577$ and $N = 52$. Thus,

$$PMT = \frac{\$2{,}500 \times 0.0010577}{(1.0010577)^{52+1} - 1.0010577}$$

$$= \frac{\$2.6442308}{0.0056542}$$

$$= \$46.77$$

Sometimes a person may know about how much they can afford to save. The question is how long it will take to save a certain sum. This can be calculated using the following equation.

$$N = \frac{\log\left[\dfrac{FV \times i}{PMT} + (1 + i)\right]}{\log (1 + i)} - 1 \qquad \textbf{(Equation 8-13)}$$

where FV, i, PMT, and N are as previously defined.

EXAMPLE: Jane Rando wants to buy an upright piano that costs $2,700. If she can put $75 per month toward the purchase, and if she deposits it in a 5¾% account, how long will it take her to save the money?

Here $n_{pmt} = 12$, since the payments are monthly. N is the number of months. In addition, $i = 0.0575/12 = 0.00479167$; $FV = \$2,700$; and $PMT = \$75$.

$$N = \frac{\log\left[\dfrac{\$2,700 \times 0.00479167}{\$75} + 1.00479167\right]}{\log 1.00479167} - 1$$

$$= \frac{\log 1.1772917}{\log 1.00479167} - 1$$

$$= \frac{0.07088}{0.00207} - 1$$

$$= 34.242 - 1 = 33 \text{ months}$$

Therefore, it will take Janet 33/12 = 2.75 years to save the money at this rate.

INFLATION AND SAVINGS

Balanced against the power of compound interest to multiply your money, however, are the effects of inflation. Inflation is a process very similar to compounding except that it works against you. At an annual inflation rate of 6%, in the year 2,000 it will take a salary of $51,000 to have the buying power equivalent to $15,000 in 1979. Similarly, a $500 television set would cost $1,700; a $4,000 auto—$13,600; a $35,000 house—$119,000; and $50 worth of groceries—$170. Despite the inflation that has occurred in the last decade, the discretionary income of many Americans has risen steadily. However, for the increasing number of retirees with fixed incomes, the shrinking dollar has ominous implications. It also has substantial effects on the value of savings.

As is discussed in Chapter 7, one way to take inflation into account is by looking at financial transactions that extend over a significant period of time in constant-value dollars. The value in current dollars of a future sum of money is given by the following

$$CV(A) = FV(B)(1 + r_{av})^{-T}$$

where $CV(A)$ is the value in year-A dollars, $FV(B)$ is the amount in year B dollars, r_{av} is the average annual inflation rate, and $T = $ Year $B - $ Year A. This equation can also take the form:

$$FV(B) = CV(A)(1 + r_{av})^T \qquad \text{(Equation 8-14)}$$

In this way equivalent future costs can be projected from current costs.

EXAMPLE: What is the value of $100,000 in 1995 expressed as 1979 dollars if the inflation rate is 6% per year?

Year A = 1979. Year B = 1995. Thus, T = 1995 − 1979 = 16 years. Average inflation, r_{av}, is 0.06. $FV(1995)$ = $100,000. Therefore,

$$CV(1979) = \$100{,}000 \, (1.06)^{-16}$$

$$= \$100{,}000 \times 0.39365$$

$$= \$39{,}365$$

EXAMPLE: A Mercury Cougar sells for about $5,000 in 1978. If inflation continues at 8% annually for the next decade, what is the equivalent 1988 price for this car?

In this case, Year A = 1978 and Year B = 1988, thus, T = 10 years, $CV(1978)$ = $5,000 and r_{av} = 0.08.

$$FV(1988) = \$5{,}000 \, (1.08)^{10}$$

$$= \$5{,}000 \times 2.1589$$

$$= \$10{,}795$$

(Multiplying the number 2.1589 by 100 gives the percent increase in prices from 1978 to 1988 with 8% annual inflation: 215.9%.)

With this foundation, we can now look at the effect that inflation has on savings. We can do this by combining Equations 8-2 and 8-14 to determine the constant value of money invested in savings. This will give the future value of money invested in a savings account in present-day dollars. First, we have to define the periodic inflation rate, r_p. This is equivalent to the periodic interest rate. If the account is compounded daily, then this will be the daily inflation rate; if it is compounded monthly, it is the monthly inflation rate. Strictly speaking,

$$r_p = (1 + r_{av})^{\frac{1}{n}} - 1 \qquad \textbf{(Equation 8-15)}$$

where n is the number of compounding periods per year. However, the difference between this expression and

$$r_p \cong \frac{r_{av}}{n} \qquad \textbf{(Equation 8-16)}$$

is extremely small. Since inflation is by nature an imprecise quantity, we may as well use the simpler expression for r_p.

EXAMPLE: Given an annual inflation rate of 6%, what is the monthly inflation rate calculated by the exact and approximate formulas (Equations 10-15 and 10-16, respectively)?

For the precise formula:

$$r_p = (1 + 0.06)^{\frac{1}{12}} - 1$$

$$= 1.0049 - 1 = 0.0049$$

For the approximate formula:

$$r_p = \frac{0.06}{12} = 0.0050$$

How great a difference is this annually? To calculate this, you must know that

$$r_{av} = (1 + r_p)^n - 1 \qquad \textbf{(Equation 8-17)}$$

For $r_p = 0.0049$

$$r_{av} = (1.0049)^{12} - 1$$

$$= 0.0604$$

(The 0.0004 is an error resulting from use of the log tables.) For $r_p = 0.005$

$$r_{av} = (1.0050)^{12} - 1$$

$$= 0.0617$$

As you can see, using $r_p = 0.005$ is actually equivalent to a 6.2% annual inflation rate. Because variations in the inflation rate of a few tenths of a percent are of doubtful significance, this approximation is acceptable.

Now that we have defined r_p, we can alter the compound interest equation to account for inflation,

$$CV(A) = P\left(\frac{1 + i}{1 + r_p}\right)^N \qquad \textbf{(Equation 8-18)}$$

where $CV(A)$ is the value of the balance in the account in Year A dollars, P is the principal in the account in Year A, and the remaining variables are as previously defined.

EXAMPLE: If \$5,000 is deposited into a 6.5% annual interest certificate compounded quarterly and the inflation rate is averaging 6% per year, what is the real value[5] of the balance of the account after 5 years? After 10 years? After 15 years?

First we must calculate r_p and i. Since r_{av} is 0.06,

$$r_p = \frac{6}{4 \times 100} = 0.15$$

$$i = \frac{6.5}{4 \times 100} = 0.016250$$

After the fifth year,

$$CV = \$5,000 \left(\frac{1.016250}{1.015000}\right)^{4 \times 5}$$

$$= \$5,000 \times 1.0249$$

$$= \$5,124.50$$

For the tenth year,

$$CV = \$5,000 \left(\frac{1.016250}{1.015000}\right)^{40}$$

$$= \$5,252.50$$

And finally,

$$CV = \$5,000 \times 1.0012315360$$

$$= \$5,383.50$$

So, in this case, the purchasing value of the money in the account has increased by only 5% in 15 years, about 1/3% per year.

EXAMPLE: What is the constant-dollar value of the account in the previous example, if the account is earning 8% annual interest?

In this case, the only change would be in i, which becomes .08/4 = 0.02. After 5 years,

$$CV = \$5,000 \left(\frac{1.02000}{1.01500}\right)^{20}$$

$$= \$5,516.50$$

---

[5]The term *real value* will be used as shorthand for constant-value dollars.

After 10 years,

$$CV = \$5{,}000 \times 1.0049261^{40}$$

$$= \$6{,}086.00$$

After 15 years,

$$PV = \$5{,}000 \times 1.0049261^{60}$$

$$= \$6{,}714.50$$

What happens when the interest rate and the inflation rate are the same? To determine this, let us set $i = r_p$ into Equation 8-18. Then,

$$CV = P\left(\frac{1+i}{1+r_p}\right)^N$$

$$= P\left(\frac{1+i}{1+i}\right)^N$$

$$= P(1)^N = P$$

When the interest rate and inflation rate are equal, the purchasing power of a savings account is static. It follows, then, that when the interest rates are lower than general inflation, the value of an account is decreasing; and when the interest rate is higher than inflation, the value is growing. How fast a savings account increases or decreases in value depends on the difference between the interest and inflation rates. Table 8-1 lists the value of a $10,000 savings account with various interest rates, inflation rates, and maturities. Its daunting array of numbers contains some interesting information about the relationship between inflation and interest rates.

Compare the growth of a savings account having a 2% interest rate and zero inflation with one having a 4% interest rate and 2% inflation. The values are within $10 of each other. Now compare these values with the balance when the interest rate is 6% and inflation 4%. It, too, is very close to the others. In all these cases the difference between the interest rate and inflation rate are the same: 2%. If you compare other rows in Table 8-1, in which the difference between the interest and inflation rates is the same, you will find that the value of the account increases at approximately the same rate. Thus, the difference between the inflation rate and the interest rate determines how the purchasing power of the money in a savings account increases or decreases.

This fact is illustrated in Graph 8-5. The 11 curves fanning out from $10,000 at 0 years represent the true value of the money in the account over 20 years for differences in interest and inflation ranging from +10% to −10%.

When the difference is 0, the value of the account remains constant. When the inflation rate is more than the interest rate, the value of the account drops off rapidly at first, but as time marches on the rate of decrease in value gradually slows down. When the interest rate is higher than the inflation rate, on the other hand, the true value of the account grows at an ever-increasing rate.

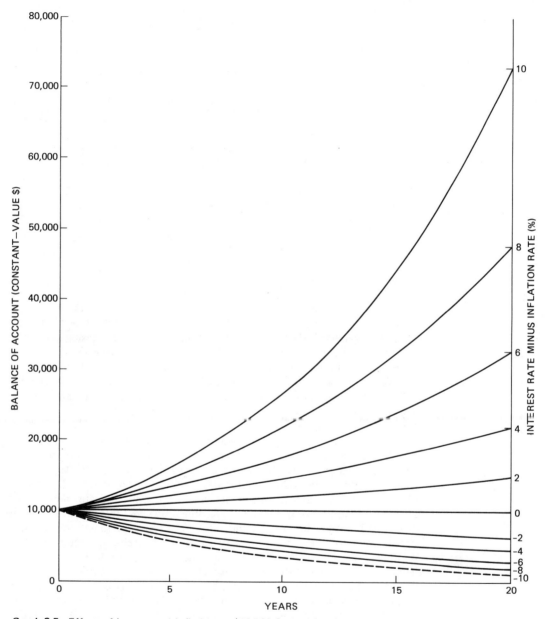

Graph 8-5 Effects of Interest and Inflation on $10,000 Savings Account

Table 8-1 Effects of Interest and Inflation Rate on a $10,000 Savings Account with Monthly Compounding

INTEREST RATE (%)	INFLATION RATE (%)	BALANCE IN CONSTANT-VALUE DOLLARS			
		5 Years	10 Years	15 Years	20 Years
2	0	11,051	12,212	13,495	14,913
	2	10,000	10,000	10,000	10,000
	4	9,051	8,191	7,414	6,710
	6	8,193	6,712	5,499	4,505
	8	7,417	5,502	4,081	3,027
	10	6,716	4,511	3,030	2,035
4	0	12,210	14,908	18,203	22,226
	2	11,048	12,207	13,488	14,903
	4	10,000	10,000	10,000	10,000
	6	9,052	8,194	7,417	6,714
	8	8,195	6,717	5,505	4,511
	10	7,421	5,507	4,087	3,033
6	0	13,489	18,194	24,541	33,102
	2	12,206	14,898	18,185	22,185
	4	11,047	12,204	13,482	14,894
	6	10,000	10,000	10,000	10,000
	8	9,054	8,197	7,421	6,719
	10	8,198	6,721	5,510	4,517
8	0	14,989	22,196	33,069	49,268
	2	13,482	18,176	24,504	33,036
	4	12,202	14,889	18,167	22,167
	6	11,045	12,200	13,475	14,884
	8	10,000	10,000	10,000	10,000
	10	9,055	8,200	7,425	6,723
10	0	16,453	27,070	44,539	73,280
	2	14,889	22,167	33,004	49,138
	4	13,475	18,158	24,468	32,970
	6	12,198	14,879	18,149	22,138
	8	11,043	12,196	13,468	14,874
	10	10,000	10,000	10,000	10,000

INFLATION AND PERIODIC SAVINGS

It is also possible to determine the effect of inflation on periodic savings. For simplicity, we will assume that the compounding period is the same as the payment period. For monthly payments, monthly compounding is assumed; for quarterly payments, quarterly compounding is assumed. As we have seen, the difference in interest compounded monthly, daily, and continuously is very small, thus if the payment period is once a month, and compounding is more frequent, this assumption will not introduce large errors.

If p is the number of payment periods per year, then we will define i, r_p, and N as

$$i = \left(\frac{APR}{100 \times p}\right)$$

(Equation 8-19)

$$r_p = \left(\frac{R}{100 \times p}\right)$$

(Equation 8-20)

$$N = p \times T$$

(Equation 8-21)

where APR is the Annual Percentage Rate, R is the annual inflation rate, and T is the time in years. Further, it is convenient to define another quantity, a, as

$$a = \frac{i - r_p}{1 + r_p}$$

(Equation 8-22)

although this quantity, a, has no intrinsic meaning, since the quotient of $i - r_p$ and $1 + r_p$ is repeated several times in the equation for the constant value of a periodic savings account, it is convenient to give it as a symbol.

Depending on the value of a, there are two different formulas for calculating the present true value of such an account. If a is 0 ($APR = R$),

$$CV(A) = PMT \times N$$

(Equation 8-23)

If a is not equal to 0,

$$CV(A) = PMT\left[\frac{(a + 1)^{N+1} - a - 1}{a}\right]$$

(Equation 8-24)

EXAMPLE: Jack and Eleanor Spratt have decided to put $50 per month for the education of their newborn baby into a long-term account that commands 8% annual interest. If they are able to continue with this savings plan, and if inflation averages 6% annually, what will be the purchasing power of this account after 18 years?

Because this is a monthly payment plan, p = 12 and PMT = $50. The APR is 8%, R is 6%, and T = 18 years. Thus,

$$i = \frac{8}{100 \times 12} = 0.00666667$$

$$r_p = \frac{6}{100 \times 12} = 0.00500000$$

$$N = 12 \times 18 = 216$$

and

$$a = \frac{i - r_p}{1 + r_p} = \frac{0.0066667 - 0.00500000}{1 + 0.00500000}$$

$$= 0.00165838$$

Since *a* is not equal to 0,

$$CV(A) = \$50 \left[\frac{1.0016583^{217} - 1.0016583}{0.0016583} \right]$$

$$= \$50 \left(\frac{0.43103482}{0.0016583} \right)$$

$$= \$50 \times 259.91348$$

$$\$12,995.67$$

The actual amount of money in the account after 18 years will be $24,165, but due to inflation this money only has the purchasing power of $13,000 in constant-value dollars of the year the account was set up.

If the inflation during this period is 8%, instead of 6%, what will the value of the educational account be?

In this case, $r_p = i = 0.0005$, so $a = 0$. Therefore,

$$CV(A) = PMT \times N = \$50 \times 216 = \$10,800$$

It is obvious from comparing the equations for interest and inflation on normal and periodic savings accounts that the situation with the latter is somewhat more complicated. Nevertheless, the difference between interest and inflation rates still determines the growth in purchasing power of the periodic savings account, as can be seen by inspecting Table 8-2. This table gives the balance in constant-value dollars of a $100 per month periodic savings account having interest and inflation rates varying from 0% to 10%. Here, too, the balances computed when there is no difference between the interest and inflation rates are within $100 of each other.

Graph 8-6 illustrates the balance of a periodic savings account as a function of time and the difference between *APR* and *R*, similar to that of a straight savings account (see Graph 8-5). The series of curves indicates the greatest growth when the difference between interest and inflation is positive and the least growth when the difference is negative.

There are some important differences between the plots in Graphs 8-5 and 8-6. Unlike the one time deposit, which declines in real value whenever the interest rate is lower than the inflation rate, periodic savings continues to grow in constant value dollars even when the inflation rate far outstrips the interest rate. In the latter case, it is a matter of how fast the value of the account grows. Also, when the inflation rate is greater than the interest rate, the constant value dollar balance of an account simply gets closer and closer to a limit which cannot be exceeded. So, when this is the case you could save forever and the value of your account would only grow to a certain, finite limit.

This limit is expressed mathematically as:

$$LIM_S = -\left(\frac{a + 1}{a} \right) PMT \qquad \textbf{(Equation 8-25)}$$

Table 8-2 Effects of Interest and Inflation Rates on a $100-Per-Month Periodic Savings Account

INTEREST RATE (%)	INFLATION RATE (%)	BALANCE IN CONSTANT-VALUE DOLLARS			
		5 Years	10 Years	15 Years	20 Years
0	0	6,000	12,000	18,000	24,000
	2	5,705	10,868	15,540	19,767
	4	5,430	9,877	13,519	16,502
	6	5,173	9,007	11,850	13,958
	8	4,932	8,242	10,464	11,955
	10	4,707	7,567	9,306	10,362
2	0	6,315	13,294	21,006	29,529
	2	6,000	12,000	18,000	24,000
	4	5,706	10,870	15,544	19,774
	6	5,431	9,880	13,525	16,512
	8	5,174	9,011	11,858	13,969
	10	4,933	8,247	10,472	11,967
4	0	6,652	14,774	24,691	36,800
	2	6,315	13,292	21,001	29,518
	4	6,000	12,000	18,000	24,000
	6	5,706	10,871	15,547	19,780
	8	5,432	9,883	13,531	16,521
	10	5,175	9,015	11,865	13,981
6	0	7,012	16,470	29,227	46,435
	2	6,651	14,769	24,678	36,772
	4	6,314	13,289	20,995	29,508
	6	6,000	12,000	18,000	24,000
	8	5,707	10,873	15,551	19,788
	10	5,433	9,886	13,537	16,531
8	0	7,397	18,417	34,835	59,295
	2	7,010	16,461	29,202	46,380
	4	6,650	14,764	24,664	36,744
	6	6,314	13,287	20,990	24,497
	8	6,000	12,000	18,000	24,000
	10	5,707	10,875	15,555	19,792
10	0	7,808	20,655	41,792	76,570
	2	7,394	18,403	34,793	59,196
	4	7,008	16,452	29,177	46,325
	6	6,649	14,758	24,651	36,717
	8	6,313	13,285	20,984	29,487
	10	6,000	12,000	18,000	24,000

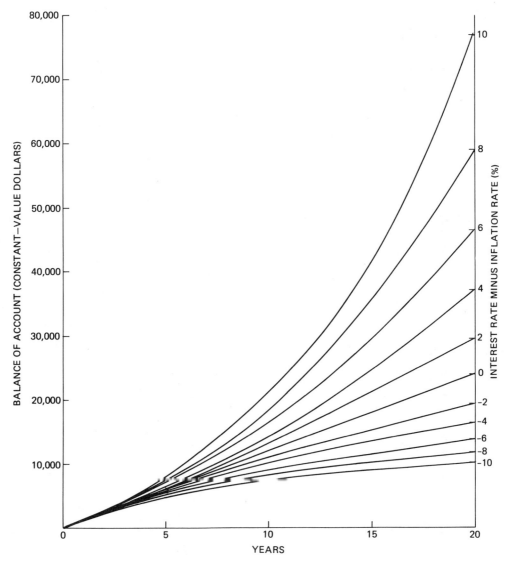

Graph 8-6 Effects of Interest and Inflation on Periodic Savings Account ($100 Per Month)

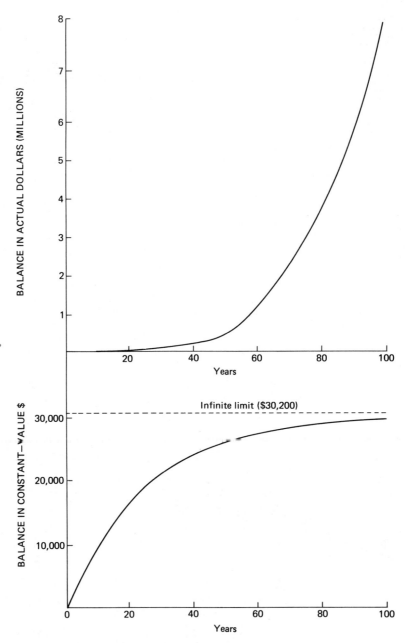

Graph 8-7 Growth of $100-per-month Periodic Savings Account in Actual and Constant-Value Dollars (Apr+ 5%; R = 10%)

EXAMPLE: If the inflation rate is 10% and the highest savings rate you can obtain is 6%, what is the constant-value limit on a periodic savings plan of $100 per month?

$$i = \frac{6}{100 \times 12} = 0.005$$

$$r_p = \frac{10}{100 \times 12} = 0.00833333$$

consequently,

$$a = \frac{0.005 - 0.00833333}{1 + 0.00833333} = -0.00330578$$

so the

$$LIM_S = -\left[\frac{1 - 0.00330578}{-0.00330578}\right] \times 100$$

$$= 301.50003 \times \$100$$

$$= \$30,150$$

Under conditions of 5% interest and 10% inflation, then, the highest value that the balance of a periodic savings plan of $100 per month can approach is $30,150 (in constant-value dollars).

Graph 8-7 illustrates dramatically how this constant-value-dollar limit works. The curve at the top traces the growth of a $100-per-month savings plan over a century. As you can see, the balance grows rapidly, and after 100 years it reaches almost $8 million. But while the money in the account is growing, its purchasing power is dropping by 10% per year, illustrated by the totally different curve plotted at the bottom of the graph. This curve grows fairly rapidly for the first 25 years; it then begins to gradually level off. By the end of the next 75 years, the purchasing power of the account is only 50% above its value after the first 25 years. If the plot were extended to 1,000 years or to 1 million years, the curve would simply creep closer and closer to the infinite limit, but never reach or surpass it.

The growth limit, as well as the true growth of periodic accounts is also related to the difference between the interest and inflation rates. This fact is illustrated by Table 8-3 on the following page.

When the inflation rate is 1% higher than the interest rate, $1 per month will get you less than $600 (in constant-value dollars). When the inflation rate is 9% higher than the interest rate, the growth of the same monthly investment is limited to $67.

You can use Table 8-3 to estimate the theoretical limit on the purchasing power of any monthly periodic savings account. When the inflation rate

Table 8-3 Limit on Periodic Savings

APR − R (%)	Limit on $1-per-Month Periodic Savings (CONSTANT-VALUE DOLLARS)
−1	$600
−2	300
−3	200
−4	150
−5	120
−6	100
−7	86
−8	75
−9	67

exceeds the interest rate, take the difference between the interest and infla-tion rates, find the corresponding $1-per-month limit, and multiply this times the dollar-per-month amount of the particular savings plan.

EXAMPLE: What is the limit on a $50-per-month periodic savings plan if the inflation rate is 8% per year and the interest rate is 6%?

$$APR - R = 6\% - 8\% = -2\%$$

From Table 8-3 the −2% limit for $1 is 300. So the limit on the $50-per-month savings balance is

$$Savings\ Limit = \$50 \times 300$$

$$= \$15,000$$

SAVINGS
WITH A BUSINESS-ANALYST CALCULATOR

Business-analyst calculators take to the problems in this chapter like a duck to water, because they are specifically designed for them. In most cases, the instruction book for the calculator will explain exactly how your machine handles these computations.

Simple Interest Some business-analyst models calculate simple interest di-rectly: enter the days in $\boxed{n}$, the *APR* in $\boxed{i}$, and the principal in $\boxed{PV}$, a special key (sometimes indicated by $\boxed{INT}$) computes simple interest. In other models you must determine simple interest as a special case of com-pound interest where $N = 1$. If the number of days is D, then the interest rate you enter in $\boxed{i}$ is $APR \times D/360$. Then keying $\boxed{PMT}$ will give you the amount of principal plus interest that must be payed at the end of the period.

EXAMPLE: You wish to borrow $1,500 for 90 days. The annual interest rate is 16%. How much simple interest must you pay for the privilege?

To solve this with a calculator that does not have a simple interest function, enter 1 into $\boxed{n}$ and $1,500 into $\boxed{PV}$. In $\boxed{i}$ you enter 16 X 90/360 = 4.

Then keying $\boxed{PMT}$ will yield $1,560. Thus, the simple interest you would pay is $1,560 − $1,500 = $60.

Compound Interest and Annuities These are the primary financial functions in business-analyst models. Generally, they are calculated using the following 5 keys:

$$\boxed{n} \qquad \boxed{i} \qquad \boxed{PMT} \qquad \boxed{PV} \qquad \boxed{FV}$$

where *n* is the number of compounding periods, *i* is the interest (as a percentage) per period, *PMT* is the periodic payment if any, *PV* is the principal, and *FV* is the future value. The keys on your calculator may be in a different order.

EXAMPLE: Maude has $7,654.30 in a savings account which offers 6.5%, compounded 360 days per year. What will be her balance 5 years from now?

In this case, *PV* = $7,654.30, *n* = 5 X 360 = 1,800, and

$$i = \frac{6.5}{360} = 0.0180556$$

Thus, *FV*, the future balance, is $10,593.47.

EXAMPLE: Henry Weaver is self-employed and is putting $100 a month into a tax-deferred annuity. If the annuity has an *APR* of 8% and is compounded monthly, how much will Henry get after 25 years?

Here *PV* = 0, and *PMT* = $100. The periodic interest rate, *i*, is 8/12 = 0.66666667, and *n* = 12 X 25 = 300. Keying $\boxed{FV}$ gives $95,102.63.

Passbook Savings Account Checking on your local savings and loan is considerably easier with a financial calculator, than it is with a 4-function calculator. Take a typical page of a passbook account bank statement.

DATE	WITHDRAWAL	INTEREST	ADDITIONS	BALANCE
JUL 12			2,000.00	2,200.00
JUL 18			832.23	2,832.23
SEP 26		32.08		2,864.31
OCT 15			703.21	3,567.52
DEC 13	500.00			3,067.52
DEC 26		44.36		3,111.88

If your calculator has a day/date function, you can use it to determine the number of days between the subsequent entries. If not, you can use the day number calendar in Appendix 4.

The passbook account in the table is advertised at a 5.5 *APR*, with the daily interest rate determined on the basis of a 360-day year, but compounded 365 days per year. This means that the periodic interest rate is 5.5/360 = 0.01527778. Enter this in $\boxed{i}$. Since the first $\boxed{PV}$ = $2,000,[6] and this remains for 5 days, $\boxed{n}$ = 5. FV = $2,001.53. To this, add a deposit of $832.23. The sum of $2,833.76 becomes the new $\boxed{PV}$. This balance remains for 70 days, giving an $\boxed{FV}$ of $2,864.22. This is $0.09 lower than the bank's computation, suggesting that the interest is computed by the bank in a slightly different manner than advertised.

The balance of $2,864.31 remains for $\boxed{n}$ = 19 days, giving an $\boxed{FV}$ of $2,872.64. The deposit of $703.21 increases the balance to $3,575.85. It stays in the account for $\boxed{n}$ = 59 days. $\boxed{FV}$ is now $3,608.22. The balance is decreased to $3,108.22 by a $500 withdrawal. The interest is credited 13 days later: $\boxed{FV}$ is $3,114.40 while the balance is $3,111.88. This suggests that the savings and loan may have made a $2.52 error.

Time Required for a Principal to Grow to a Specified Amount This is another computation made extremely easy with the advanced calculator. Entering the principal in $\boxed{PV}$, the future value of the account desired into $\boxed{FV}$, and the interest rate per period into $\boxed{i}$, the number of periods required to achieve *FV* is calculated by executing $\boxed{n}$.

EXAMPLE: Janet has $15,000 in a 7.25%, 4-year certificate, compounded annually. She would like to know how long it will take for the account to double. In this case $\boxed{PV}$ = $15,000, $\boxed{i}$ = 7.25, and FV = $30,000. Then $\boxed{n}$ = 9.9031817 years.

Interest Rate, Given Principal, Period, and Final Value If you wish to know what interest rate you must have for a savings account or investment to grow to a specified value in a given amount of time, it is only necessary to enter the present value, the desired future value, and the number of periods. Executing $\boxed{i}$ will give the interest rate.

EXAMPLE: In previous example, Janet would like to know what annual interest rate is necessary to make her money grow to $40,000 in 10 years, and whether there is much difference between annual and monthly compounding.

---

[6]This simplified notation is used throughout. In this case, $\boxed{PV}$ = $2,000 means: (a) *PV* = $2,000, *and* (b) $2,000 is to be entered into the key marked $\boxed{PV}$.

For annual compounding, since $\boxed{PV}$ = \$15,000, $\boxed{FV}$ = \$40,000, and $\boxed{n}$ = 10, then $\boxed{i}$ = 10.305425%.

For monthly compounding, $\boxed{PV}$ and $\boxed{FV}$ remain the same but $\boxed{n}$ = 120. In this case $\boxed{i}$ computes as 0.8207071%, and the annual percentage rate is 12 X 0.8207071 = 9.8484852.

Periodic Savings The equations for periodic savings are substantially more complicated than those for straight compounding. However, they are no more difficult to solve using the business-analyst calculator. Here, the periodic savings amount is entered into the $\boxed{PMT}$ key. The periodic interest rate for the period between payments is entered into $\boxed{i}$. Then keying in various numbers of periods in $\boxed{n}$ and executing the $\boxed{FV}$ key gives the balance of the account.

The business-analyst calculator can also handle an account that starts with a given prinicpal and to which periodic payments are then made. In this case, enter the principal into $\boxed{PV}$.

EXAMPLE: Lester is thinking about signing up for a tax-deferred annuity at the non-profit company where he works. The company will match \$1 for every \$2 he puts in. Lester thinks he can manage \$25 a month. If the *APR* on the account is 7.25%, what will this annuity amount to in 10, 15, and 20 years?

Here $\boxed{PV}$ = 0, and $\boxed{PMT}$ = \$25 + (1/2 X \$25) = \$37.50. The periodic interest rate, $\boxed{i}$, = 7.25/12 = 0.60416667.

When n = 120, FV = \$6,580.75.
When n = 180, FV = \$12,147.87.
When n = 240, FV = \$20,138.63.

Inflation and Savings Unfortunately, calculator manufacturers have not yet caught up with the realities of inflation: Even advanced-model calculators are not set up to take inflation explicitly into account. Fortunately, the mathematical similarity between inflation and compounding makes it possible to handle inflation rather simply.

To compute inflationary effects, we need first to define a surrogate interest rate, A, which takes it into account.

$$A = \frac{I_p - R_p}{100 + R_p} \times 100$$

(Equation 8-26)

where I_p is the periodic interest rate (as a percentage) and R_p is the periodic inflation rate (as a percentage). A is a percentage also because this is the form which most calculators employ. I_p and R_p must apply for the same period. For monthly compounding, as an example, $I_p = APR/12$ and $R_p = R/12$.

EXAMPLE: What is the purchasing power of a savings account with a principal of $10,000 after 5 years if the interest rate is 8¾%, compounded quarterly, and inflation averages 9% per year?

First, we must deteremine A. $I_p = 8.75/4 = 2.1875$. $R_p = 9/4 = 2.25$. Then,

$$A = \frac{2.1875 - 2.25}{100 + 2.25} \times 100 = -0.06112469$$

Enter A into $\boxed{i}$, $10,000 into $\boxed{PV}$, and $5 \times 4 = 20$ into $\boxed{n}$. Then, determining the future value (in constant-value dollars) with $\boxed{FV}$ yields $9,878.46. Thus, the purchasing power of the money in the account has slightly decreased.

EXAMPLE: Using the annual interest rate and inflation rate from the previous example, what is the annual growth (in constant-value dollars) of a periodic savings account that begins with $1,000 and adds $50 per month?

Because the compounding period here is monthly rather than quarterly, $I_p = 0.72916667$, and $R_p = 0.75$. Thus,

$$A = \frac{0.72916667 - 0.75}{100 + 0.75} \times 100 = -0.02067825$$

As before, A is entered into $\boxed{i}$. Now $1,000 is $\boxed{PV}$, and the periodic payment, $\boxed{PMT}$, is $50. Then,

when $\boxed{n} = 12$, $\boxed{FV} = 1,595.84$;

when $\boxed{n} = 24$, $\boxed{FV} = 2,192.20$; and

when $\boxed{n} = 36$, $\boxed{FV} = 2,786.00$;

and so on.

By entering I_p in $\boxed{i}$, we can determine the balance in actual rather than in constant-value dollars. Doing this, we get the following values:

for $\boxed{n} = 36$, $\boxed{FV} = 3,348.80$;

for $\boxed{n} = 24$, $\boxed{FV} = 2,496.71$; and

for $\boxed{n} = 12$, $\boxed{FV} = 1,715.75$.

PROBLEMS

1   On January 1, Chris takes out a $4,000-, 8-year certificate. The interest rate is 8½% per year, compounded annually. What is the value of the certificate after 8 years? After 16 years?

2 Joan has $1,000 in a passbook savings account. The interest rate is 5¾%, compounded monthly. She has priced modular sofas, and has decided she must pay $1,300 for the type she likes. When can she buy the sofa if she waits for her account to grow to this amount?

3 What is the annual interest earned by $50,000 invested at an *APR* of 9¼%, compounded annually?

4 How much interest does a $2,000 certificate earn in the first 12 months? The 6½% interest is compounded quarterly.

5 Calculate the interest earned from January 1 to March 31 on an account earning 0.1437% daily interest.

Beginning balance: $5,000

Deposits	Withdrawals
Jan 5: $750	Jan 20: $1,000
Jan 12: $1,230	Feb 20: $1,000
Feb 23: $554	Mar 20: $1,000
Mar 7: $1,255	
Mar 8: $970	

6 When their first child is born, Ed and Marie resolve to put $20 per month into a savings account for the child's education. If this money earns an average of 8% per year, how much will be in the account on their child's eighteenth birthday? If the inflation rate averages 6% for this period, what will the constant-dollar value of the account be?

7 George wants to buy a new washer and dryer a year from now. He estimates their total cost at $800, and his savings account earns 5½% annually, compounded monthly. How much must he put aside each month to save up the money?

8 Sam is thinking about several ways to invest the $25,000 he inherited. In a savings account he can get 8½% annual interest. Bonds will earn 9%, but they are more difficult to convert to cash in time of need. Common stocks can get about 10%, but they are riskier. If inflation is running at 7%, what will be the purchasing power of his money with the three types of investments after 5 years? After 10 years?

9 What is the present value of a periodic savings account after 10 years when the monthly payments are $150 per month, the interest rate is 7.25%, and the inflation rate is 6%? What is the actual balance of such an account?

10 If George puts $2,500 per year into time certificates with annual earnings of 8.5%, how much money will he have saved in 25 years? With 7% annual inflation, how much will this amount be worth in constant-value dollars?

11 Determine the theoretical limit on the value of a periodic savings plan with $300 monthly payments if the interest rate is 8% and the inflation rate is 10%.

9

Borrowing

TRUE INTEREST RATES

In today's intricate financial world, buying money is far from a straight-forward matter. There are hundreds of ways to borrow money, each with its own advantages and disadvantages. You can go to relatives or friends, your employer, your insurance company, a full-service bank, a loan company, a credit union, a pawnbroker, or a loan shark. You can take out a second mortgage on your home or run up a charge account balance. You can borrow money for a month, a year, or 35 years. In fact, borrowing is a veritable labyrinth, one which your calculator can help you cut through.

One key to understanding what various expressions mean in terms of money is the Annual Percentage Rate, or APR.[1] This is simply the total cost of the loan divided by the product of the amount loaned times the number of years for which it is loaned.

$$APR = \frac{C_L}{P \times T} \times 100 \qquad \text{(Equation 9-1)}$$

where C_L is the total cost of the loan, P is the principal or amount loaned, and T is the period of the loan in years. It is not always easy to determine C_L. In many cases it is more than interest; it may also include credit charges, service charges, cost of required insurance, and other types of fees limited only by the ingenuity of the lender.

[1] Also called the true annual interest rate.

EXAMPLE: You take out a personal loan for $1,000 for 6 months, and you repay $1,060. The C_L = $1,060 − $1,000 = $60; P = $1,000; and T = 6/12 = 0.5. Thus,

$$APR = \frac{60}{1000 \times 0.5} \times 100 = 12\%$$

In the past, lenders used a number of different interest rates. Often these served the purpose of making the amount of interest seem less than it actually was. This became such a problem that the U.S. Congress intervened. Today the Truth-in-Lending Act requires that loans be quoted with an annual percentage rate (APR). While this is an improvement, for certain types of loans it makes it difficult to figure the total amount of interest you will pay.

Before the legislation requiring the quotation of the APR, two other types of interest rates were in common use. These are the *add-on* and *discount rates*; some lenders continue to use them. Therefore, it is important to know how they can be converted to annual percentage rates.

PREPAYMENT CHARGES

So far we have talked only about interest, but there are several other charges lenders frequently demand that may considerably increase the cost of a loan. One of the most inequitable is the prepayment penalty. In some cases paying a loan off early makes an interest rate substantially higher than if it is paid off according to the original schedule. Of course, if a loan is paid off almost immediately, the bank must add an additional charge to cover its expenses in making out the loan in the first place. But usually these expenses have been recovered in the first few months interest. Still many lenders insist on a prepayment penalty if a loan is paid off any time before its maturity.

The preferable prepayment method is the *actuarial* method. The bank calculates how much interest is due at the time of any given payment. There is no additional prepayment penalty. More lenders are adopting this approach.

LATE FEE

Many banks charge a fee if any payment is 10 to 15 days overdue. This is usually 4% to 6% of the amount of the installment payment. Instead of a flat percentage some lenders calculate the extra charge as the added interest due for the period that the payment is late. Still other banks add both types of charges.

INSURANCE

Banks often require borrowers to take out credit life insurance that ensures complete payment of the loan in case the borrower dies. These fees, if they are paid through the bank, must be included in the total cost of the loan in calculating the annual percentage rate.

This insurance is generally regulated by the states, and there are variations in premiums and amount of coverage. When sold through banks, it is, in general, expensive. Thus, comparison shopping for the insurance policy the bank demands may save you some money.

INSTALLMENT BUYING

Most of the purchases of durable goods that people make today, like furniture, automobiles, and appliances, are bought "on time" or with installment loans. The financial innovation of installment buying and its proliferation into a major form of lending has enabled many people to enjoy various material benefits without the vicissitudes of saving. At the same time it has made it much easier for an individual or family to borrow themselves to the brink of bankruptcy.

Installment buying is a two-edged sword. Therefore, it is extremely important to understand the terms of a given contract and what the trade-offs are before taking out such a loan. A large amount of money is required to get what we want immediately, rather than save up for it. This was illustrated by an analysis done by Frederick E. Waddell.[2] Mr. Waddell assigned unit prices to 9 durable items typically bought on time: refrigerator, range, washing machine, automatic toaster, electric sewing machine, vacuum sweeper, living room rug, television set, and automobile. He multiplied the prices by the number of each product a family was likely to use during its life span. The price of these goods was estimated at $31,005. The total cost of credit for buying them was $8,129. However, if a family saved up the money to buy these items rather than getting them on credit, they would be ahead by more than $32,000 because of the interest their money would have earned.

The calculator can increase your understanding of the installment buying process by helping you determine the size of the payments, the amount of interest you pay with each payment, the balance remaining after so many payments, and the accumulated interest. The formula for finding the size of the payments, *PMT*, on an installment loan is:

$$PMT = P\left(\frac{i}{1 - (1 + i)^{-N}}\right) \qquad \text{(Equation 9-2)}$$

where P is the principal of the loan, i is the periodic interest rate,[3] and N is the total number of payments.

EXAMPLE: You are thinking about taking out a loan for adding a room onto your home. You think you can get a 4-year loan at 10% annual interest. You want to get some idea of what the payments

---

[2] Frederick E. Waddell, *"A-Borrowing, A-Sorrowing," Journal of Consumer Affairs*, 4, no. 1 (1970), pp. 31-45.

[3] As in i for the compound interest, i is the *APR* expressed as a decimal and divided by the number of payment periods per year.

would be for the addition costing $3,000 or for the more finished job costing $7,500.

The payments for the cheaper job would be:

$$PMT = \$3,000 \left[\frac{\frac{0.10}{12}}{1 - \left(1 + \frac{0.10}{12}\right)^{-48}} \right]$$

$$= \$3,000 \left[\frac{.00833}{0.32848} \right]$$

$$= \$3,000 \times 0.0253708$$

$$= \$76.11$$

While for the more expensive job, the payments would increase to:

$$PMT = \$7,500 \times 0.0253708 = \$190.28$$

(Once you have calculated the quantity in brackets for a given interest rate and period of time, you can get the monthly payment by multiplying any amount you may wish to borrow by the same quantity.

EXAMPLE: What if our would-be borrower really needed the $7,500, but could only afford to pay $200 per month. For how long must he try to get a loan? Still assume a 10% annual interest rate.

The formula that expresses the number of periodic payments, given the size of the loan, the size of the payments, and the interest rate, is

$$N = \frac{-\log\left[1 - i\left(\frac{P}{PMT}\right)\right]}{\log(1+i)} \qquad \textbf{(Equation 9-3)}$$

For this case,

$$N = \frac{-\log\left[1 - 0.00833\left(\frac{\$7,500}{\$200}\right)\right]}{\log(1.00833)}$$

$$= \frac{-\log(1 - 0.31238)}{\log 1.00833}$$

$$= \frac{-\log 0.68763}{\log 1.00833}$$

Turning to the log tables, we find

$$N = \frac{+\ 0.16265}{0.00360}$$

$$=\ 45.15$$

This means that it would take 45 monthly payments of $200 each (with the final payment being slightly larger), in order to pay off the loan.

TOTAL INTEREST

While interest rates are useful for comparing different loans, the *bottom line* is the total number of dollars that the loan will cost you. It is difficult to go directly from *APR* to the total interest for an installment loan. But determining the total cost of a loan is direct if you know the size and number of payments.

First, you must calculate the total amount of money you will pay back to the lender over the course of the loan. This is

$$Total\ Cost\ =\ PMT \times N \qquad \text{(Equation 9-4)}$$

Now the total interest, *TI*, is the difference between the total outlay from the previous equation and the principal of the loan:

$$Total\ Interest\ =\ Total\ Cost\ -\ P$$

or

$$TI\ =\ (PMT \times N)\ -\ P \qquad \text{(Equation 9-5)}$$

EXAMPLE: How much total interest would be paid for the $3,000 and $7,500 home improvement loans from the example on page 123? The monthly payments on these 4-year loans were $76.11 and $190.28, respectively. In this case, *N* would be 4 X 12 = 48. For the smaller loan,

$$TI\ =\ (\$76.11 \times 48)\ -\ \$3,000$$

$$=\ \$653.28$$

For the larger loan,

$$TI\ =\ (\$190.28 \times 48)\ -\ \$7,500$$

$$=\ \$1,633.44$$

BALANCE REMAINING

Most people who have been involved with mortgages or other long-term installment loans realize that at first much of the money they pay goes toward paying off the interest, not the principal. The process of paying off such a loan is similar to a snowball rolling downhill. The amount of principal you pay off at first is small, but as you continue paying, the amount applied to the principal grows at an ever-increasing rate.

Consider the case of a $7,500, 5-year loan at a 10% annual interest rate. The relationship between principal and interest is shown on Graph 9-1. The straight dotted line connecting $7,500 (the start of the loan) and $0 (the end of the loan) represents how the balance would decrease if it were reduced by an equal amount each month. The slightly curving solid line above it illustrates the way the principal actually decreases. Until the very end, the balance is always above the dotted line. The reason for this is illustra-

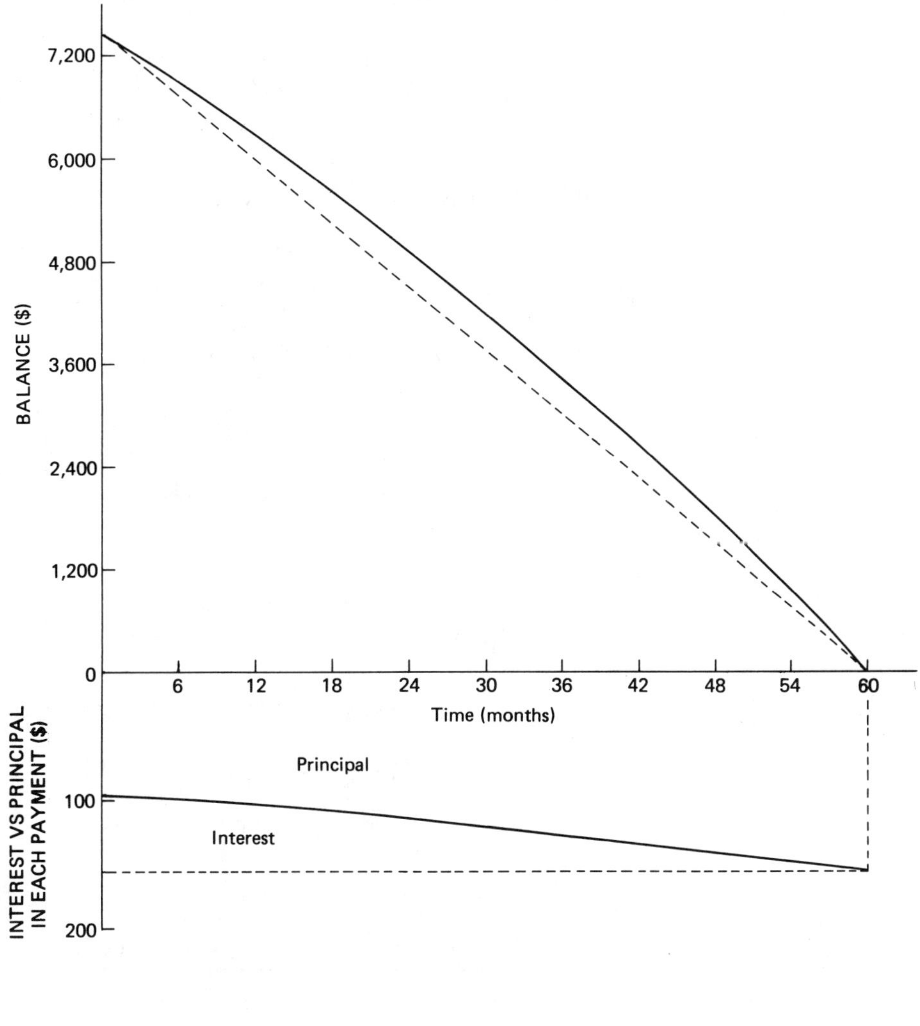

Graph 9-1 Balance of $7,500 Loan for Five Years at 10% Annual Interest

ted by the curve at the bottom of the graph. This shows the amount from each payment that goes to pay interest and to decrease the principal. The interest portion starts fairly large and gradually decreases because it is computed from the amount of principal outstanding: When the principal is large, the interest portion is also large; as the principal decreases, so does the interest.

It is possible to calculate the balance of an installment loan at any payment period, provided we know: the initial value, P; the size of the payments, PMT; and the periodic interest rate, i. On payment k, the balance, B_k, is

$$B_k = (1+i)^k \left[PMT \left(\frac{(1+i)^{-k} - 1}{i} \right) + P \right] \qquad \text{(Equation 9-6)}$$

EXAMPLE: You have been paying the loan on your automobile now for 1 year and you wonder how much more principal you have to pay. You've gotten a little ahead and are thinking about paying it off.

The loan was for $5,500 at 11% for 24 months. The monthly payments are $256.34. The balance after 12 months would be

$$B_{12} = \left(1 + \frac{0.11}{12}\right)^{12} \left[\$256.34 \left(\frac{\left(1 + \frac{0.11}{12}\right)^{-12} - 1}{0.11/12} \right) + \$5,500 \right]$$

But 0.11/12 equals 0.00916667, so

$$B_{12} = (1.00916667)^{12} \left[\$256.34 \left(\frac{(1.00916667)^{-12} - 1}{0.00916667} \right) + \$5,500 \right]$$

Using logs to evaluate 1.00916667^{12} gives

$$B_{12} = 1.1157 \left[\$256.34 \left(\frac{\left(\frac{1}{1.1157}\right) - 1}{0.00916667} \right) + \$5,500 \right]$$

Thus,

$$B_{12} = 1.1157 \left[\$256.34 \frac{-0.10370}{.00916667} + \$5,500 \right]$$

$$= 1.1157 \left[\$256.34 \times -11.3129099 + \$5,500 \right]$$

$$= 1.1157 \left[-\$2,899.95 + \$5,500 \right]$$

$$= 1.1157 \times \$2,600.04$$

$$= \$2,900.87$$

There is half the principal remaining plus an additional $150.87.

INTEREST BETWEEN PAYMENTS

If a person wishes to determine the amount of interest paid during a specific period of a loan—for a certain year, for instance—the calculations, although difficult, are far from impossible.

EXAMPLE: A $10,000 loan was secured at 10% for 5 years to pay for a new boat. The first monthly payment of $212.47 was paid on August 1, 1979. How much interest did the new skipper pay on his boat in 1979?

To solve such a problem, we need the following formula:

$$I_{j-k} = B_k - B_{j-1} + (k - j + 1)\ PMT \quad \textbf{(Equation 9-7)}$$

here, the j and k are payment periods, and B_k and B_{j-1}, respectively, are the balances at payment k and one payment before payment j. Since the first 5 payments were made in 1979, I_{j-k} is I_{1-5}. Therefore, we first need to calculate B_5 and $B_{1-1} = B_0$.

Doing this:

$$B_5 = (1 + 0.008333)^5 \left[\$212.47 \left(\frac{(1 + 0.0083333)^{-5} - 1}{0.008333} \right) + \$10,000 \right]$$

$$= (1.008333)^5 \left[\$212.47 \left(\frac{\dfrac{1}{1.0083333^5} - 1}{0.0083333} \right) + \$10,000 \right]$$

$$= 1.0424 \left[\$212.47 \left(\frac{0.959324636 - 1}{0.00833333} \right) + \$10,000 \right]$$

$$= 1.0424 \left[\$212.47 \left(\frac{-0.040675}{0.00833333} \right) + \$10,000 \right]$$

$$= 1.0424 \left[(\$212.47 \times -4.88104394) + \$10,000 \right]$$

$$= 1.0424 \left[(\$10,000 - \$1,037.71) \right]$$

$$= 1.0424 \times \$8,962.92$$

$$= \$9,342.95$$

and

$$B_0 = (1.0083333)^0 \left[\$212.47 \left(\frac{1.008333^{-0} - 1}{0.0083333} \right) + \$10,000 \right]$$

but, since any number to the zero power is one, then

$$B_0 = 1\left[\$212.47\left(\frac{1-1}{0.008333}\right) + \$10,000\right]$$

$$= \$10,000$$

Obviously, the balance before the first payment is **P**. We could have reasoned this out without the calculations, but it serves as a nice check on our formula.

Now we are ready to calculate the interest.

$$I_{1-5} = B_5 - B_0 + \left[(5 - 1 + 1) \times \$212.47\right]$$

$$= \$9,342.95 - \$10,000 + (5 \times \$212.47)$$

$$= \$9,342.95 - \$10,000 + \$1,062.35$$

$$= \$405.30$$

This may be too much trouble for most people, especially since the lender often supplies a yearly tabulation of interest paid for tax purposes. However, this same formula can also give you the amount of interest paid on a specific payment. You do this by setting $j = k$. Then,

$$I_k = B_k - B_{k-1} + PMT \qquad \textbf{(Equation 9-8)}$$

gives the amount of interest paid on payment k.

EXAMPLE: The new skipper from the previous example wants to determine how much interest he paid with his fifth payment. This can be expressed as

$$I_5 = B_5 - B_4 + \$212.47$$

Since we have already calculated B_5 and found it to be $9,343.47, all that remains is to determine B_4. This is

$$B_4 = (1.0083333)^4\left[\$212.47\left(\frac{1.0083333^{-4}-1}{0.008333}\right) + \$10,000\right]$$

$$= 1.0338\left[\$212.47\left(\frac{0.967305088 - 1}{0.0083333}\right) + \$10,000\right]$$

$$= 1.0338\left[\$212.47\left(\frac{-0.032694912}{0.0083333}\right) + \$10,000\right]$$

Table 9-2 Conversion Factors for Total Interest from Principal

ANNUAL PERCENTAGE RATE	MATURITY (YRS)			
	20	25	30	35
8	1.01	1.32	1.64	1.98
9	1.16	1.52	1.90	2.29
10	1.32	1.73	2.16	2.61
11	1.48	1.94	2.43	2.94

EXAMPLE: For a loan of $30,000 at 10% annual interest with a 25-year maturity, the factor is 1.73. Therefore, the total interest is just $30,000 × 1.73 = $51,900. Compare this with an 11% loan of the same value with a 20-year maturity. Here the total interest is less: $30,000 × 1.48 = $44,400.

The example above illustrates another important fact about mortgages. The maturity is just as important as the interest rate in determining the total amount of interest you pay. Look at Table 9-2 again. Note that the factors in the 35-year column are almost twice those in the 20-year column. This means that the interest paid on a given loan with a 35-year maturity is about double that paid on one with a 20-year maturity. This is a greater percentage increase than that over the 3 percentage points of annual interest. The range between 8% and 11% is about 150%.

Taking both interest and maturity into account, the amount of interest you pay can range from an amount equal to the loan value up to almost three times the value.

INFLATION
AND INSTALLMENT BUYING

Borrowing is often considered "akin to sin," while savings is considered a virtue. In Chapter 8, we saw how inflation diminishes the financial advantages of savings. Similarly, we would expect that inflation makes borrowing less costly because the purchasing power of each dollar you borrow is greater than those you pay back over the maturity of the loan. During inflationary times, it appears to be a sensible strategy to borrow to purchase items that increase in value at a rate greater than or equal to the inflation rate, for example, real estate. Indeed, some experts now recommend that people get the largest mortgage possible when they buy a new home or property.

Of course, such advice is based on the general feeling that inflation will continue at a significant rate for the remainder of the century. However, economists have shown themselves singularly unable to predict the course of the U.S. economy, so there is a considerable risk in attempting to predict economic conditions for more than a few years into the future. It is not impossible that the nation's inflation rate could drop dramatically 5 years,

10 years, 15 years, or 20 years from now. Still, this is considered highly unlikely.

Exactly how does inflation affect the real cost of installment borrowing? We can examine this question with a fair amount of precision by adapting the basic installment loan equations to take inflation into account. As we have previously defined,

$$Average\ Annual\ Inflation\ Rate\ =\ R$$

and, if p is the number of payments per year, then

$$Periodic\ Inflation\ Rate\ =\ r_p\ =\ \frac{R}{100 \times p}$$

With this basic underpinning, we can now adapt Equation 9-4 to express the total amount of money paid on a loan in constant-value dollars.

$$Total\ Real\ Cost\ =\ \left[PMT\ \frac{(1 + r_p)^{N+1} - 1}{r_p (1 + r_p)^N} \right] \qquad \text{(Equation 9-9)}$$

Where N is the total number of payments.

EXAMPLE: What is the total real cost, **TRC**, of a 9.5% mortgage of $40,000 with a 25-year maturity if the inflation rate is 4%? 6%? 8%? Monthly payments are $349.48.

In every case, the total number of payments, **N**, is $p \times T$, or

$$N\ =\ 12 \times 25\ =\ 300$$

For 4% inflation,

$$r_p\ =\ \frac{4}{100 \times 12}\ =\ 0.00333333$$

and

$$1 + r_p\ =\ 1.0033333$$

Then,

$$TRC\ =\ \$349.48 \left[\frac{1.0033333^{300+1} - 1}{0.0033333\ (1.003333)^{300}} \right]$$

$$=\ \$349.48 \left(\frac{2.7228460 - 1}{0.0033333 \times 2.7138} \right)$$

$$=\ \$66,557.77$$

For 6% inflation,

$$r_p = \frac{6}{100 \times 12} = 0.00500000$$

and

$$1 + r_p = 1.0050000$$

As a result,

$$TRC = \$349.48\left(\frac{1.005^{301} - 1}{0.005 \times 1.005^{300}}\right)$$

$$= \$349.48\left(\frac{3.487325}{0.0223250}\right)$$

$$= \$349.48 \times 156.2071669$$

$$= \$54,591.28$$

At an 8% inflation rate,

$$r_p = \frac{8}{100 \times 12} = 0.00666667$$

and

$$1 + r_p = 1.0066667$$

Thus,

$$TRC = \$349.48\left(\frac{1.0066667^{301} - 1}{0.00666667 \times 1.0066667^{300}}\right)$$

$$= \$349.48\left(\frac{6.3891349}{0.0489347}\right)$$

$$= \$45,629.69$$

The following chart summarizes our calculations:

INFLATION RATE (%)	TOTAL REAL COST
0	104,844
4	66,558
6	54,591
8	45,630

It is clear that even a relatively modest inflation rate substantially decreases the value of the dollars that you repay the lender.

This raises the question of how much such a loan actually costs in an inflationary time. Since the money has the purchasing power of the year in which it is borrowed, therefore, the total real interest, TRI, of the loan is

$$TRI = TOTAL\ REAL\ COST - P \qquad \text{(Equation 9-10)}$$

EXAMPLE: What is the total real interest of the loan in the previous example with 4%, 6%, and 8% inflation rates?

For 4% inflation:

$$TRI = \$66{,}558 - \$40{,}000 = \$26{,}558$$

For 6% inflation:

$$TRI = \$54{,}591 - \$40{,}000 = \$14{,}591$$

For 8% inflation:

$$TRI = \$45{,}630 - \$40{,}000 = 5{,}630$$

So, in terms of real cost, inflation can have a tremendous effect on installment loans.

While inflationary effects are most pronounced on long-term loans such as mortgages, they also alter the true cost of shorter-term purchases. This is illustrated in the following example.

EXAMPLE: What is the effect of a 6% inflation rate on the real cost of a $7,500, 5-year loan with an annual interest rate of 10%? The monthly payments are $159.35.

To answer this question, let us first determine the total interest in actual dollars using Equation 11-8. $N = 12 \times 5 = 60$. Thus,

$$Total\ Interest = (\$159.35 \times 60) - \$7{,}500$$

$$= \$9{,}561.00 - \$7{,}500$$

$$= \$2{,}061$$

With a 6% annual inflation rate, $r_p = 0.00500000$, and

$$TRC = \$159.35 \left(\frac{1.005^{61} - 1}{0.005 \times 1.005^{60}} \right)$$

$$= \$159.35 \left(\frac{1.3556 - 1}{0.005 \times 1.3488} \right)$$

$$= \$159.35 \left(\frac{0.3556}{0.006744} \right)$$

$$= \$159.35 \times \$52.72835$$

$$= \$8,402.48$$

and the total real interest is

$$TRI = \$8,402.26 - \$7,500 = \$902.26$$

The result of a 6% inflation rate is to cut the constant-value cost of the loan by more than 50%.

Now that we have a formula combining interest and inflation for installment buying, what can we learn about the relationship between them?

First, let's look at the total real cost of the loan in the previous example under different inflation rates:

Table 9-3 Total Real Interest of a $7,500, 5-Year Loan at 10% Annual Interest

ANNUAL INFLATION RATE (%)	TOTAL REAL INTEREST (CONSTANT VALUE DOLLARS)
0	2,061
2	1,749
4	1,313
6	902
8	519
10	159
12	−177

As expected, each increase in the inflation rate decreases the total real cost of a loan substantially. When the interest rate and inflation rate are equal, the loan does not cost much, but it does have a slight real cost. This suggests that inflationary effects are not quite as strong on installment loans as they are on savings accounts: When the interest and inflation rates are equal, recall that the purchasing power of a savings account remained static so the saver was not gaining a financial advantage. In the case of the installment loan, however, the lender still makes a slight constant-value "profit."

Notice that when the inflation rate is 12%, the total real interest is a negative number. This means that the cumulative buying power of the loan payments is less than that of the face value of the loan. This does not necessarily mean that the borrower has made money: To have gained financial advantage the borrower must have purchased something that is increasing in value at a rate equal to inflation, such as property.

Under what conditions is the total real interest of an installment loan equal to zero? The answer to this question sheds some interesting light on the interplay between interest and inflation. It turns out that it is not only the interest rate but also the maturity of the loan that determines the level of inflation required to drive the total real interest of a loan to zero. Following is a formula expressing the relationship between the periodic interest rate, i, the periodic inflation rate, r_p, and the total number of payments for a loan, N, when the total real cost is very close to zero:

$$r_p = \frac{i(N+1)}{N} + \frac{1}{N^2} \qquad \text{(Equation 9-11)}$$

or, alternately,

$$i = r_p \frac{N}{N+1} - \frac{1}{N(N+1)} \qquad \text{(Equation 9-12)}$$

EXAMPLE: If the inflation rate is running at 7%, at what interest rate would the total real cost of a 5-year monthly installment loan equal zero?

For this loan N = 12 payments per year X 5 years = 60 payments, and

$$r_p = \frac{7}{100 \times 12} = 0.00583333$$

Thus,

$$i = \left(0.005833 \times \frac{60}{61}\right) - \frac{1}{60 \times 61}$$

$$= (0.005833 \times 0.98360656) - 0.00027322$$

$$= 0.00573770 - 0.00027322$$

$$= 0.00546448$$

We can convert i to an annual percentage rate by multiplying it by 1,200. Thus

$$APR = 0.00546448 \times 1,200 = 6.6\%$$

The significance of this calculation is that, if you can put the principal to good use, you can borrow money for 6.6% interest or less and come out ahead in purchasing power.

Perhaps a more valuable way to look at this relationship is to ask what rate of inflation causes a loan of a specific annual percentage rate and maturity to have a total real cost of zero. Then, if the inflation rate is higher than this value, the real cost of the loan will be negative, and if the inflation rate is lower, the real cost of the loan will be positive. Graph 9-2 illustrates this for annual percentage rates from 5% to 12%. For short loans of a year or less, it takes a horrendous inflation rate to bring the total real cost down to zero. The shorter the loan, the less effect inflation has on its cost. For a two-year loan, inflation must be about 25% higher than the interest rate to create this condition. But for a five-year loan, the inflation rate need only be ½% higher than the interest rate to reduce the constant-value cost to nothing. For longer maturity loans, when the interest and inflation rates are equal, the total real cost approaches zero.

As you have no doubt noticed, computing the total real interest is a bit tedious. Fortunately, there is a short cut. It so happens that the total real interest is a set proportion of the principal for a given inflation rate, interest

Graph 9-2 Relationship Between Interest Rate, Inflation Rate, and Maturity when Total Real Interest is Zero

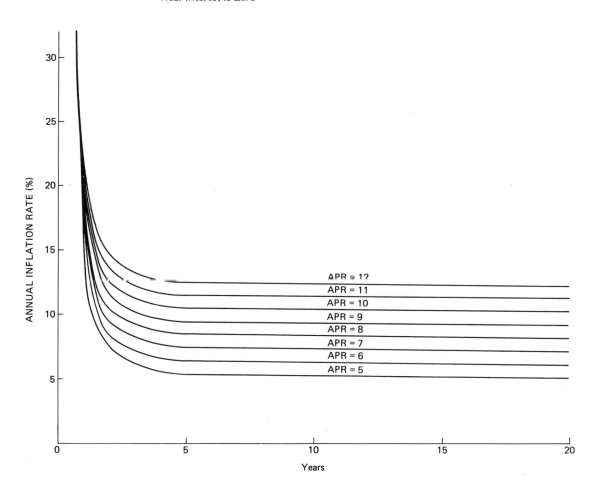

Table 9-4 Conversion Factors for Total Real Cost of Mortgages of Typical Maturities

ANNUAL INFLATION RATE (%)	ANNUAL INTEREST RATE (%)	MATURITY (YEARS)			
		20	25	30	35
0	8	1.01	1.32	1.64	1.98
	9	1.16	1.52	1.90	2.29
	10	1.32	1.73	2.16	2.61
	11	1.48	1.94	2.43	2.94
2	8	0.66	0.83	0.99	1.15
	9	0.79	0.99	1.18	1.37
	10	0.92	1.15	1.38	1.60
	11	1.05	1.32	1.59	1.84
4	8	0.39	0.47	0.54	0.61
	9	0.49	0.60	0.69	0.78
	10	0.60	0.73	0.85	0.95
	11	0.71	0.87	1.00	1.13
6	8	0.18	0.21	0.23	0.25
	9	0.26	0.31	0.35	0.38
	10	0.36	0.42	0.47	0.52
	11	0.45	0.53	0.60	0.65
8	8	0.01	0.01	0.01	0.01
	9	0.08	0.10	0.10	0.11
	10	0.16	0.19	0.20	0.22
	11	0.24	0.28	0.31	0.33
10	8	−.12	−.14	−.16	−.17
	9	−.06	−.07	−.08	−.08
	10	0.01	0.01	0.01	0.01
	11	0.08	0.09	0.09	0.10

rate, and maturity. Therefore, all you need to do is calculate the *TRI* for any principal and then divide it by that principal. This will give you a factor by which you can multiply any other principal to get the *TRC*. Of course, this only applies for a given inflation rate, interest rate, and maturity. If you change one of these factors, you must recalculate the proportion.

Table 9-4 lists these conversion factors for a range of inflation rates, interest rates, and maturities typical of mortgages. To estimate total real cost for a given mortgage using this table, find the factor corresponding to the inflation rate, interest rate, and maturity closest to the case you are considering. Multiply this factor times the principal of the loan and the product will give you an approximate value of the total real cost.

EXAMPLE: What is the total real interest of a $35,000 mortgage with a 10% annual interest rate and a 30-year maturity when the inflation rate averages 6% per year for the period?

From Table 9-4, the proper conversion factor for this case is 0.47, so

$$TRI = 0.47 \times \$35{,}000 = \$16{,}450$$

How does this change if the maturity is increased to 35 years? Turning to the table again, the new conversion factor is 0.52, and

$$TRI = 0.52 \times \$35{,}000 = \$18{,}200$$

Besides its utility for finding total real interest, Table 9-4 illustrates another of inflation's effects on long-term borrowing. With zero inflation, the total interest on a 25-year mortgage is almost twice that of a 20-year mortgage; but even with a modest 2% inflation, the real cost difference between the 2 mortgages is reduced to 50%. In general, the smaller the difference between the inflation rate and the interest rate, the less effect the length of the loan has on its constant-value-dollar cost.

VARIABLE-RATE MORTGAGES

Because the nation's lenders have in their portfolios a large proportion of old, low-interest mortgages on which they are, in essence, losing money, a shortage of mortgage money has developed in many parts of the country. To rectify this situation, and, of course, to increase their profits, banks and thrifts (Savings and Loans) have increasingly begun to offer *variable-rate* mortgages. In these mortgages the lender is free to change the interest rate to reflect the situation in the market place. Although they talk about the possibility of decreasing rates in the future, it is difficult to imagine how rate decreases would outweigh the increases. To make this type of mortgage attractive, they are generally offered at a slightly reduced interest rate.

Lenders generally argue that variable-rate mortgages are fair and will ensure a steady supply of money to finance mortgages in the future. Consumer interests, however, take quite a different view. In a 1973 report prepared by the staff of the House Committee on Banking and Currency, variable-rate mortgages were attacked because they put all the risk onto the shoulders of the borrower, and because they may tend to discourage home ownership.

In the federal regulations authorizing variable-rate mortgages in 1979, certain limits on rate changes are included. The rate can not be adjusted more than once per year; it can not be raised more than ½% at a time. The maximum total increase over the life of the loan is 2½%. There are no limitations on rate decreases. Finally, a savings and loan bank that offers you a variable-rate mortgage must also offer you one at a fixed rate.

To understand some of the implications of variable-rate mortgages, let's look at a mortgage that begins at a given interest rate, and then after a certain period the interest rate is increased.

EXAMPLE: A family has the option of getting a $40,000, 30-year mortgage at 8¾% fixed interest or at 8½% variable interest. They choose the variable-rate loan. Ten years later the bank increases their rate to 9¾%. Assuming no further adjustments in the interest rate, how much interest will the family pay in each case?

First, consider the fixed-rate case. Using Equation 9-2 we can calculate the monthly payments and use this to determine total interest.

$$PMT = P \left(\frac{i}{1 - (1 + i)^{-N}} \right)$$

In this case, P = $40,000; i = 0.0875/12 = 0.00729167; and N = 360 months. Thus,

$$PMT = \$40,000 \left(\frac{0.00729167}{1 - (1.00729167)^{-360}} \right)$$

$$= \$40,000 \left(\frac{0.00729167}{1 - 0.073131} \right)$$

$$= \$40,000 \left(\frac{0.00729167}{0.92686851} \right)$$

$$= \$40,000 \times 0.00786699$$

$$= \$314.68$$

The total interest they would pay is

$$TI = (PMT \times N) - P$$

then,

$$TI = (\$314.68 \times 360) - \$40,000$$

$$= \$73,284.80$$

If you wish, you can adjust this for a 6% inflation rate: r_p = 0.06/12 = 0.005

$$TRI = \$314.68 \left(\frac{(1.005)^{361} - 1}{0.005 \, (1.005)^{360}} \right) - \$40,000$$

$$= (\$314.68 \times 167.79410) - \$40,000$$

$$= \$12,801$$

For the variable-interest case, we must first determine the balance after the first 10 years and the amount of interest paid up to that point. Then we will deal with the situation after the interest rate is raised. From Equation 9-6 we get

$$B_k = (1+i)^k \left[PMT \left(\frac{(1+i)^{-k} - 1}{i} \right) + P \right]$$

For 10 years, $k = 120$, and the rest of the variables remain the same as above.

$$B_{120} = 1.00729167^{120} \left[\$314.68 \left(\frac{1.00729167^{-120} - 1}{0.00729167} \right) + \$40,000 \right]$$

$$= 2.3913 \left[\$314.68 \, (-79.792067) + \$40,000 \right]$$

$$= 2.3913 \times \$14,891.03$$

$$= \$35,608.93$$

To figure the interest already paid we need Equation 9-7.

$$I_{j-k} = B_k - B_{j-1} + (k - j + 1) \, PMT$$

In this case $k = 120$ and $j = 1$. The second balance we need is B_0, which is just P. Thus,

$$I_{1-120} = \$35,608.93 - \$40,000 + (120 - 1 + 1) \, \$314.68$$

$$= -\$4,391.07 + (120 \times \$314.68)$$

$$= \$37,761.60 - \$4,391.07$$

$$= \$33,370.53$$

At this point, inflation has been continuing at a substantial clip. Interest rates have been rising and mortgage money is scarce, so the bank decides to raise the rate to 9¾%. The balance is now $35,608.99, due in another 20 years. To do our calculations, we consider this as a new loan of $35,608.99, $i = 0.0975/12 = 0.008125$, and $N = 240$ months. Then,

$$PMT = \$35,608.99 \left(\frac{0.008125}{1 - (1 + 0.008125)^{-240}} \right)$$

$$= \$35,608.99 \left(\frac{0.008125}{1 - 0.14340001} \right)$$

$$= \$35,608.99 \left(\frac{0.008125}{0.85659999} \right)$$

$$= \$35,608.99 \times 0.00948517$$

$$= \$337.76$$

Suppose, however, they do not feel they can afford the extra $277 per year in mortgage payments and the bank offers to let them keep paying the same amount by extending the length of the loan. Using Equation 9-3, we can determine how much longer our home-owners must pay.

$$N = \frac{-\log 1 - \left(\dfrac{0.008125 \times \$35{,}608.99}{\$314.68}\right)}{\log (1.008125)}$$

$$= \frac{-\log (1 - 0.91941987)}{\log (1.008125)}$$

$$= \frac{-\log (0.080580133)}{\log (1.008125)}$$

Looking up these values in the log tables, we find

$$N = \frac{-(-1.0937720)}{0.0035144}$$

$$= 311$$

This is almost 26 years, so the increased interest rate would add an extra 6 years of mortgage payments.

Now we can calculate the total interest these people would pay with increased payments or by extending the loan. For the former,

$$Total\ Interest = (\$337.76 \times 240) - \$35{,}608.99$$

$$= \$45{,}453.41$$

and for the latter,

$$Total\ Interest = (\$314.68 \times 311) - \$35{,}608.99$$

$$= \$62{,}256.49$$

Adding the interest paid for the first 10 years of the loan gives grand totals of $78,824.00 and $95,627.08. This compares with $73,284.91 for the fixed-rate loan.

Thus, in this hypothetical example at least, the borrowers would have been better off with a fixed-rate loan. Given even a conservative inflation rate, of course, much of this difference would be in dollars of reduced value.

To make a more equitable comparison between these 2 cases, let us adjust the variable-rate mortgage case for a 6% inflation rate as we did for the fixed mortgage. For simplicity, let us only consider the extended mortgage case.

Our starting place is Equation 9-9.

$$TRC = PMT \left[\frac{(1 + r_p)^{N+1} - 1}{r_p (1 + r_p)^N} \right]$$

The extended loan would have lasted a total of 120 plus 311 months, so N is 431. As in the fixed-interest case, $r_p = 0.005$. Therefore,

$$TRI = \$314.68 \left(\frac{(1.005)^{432} - 1}{0.005 (1.005)^{431}} \right) - \$40,000$$

$$= (\$314.68 \times 177.69647) - \$40,000$$

$$= \$15,917.52$$

This compares with \$12,264.93 in the fixed-interest case, so the variable-interest mortgage ends up being about 25% more expensive in constant-value dollars as opposed to the 30% increased cost when calculated in actual dollars.

Coupled with the added expense of the variable-rate loan in the preceding example is the possibility that the interest rates can be varied as often as the lender sees fit. Because a mortgage is generally a family's biggest financial transaction, it is carefully budgeted. Thus, the outlook of arbitrary changes in the future is not very popular.

SAVING VERSUS BORROWING

A number of American politicians, economists, and general spokesmen are bemoaning the decline of thrift and the upsurge of debt financing in the United States in the late 1970s and early 1980s. We have become a spend-thrift nation, many would have us believe. Generally overlooked in such comments of moral indignation, and in a number of economic forecasts, however, is the fact that in today's financial climate putting money into savings is a losing proposition, and the real cost of borrowing is substantially less than it seems. Actually, the financial acumen of large numbers of Americans is at work in this shift, not some new strain of economic irresponsibility surfacing in our national character.

The effects of inflation on both saving and borrowing have been explored in this and in the previous chapter. Now it is time to put the two together. Suppose you have a major, necessary purchase coming up—a new car, appliance, or similar item—and you don't have the money for this purchase. You have two choices: either save the money and buy the item for cash in a certain period of time, or making the purchase and paying on time. If you buy on time, you will pay a substantial amount greater than the purchase price because of the interest you pay on the loan and the interest you lose from not putting this money to work in a savings account. On the other hand, if you put your money into a savings account every month for that same period of time, then the chances are that the cost of the item will have risen, pushed higher by inflation.

A direct way of comparing these two options is to ask, "Under what circumstances are the monthly payments into a savings account necessary to purchase an item in N periods, less than or equal to the monthly payments of a loan with the same maturity necessary to purchase the item immediately?" However, there are some pitfalls to this approach. First, various categories of products are affected by inflation to varying degrees. Innovations in some product lines such as consumer electronics are keeping the rate of price inflation considerably below that of the general inflation rate. Housing, in many parts of the country, on the other hand, appears to be leading the other way. It is possible to compensate for this to a degree, by finding the detailed breakdown of inflation by sector in the Consumer Price Index and then using the best approximation. Second, the longer the time period assigned to such a comparison the more uncertain the inflation rate will be. Third, there is the cost of federal and state income tax. Because one must pay tax on savings account interest and yet can deduct that paid on loans, the tax structure also makes borrowing more desirable than otherwise would be the case.

Savings at reasonable interest rates is an alternative that is considerably more in the borrower's best interest than is the variable-rate mortgage. Because savings accounts are a major source of money for mortgages, an alternate way to ensure adequate funds for new mortgages is to keep savings interest rates in step with current financial realities. Otherwise the economic pressure on individuals will continue to favor borrowing over savings. There are a number of authorities who feel that the interest rates given on savings accounts have lagged far behind inflation. The dramatic effects which inflation has on savings accounts is covered in Chapter 8.

With these qualifications in mind, let us sharpen our question further. Given an inflation rate and an interest rate for borrowing, what savings interest rate is needed to make the savings approach financially superior? Interestingly enough, the answer to this question is independent of the amount of money in question, except when it affects the interest rates involved. The answer does, however, depend on the length of time involved.

The following expression allows us to answer our question. It is only an approximation, but is good to within ½% for current interest and inflation rates.

$$i_s = \frac{2}{N(N+1)i_1} \left[(i + r_p)^N - \left(\frac{1 + r_p{}^N}{1 + i_1} \right) - Ni_1 \right]$$ (Equation 9-13)

where i_s is the periodic interest rate for savings, i_1 is the periodic interest rate for a loan, r_p is the periodic inflation rate, and N is the number of periods.

EXAMPLE: Harold is thinking about buying a new car. Interest rates are running at 18% per annum. Typical maturities for auto loans are 24 months, and the estimate for the current annual inflation rate is 20%. What interest rate must Harold obtain to make it worthwhile to wait 2 years before purchasing an automobile?

An interest rate of 18% makes i_1 = 18/1,200 = 0.015. N = 24, and r_p = 20/1,200 = 0.0166667. Therefore,

$$i_s = \frac{2}{24 \times 25 \times 0.015} \left[1.0166667^{24} - \left(\frac{1.0166667}{1.015} \right)^{24} - 24 \times 0.015 \right]$$

$$= 0.0192783$$

which is equivalent to an **APR** of 23%. In Harold's case, then, financing would appear to be superior to saving under these circumstances.

Each of the following graphs illustrates the relationship between the interest rates on savings and on loans of 1- to 5-year maturities, given a different annual inflation rate. Several general conclusions can be drawn from these graphs:

Graph 9-3 5% Inflation Rate

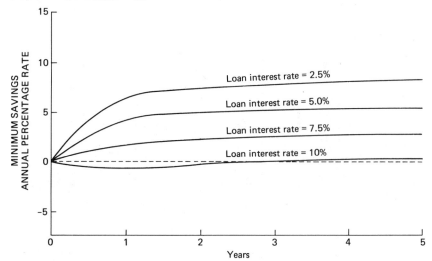

Graph 9-4 10% Inflation Rate

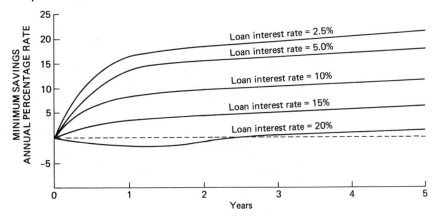

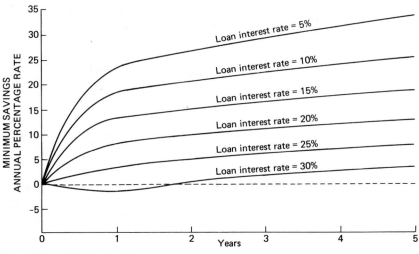

Graph 9-5 15% Inflation Rate

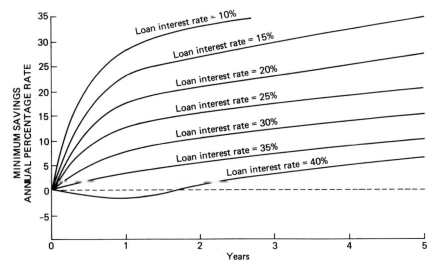

Graph 9-6 20% Inflation Rate

1. When the cost of borrowing money is twice the inflation rate, it is almost always better to save rather than to borrow.

2. When the interest rate on loans and the inflation rate are about the same, the interest rate on savings must be comparable or better to make savings advantageous. Historically, the prime lending rate has trailed the inflation rate by a few points. In this case savings rates greater than the cost of money are needed to make thrift cost-effective—an unrealistic situation because savings rates trail lending rates by a considerable margin.

3. In periods of relatively high inflation, the longer the time in question, the greater the advantage of borrowing over saving.

This explains quite clearly why the Federal Reserve Board's actions in late 1979 and early 1980 of increasing interest rates toward 20% per year did not dampen the demand as anticipated. The inflation rate during this period was 13% to 20%, and the savings rate was up to 10%. As you can clearly see, even in these conditions borrowing was still the least costly strategy. Ironically, the Fed's actions actually fed the economy's inflationary fires rather than dampening them as expected. The increased cost of money forced many businessmen to raise their prices. As indicated by the 15% and 20% inflation rate graphs, it would take lending rates of 20% to 30% to revitalize 10% savings accounts.

COMPUTING BORROWING WITH BUSINESS-ANALYST CALCULATOR

Utilizing the same row of keys employed for compound interest calculations plus a few others, the business-analyst calculator makes short work of most computations in this section.

Installment Payments Determining the size of monthly installment payments on a loan is generally the most important single consideration in deciding whether or not one can afford to buy on time. To do this, enter the number of periods in the loan $\boxed{\text{n}}$, the periodic interest rate as a percentage $\boxed{\text{i}}$, and the amount of money you are borrowing $\boxed{\text{PV}}$. With these values stored in the calculator, keying $\boxed{\text{PMT}}$ will give you the payments required.

EXAMPLE: You are thinking about taking out a home-improvement loan in order to add a new room to your house. You have gotten some estimates from local contractors and have to decide between 2 options: a bare-bones, $3,000 job or a more finished $7,500 addition. Interest on home improvement loans is 18% *APR* with a maturity of 4 years. How much are the monthly payments for both options?

Enter: the number of periods, *n*, which is 4 X 12 = 48 and the periodic interest rate, I_p = 18/12 = 1.50.

For the inexpensive option: enter $3,000 in $\boxed{\text{PV}}$ and key $\boxed{\text{PMT}}$, getting $88.12.

For the expensive option: enter $7,500 in $\boxed{\text{PV}}$ and key $\boxed{\text{PMT}}$ getting $220.31.

Total Interest The best way to calculate this, even with a business-analyst calculator, is by using Equation 9-5.

Accumulated Interest, Principal Portion of Payments, Remaining Balance With a four-function calculator, these computations are fairly time consuming. The business-analyst calculators simplify them considerably. Once the vital statistics for a given loan have been entered and the periodic payment determined, another key or two gives this information. On calculators, the labels and keystrokes involved in these special functions vary considerably more than those functions previously discussed. Consult the owner's manual for your specific model. The following discussion is based on the approach taken by Texas Instruments.

These calculators have a $\boxed{\text{P/I}}$ (Principal/Interest) key. If you enter a payment number in the display and activate this key, it computes how much of the specified payment is applied toward the principal of the loan and how much interest is paid. The principal is displayed and the interest is accessed by subsequently pushing the $\boxed{\text{x} \curvearrowright \text{y}}$ key. To get the accumulated interest and the balance remaining on the loan, a key labeled $\boxed{\text{Acc/Bal}}$ is used. Once again, a payment number is entered in the display. When $\boxed{\text{Acc/Bal}}$ is pressed, the accumulated interest paid up to and including the specified payment is calculated. The balance remaining on the loan is displayed by pushing the $\boxed{\text{x} \curvearrowright \text{y}}$ key.

Interest paid between 2 particular periods is determined by first computing the interest accumulated by the first payment period, storing this in the accessible memory, computing the interest accumulated by the later period, recalling the earlier figure, and subtracting.

EXAMPLE: An automobile loan has a principal of $5,500, an annual interest rate of 11%, and a 24-month maturity. The montly payment is $256.34.

Enter the appropriate values in $\boxed{\text{n}}$, $\boxed{\text{i}}$, $\boxed{\text{PV}}$, and $\boxed{\text{PMT}}$.
How much interest do you pay on the first payment?

To determine this, put 1 into the display and key $\boxed{\text{P/I}}$. After a fraction of a second, the number 205.93 is displayed. This is the amount of principal paid. Keying $\boxed{\text{x} \curvearrowright \text{y}}$ gives the interest: $50.42.

The first 7 payments of the loan are due in 1981. In order to calculate the amount of interest paid during 1981 for income tax purposes, first enter the number 7 in the display. Keying $\boxed{\text{Acc/Bal}}$ gives $312.66, the total interest paid in 1981. To get the balance of the loan, push $\boxed{\text{x} \curvearrowright \text{y}}$. The balance, $4,018.26, is then displayed.

The next 12 payments, numbers 8 through 20, are due in 1982. To determine the interest paid during this year, store the interest paid in 1981, $312.66, in the memory. Enter the number 20 in the display. Key $\boxed{\text{Acc/Bal}}$. The accumulated interest to that point is $629.16. Subtracting the stored amount gives $316.50, the total interest paid in 1982.

Inflation and Installment Buying As was the case with compound interest, business-analyst calculators are not explicitly set up to handle inflationary effects. The primary purpose of looking at installment loans in constant-value dollars is to get some idea of the true cost of borrowing. Even with a moderate inflation rate, calculations of the cost of a loan in nominal dollars substantially overstates the real cost.

Here we use Equation 9-10, as we did with the 4-function calculator.

$$TRI = PMT \left[\frac{(1 + r_p)^{N+1} - 1}{r_p (1 + r_p)^N} \right] - P$$

where *TRI* is the total real interest, *PMT* is the monthly payment, r_p is the periodic inflation rate as a decimal, *N* is the total number of payments, and *P* is the principal of the loan. With a business-analyst model, however, this calculation is much easier than it is with a 4-function calculator. If you haven't done so already, you can use the built-in functions to determine *PMT*. The $\boxed{y^x}$ key easily calculates the numbers-to-powers.

EXAMPLE: What is the interest in constant-value dollars that you must pay on a 9.5% mortgage with a principal of $40,000 and a maturity of 25 years if the inflation rate is 4%? 10%?

In this case, *N* = 25 X 12 = 300; *I* = 9.5/12 = 0.79166667; and *PV* = $40,000. Thus,

$$PMT = \$349.48$$

With an annual inflation rate of 4%, r_p = 4/1,200 = 0.00333333. It is a good idea to store r_p in memory because it will be used 3 times. *N* is stored in the financial register from determining *PMT* and can be recalled as needed.

$$TRI = \$349.48 \left[\frac{1.0033333^{301} - 1}{0.00333333 \, (1.0033333)^{300}} \right] - \$40,000$$

$$= \$26,559.33$$

With an annual inflation rate of 10%, r_p = 10/1,200 = 0.0083333 and

$$TRI = \$349.48 \left[\frac{1.0083333^{301} - 1}{0.0083333 \, (1.0083333)^{300}} \right] - \$40,000$$

$$= -\$1,191.21$$

PROBLEMS

1   A $10,000, 5-year loan costs $6,000 in interest and the lender requires a $50-per-year life insurance policy. What is the *APR* of the loan?

2   What are the quarterly payments for a $20,000, 10-year loan at 10¼%?

3   What are the monthly payments for a $46,000, 30-year mortgage at 11% annual interest?

4 How many months will it take to pay off a $13,000 loan at 6% annual interest if the monthly payments are $215.45?

5 What is the total interest a person must pay for a $60,000 mortgage at 10¾% for 25 years if the monthly payments are $577.25?

6 For the mortgage in problem 9, what is the unpaid balance and the interest paid after the first 5 years?

7 How much interest will Reginald pay with the seventy-second payment of a $52,000, 8¼%, 30-year mortgage?

8 For the mortgage in problem 9, what is the total real interest of the loan assuming a 6% average annual inflation rate? Assuming an 8% annual inflation rate?

9 What inflation rate reduces to about zero the total real interest of a $15,000, 12% loan with a 5-year maturity and monthly payments?

10 What inflation rate reduces to about zero the total real cost of a $35,000, 30-year mortgage of 11%?

10

Energy
and Home Insulation

While the future economics of energy in America is clouded by politics and a number of other uncertainties, one fact is generally accepted: Energy will continue to become more and more expensive. Whether you are simply concerned about rising heating bills, or if you believe that the oil companies and politicians have conspired to drive up oil prices, or if you feel that the time has come for a new energy ethic, your best strategy is the same: conservation. The U.S. government has estimated that approximately 40 million American homeowners would save money if they added insulation, storm windows, or weather stripping. Are you one of these? This chapter will help you determine the trade-off between the cost of insulating your house and the resulting fuel savings.

The importance of making your own determination rather than relying on the advice of professional home insulators was pointed out in the February, 1978 issue of *Consumer Reports*. Consumer's Union investigators concluded that "insulation is being oversold as a conservation tool. If your house already has some insulation, adding more may not be the best course to follow, because the money invested will often yield a surprisingly small saving of energy and money."

The energy it takes to heat your house depends on a number of things: The climate you live in, the temperature you maintain in the house, and how fast heat leaks from inside to outside. The cost of heating your house also depends on the type of heat you have (natural gas, oil, electric resistance, heat pump, etc.) and the efficiency of your furnace. It is unlikely that anyone but you will have the inclination to realistically determine the cost-effectiveness of the different energy-saving options. Insulation businesses have a vested interest in selling you the greatest amount of insulation possible, and to do so they all too frequently exaggerate the payoff.

HOW MUCH ENERGY
DOES YOUR HOME USE?

To determine how much energy your home uses, first determine how quickly your house loses energy. To do so, climate must be taken into account. The best method for doing this was devised by the American Society of Heating, Refrigeration, and Air Conditioning Engineers (ASHRAE). The key concept in this approach is something called a *degree day*.

DEGREE DAYS

A degree day measures climate by combining days and the average temperature. If you keep your house at 65° F, and if the average outside temperature for one day is 64° F, then this is considered to be a one-degree day. If the average temperature is 25° F for one day, this is a 40-degree day. Degree days are accumulated throughout the heating season. Seasonal averages range from 2,000 degree days in Birmingham, Alabama, to 10,000 degree days in Duluth, Minnesota. This can be expressed mathematically as

$$Degree\ Days\ =\ \sum_{i=1}^{n} (65\ -\ T_i) \qquad \text{(Equation 10-1)}$$

where T_i is the average temperature on the ith day of the season which lasts n days.

Fortunately, this is not something you must keep track of yourself. The U.S. Weather Service keeps a record of the number of degree days in various parts of the country. Many local newspapers publish degree days along with the daily weather report. Another source of this information is the U.S. Department of Commerce, which publishes a pamphlet entitled "Monthly Normals of Temperature, Precipitation and Heating and Cooling Degree Days." Pamphlets for your state can be obtained by writing the National Climatic Center, Federal Building, Asheville, North Carolina 28801 and cost $0.25 each.

YOUR HOME'S HEAT LOSS

The concept of degree days makes it possible to define a measure of how easily heat leaks out of your house that is largely independent of the climate where you live. Thus, if your home were magically transported to some other clime (where would you choose?) this measure of heat loss would enable you to calculate how much heat your home would require in this totally different location.

Before we can do this, however, we must have some way to measure energy. There are many measures of energy. Here we will use British Thermal Units, or BTUs. A BTU is the amount of heat required to raise the temperature of 1 pound of water (a little less than a pint) one degree Fahrenheit. The number of BTUs in a gallon of heating fuel, then, is the number of pounds of water that would be heated one degree Fahrenheit by the heat released when

Table 10-1 Home-Heating Systems

HEATING SYSTEM	TYPICAL EFFICIENCY (E)	FUEL UNIT	BTUs PER UNIT (Q)
Natural gas	0.60	therm*	100,000
Fuel oil	0.60	gal	140,000
Electric furnace	0.95	kwh**	3,413
Electric baseboard	1.00	kwh	3,413
Electric heat pump	1.50-2.00	kwh	3,413

*A therm is a unit of about 100 cu ft of gas, about the same as a CCF or one tenth of an MCF, other common units for measuring natural gas.
**Kwh is the abbreviation for kilowatt-hour.

the fuel is completely burned. Table 10-1 lists the amount of energy provided by common home-heating systems.

To determine your home's heat loss, you first need to dig out the records of how much fuel (or electricity) you used last winter. If you use oil or natural gas, simply total the number of gallons of heating oil or natural gas you used during the winter. If you use electric heat it is much more difficult to determine how much is used for heating and how much for other uses. The consumer relations department in your electric utility should have guidelines for determining the proportion of electricity used in space heating in your particular region. For those who use more than one type of heating system in their home, the problem is excessively difficult. If, like most people, you have only one type of heating system the problem is solved directly. To begin, find your heating system on Table 10-1. For each heating system listed in the table are its typical efficiency, E, and Q, the number of BTUs per therm, gallon, or kilowatt-hour. With E, Q, your home's energy consumption, F, for a specific heating season, and the number of degree days, D, during this period, we are ready to compute your home's heat loss. The appropriate formula is

$$Heat\ Loss = \frac{FQE}{D}$$ (Equation 10-2)

EXAMPLE: Peter owns a small house in the Boston area. Going over his records for a recent winter he found that his oil-fired furnace burned 1,329.2 gal. A call to the local weather station established that this was during a 6,321-degree-day season. Turning to Table 10-1, Peter finds that the efficiency for an oil-fired furnace is about 0.6 and that there are 140,000 BTUs per gal in home-heating oil. Therefore, F = 1,329.2 gal; Q = 140,000 BTUs per gal; E = 0.60; and D = 6,321 degree days. Then,

$$Heat\ Loss = \frac{1,329.2 \times 140,000 \times 0.60}{6,321}$$

$$= \frac{111,652,800.00}{6,321} = 17,663.8\ \text{BTUs per degree day}$$

Unfortunately, there is no standard for heat loss, so it is difficult to judge whether a specific house is unreasonably leaky. This is because heat loss depends on the size of the house, how windy the site is, and other specifics that can have a large effect on a structure's heat loss.

EXAMPLE: What if Peter's wife, Sue, is extremely sensitive to the cold. She keeps the house at a toasty 72° F all day. However, they turn the thermostat down to 60° F at night. How can Peter take this into account?

The degree-day approach to calculating heat loss is an approximation. It assumes that the average temperature in a building is 65° F. In so doing, it understates the temperature during the day and overstates it during the night.

If T_{day} is the temperature the house is kept at during the day and h_d the number of hours it is kept at this temperature, and if T_{night} is the temperature the house is kept at during the night and h_n the number of hours it is kept at this temperature, then the average temperature, T_{av}, is

$$T_{av} = \frac{(T_{day} \times h_d) + (T_{night} \times h_n)}{24} \qquad \text{(Equation 10-3)}$$

In Peter's case, T_{day} is 72° F and T_{night} is 60° F. Assuming h_d is 16 hr and h_n is 8 hr, then

$$T_{av} = \frac{(72 \times 16) + (60 \times 8)}{24}$$

$$= \frac{1152 + 480}{24}$$

$$= \frac{1632}{24}$$

$$= 68° \text{ F.}$$

The average temperature in Peter's and Sue's home is 3° higher than that assumed in the degree-day computation.

Recall that the formula for degree days is

$$Degree\ Days = \sum_{i=1}^{n} (65 - T_i)$$

If we were to substitute 68 for 65 in this equation, the number of degree days each day would be just 3 more than when 65° were used. If the heating season is 9 months (270 days), then this is equivalent to adding 270 × 3 = 810 degree days to the season. Therefore, if Peter substituted 6,321 + 810 = 7,131 degree days in the equation, he would get a more accurate figure for the total heat loss of his house.

Whatever your home's heat loss, it is possible to determine how much you can save by adding more insulation or by installing storm windows. This can be done by calculating your energy cost and then determining the amount a given conservation step will reduce this cost.

THE PRICE YOU PAY FOR ENERGY

What price do you pay for the energy you use to heat your home? While you may very well know the price per gallon, per therm, or per kilowatt-hour, you may not know the cost of energy per BTU. Because a BTU is a fairly small unit when it comes to home heating, the following equation will allow you to determine the price you pay per million BTUs. (A million BTUs is commonly abbreviated as MMBTUs.)

$$BTU \ Cost = \frac{Price \ per \ Unit \ \times \ 1,000,000}{Q \times E} \qquad \textbf{(Equation 10-4)}$$

The *Price per Unit* is the price per gallon, therm, or kilowatt-hour, depending on the type of heating system you have. If you use electric heat, you should take the lowest kilowatt-hour cost provided your utility company uses a declining rate schedule and charges lower rates the more electricity you use. Be sure to include tax and fuel adjustment charges as part of the cost.

EXAMPLE: Norman and Nancy live in Washington, D.C. They heat their home with natural gas, which costs them $0.20 per therm. What is their cost per million BTUs?

In this case, *Price per Unit* = $0.20; *Q* = 100,000 BTUs per therm; and *E* = 0.60. Thus,

$$BTU \ Cost = \frac{\$0.20 \ \times \ 1,000,000}{100,000 \ \times \ 0.60}$$

$$= \frac{\$200,000}{60,000}$$

$$= \$3.33 \ per \ \textbf{MMBTU}$$

EXAMPLE: The Jones family uses oil heat. The current cost is $0.43 per gallon. Are they paying more or less per MMBTU than Norman and Nancy?

For the Jones family, *Price per Unit* = $0.43; *Q* = 140,000; and *E* = 0.60. This means

$$BTU \ Cost = \frac{\$0.43 \ \times \ 1,000,000}{140,000 \ \times \ 0.60}$$

$$= \frac{\$430,000}{84,000}$$

$$= \$5.12 \ per \ \textbf{MMBTU}$$

so the Jones family is paying over 50% more for their energy than Nancy and Norman.

FUEL COSTS
OF DIFFERENT HEATING SYSTEMS

EXAMPLE: Margaret lives in an old house in Seattle. The furnace is on its last legs. She is trying to decide whether she should replace it with an oil, natural gas, or electric furnace. She wants to determine what her fuel bills with each type of furnace are likely to be. She has called around and gotten the following rates:

Natural gas: $0.23 per therm
No. 2 fuel oil: $0.38 per gal
Electricity: $0.025 per kwh

Next she calculates her cost per million BTUs using Equation 10-4.

$$BTU\ Cost\ \text{(gas)} = \frac{\$0.23 \times 1,000,000}{100,000 \times 0.60}$$

$$= \$3.83\ \text{per MMBTU}$$

$$BTU\ Cost\ \text{(oil)} = \frac{\$0.38 \times 1,000,000}{140,000 \times 0.60}$$

$$= \$4.52\ \text{per MMBTU}$$

$$BTU\ Cost\ \text{(electric)} = \frac{\$0.025 \times 1,000,000}{3,413 \times 0.95}$$

$$= \$7.71\ \text{per MMBTU}$$

She has calculated that her house has a heat loss of 22,500 BTUs per degree day. From Table 10-2 Margaret finds that Seattle averages 5,185 degree days per season. To get the total amount of energy she must multiply the heat loss per degree day times the total number of degree days. To express this in MMBTUs, it must then be divided by 1 million.

$$Annual\ Heat\ Loss = \frac{Heat\ Loss \times D}{1,000,000}$$ **(Equation 10-5)**

In Margaret's case, **Heat Loss** = 22,500 BTUs per degree day and D = $5,000. Then,

Table 10-2 Seasonal Heating Degree Days for Selected U.S. Cities—30-Year Average

STATE/CITY	SEASONAL AVERAGE DEGREE DAYS	STATE/CITY	SEASONAL AVERAGE DEGREE DAYS
Ala/Mobile	1,684	Nev/Reno	6,022
Alaska/Juneau	9,007	N.H./Concord	7,360
Ariz/Phoenix	1,552	N.J./Atlantic City	4,946
Ark/Little Rock	3,354	N.Mex/Albuquerque	4,292
Cal/Los Angeles	1,819	N.Y./Albany	6,888
Sacramento	2,843	Buffalo	6,927
San Francisco	3,042	New York	4,848
Col/Denver	6,016	N.C./Charlotte	3,218
Conn/Hartford	6,350	Raleigh	3,514
Del/Wilmington	4,940	N.Dak/Bismarck	9,044
D.C./Washington	4,211	Ohio/Cincinnati	4,844
Fla/Jacksonville	1,327	Cleveland	6,154
Miami	206	Columbus	5,702
Ga/Atlanta	3,095	Okla/Oklahoma City	3,695
Hawaii/Honolulu	0	Ore/Portland	4,792
Idaho/Boise	5,833	Pa/Philadelphia	4,865
Ill/Chicago	6,127	Pittsburgh	5,930
Peoria	6,098	R.I./Providence	5,972
Ind/Indianapolis	5,577	S.C./Columbia	2,598
Iowa/Des Moines	6,710	S.Dak/Sioux Falls	7,838
Kans/Wichita	4,687	Tenn/Memphis	3,227
Ky/Louisville	4,645	Nashville	3,696
La/New Orleans	1,465	Tex/Dallas-Ft Worth	2,382
Maine/Portland	7,498	El Paso	2,678
Md/Baltimore	4,729	Houston	1,434
Mass/Boston	5,621	Utah/Salt Lake City	5,983
Mich/Detroit	6,228	Vt/Burlington	7,876
Sault Ste. Marie	9,193	Va/Norfolk	3,488
Minn/Duluth	9,756	Richmond	3,939
Minneapolis	8,159	Wash/Seattle	5,185
Miss/Jackson	2,300	Spokane	6,835
Mo/Kansas City	5,161	W.Va/Charleston	4,590
St. Louis	4,750	Wis/Milwaukee	7,444
Mont/Great Falls	7,652	Wyo/Cheyenne	7,255
Nebr/Omaha	6,049	P.R./San Juan	0

Source: U.S. National Oceanic and Atmospheric Administration, Comparative Climatic Data

$$Annual\ Heat\ Loss = \frac{22,500\ \text{BTUs per degree day} \times 5,185\ \text{degree days}}{1,000,000}$$

$$= 116.7\ \text{MMBTU}$$

The next step is to calculate average annual heating costs. To do this, multiply the **Total Heat Loss** times **BTU Cost** for gas, oil, and electric, respectively.

157          $Annual\ Heating\ Cost$ (gas) $= 116.7 \times \$3.83$

$$= \$446.96$$

$$\textit{Annual Heating Cost} \text{ (oil)} = 116.7 \times \$4.52$$

$$= \$527.48$$

$$\textit{Annual Heating Cost} \text{ (electric)} = 116.7 \times \$7.71$$

$$= \$899.76$$

Assuming a 15-year lifetime for the furnace, Margaret could pay anywhere from $6,704 to $13,496 for heating assuming prices remain constant. Now she can balance these fuel-cost figures against the initial price of the different units.

HEAT CONDUCTION AND RESISTANCE

In one episode of television's "All in the Family," a fast-talking con artist convinces Archie Bunker that his house is losing energy like a sieve. He does this with a light meter, which he says measures heat loss. With this simple tactic he gets Archie to purchase a load of worthless siding. While this is a humorous satire, the point it is based on—that energy is a mysterious quantity to most people—is the patent truth. Energy is invisible. It takes many forms. It is the dynamic force of the universe. It is absolutely essential to life.

Yet despite the importance of energy, its nature is poorly understood. Our entire lives are surrounded by the invisible ebb and flow of energy tides. These heat tides flow as inevitably from hot objects to cooler ones as water runs downhill. From the 5,000° F flame in your furnace, it flows outward into the cooler air stream blown past it. The 100° hot air then blows out from the hot air vents in the floor, mixing with the cooler air in the room to produce a comfortable thermal cocoon. But heat is continually seeping out through the walls, windows, doors, roof, and every crack and cranny in your home, carrying its load of energy into the great outdoors and warming it infinitesimally. It is replaced by cold, outside air, which must be warmed. Heat travels in three basic ways: conduction, convection, and radiation.

Conduction

Conduction is the transfer of energy in solid objects. A flame heats the bottom of a frying pan sitting on a burner. The heat spreads throughout the metal in the pan and up the handle by conduction. The energy from the flame causes the metal atoms in the pan's bottom to vibrate more rapidly. As these excited atoms come into contact with their neighbors, they cause them to vibrate more rapidly as well. In this way the energy spreads.

Some materials conduct energy more readily than others. Metals are some of the best conductors. Wood and plastic are much poorer than metals. That is why they are commonly used on frying pan handles: They resist the spread of thermal energy by conduction.

Convection

Convection is the transfer of heat by liquids or gases. Because of their fluid nature, liquid and gas molecules can flow from hotter to cooler places. As they do so, they carry energy with them. The forced-air furnace is an example of convection in action. The hot air carries the heat energy from the furnace throughout the house. Similarly, infiltration—the flow of cold, outside air into a building through cracks—is a convective process.

Radiation

Solar energy is a prime example of radiation. Deep within the sun, nuclear reactions release tremendous amounts of energy. This is transferred from the star's core to its outermost layers by conduction and convection. Once this energy reaches the outer limits of the sun, most of it is converted into electromagnetic radiation—familiar to us as light—and so it can cross the void of space to reach and warm the Earth.

While the above is an example of radiation on a cosmic scale, this same phenomenon is taking place all around us. We are not as aware of it, however, because the radiation given off by warm objects, such as radiators, is in the infrared portion of the electromagnetic spectrum, which we cannot see. Instead, we sense infrared radiation as heat. This is the source of the warmth from a fireplace. If you could see in the infrared, and you went outside on a cold day and looked at your house, it would seem to glow. Your house acts as a large radiator: Its warm surfaces emit a steady stream of infrared radiation to colder surroundings.

In addition to these 3 mechanisms for heat transfer, infiltration can also contribute to the total heat loss of your house. While infiltration is often the major source of heat loss, it is also the least expensive to fix. Federal energy experts say there is no doubt that weatherstripping is cost effective almost everywhere. So if you have not done this you probably should.

Except for extremely leaky buildings, conduction is a major conduit of energy loss. The rate at which the walls, roof, and windows of a house conduct energy controls the total heat loss. The measure of conductivity is called thermal transmittance and is designated by U. This is the number of BTUs that flow through a square foot of material per degree difference between one side and the other. One of the characteristics of thermal conductivity is that the greater the temperature difference between 2 points, the faster the energy flows. The ability of a material to slow the transfer of heat is called thermal resistance and is labeled R. This is what is referred to when building contractors or the sellers of insulation talk about R *values*. The higher the R value, the greater the thermal resistance. Insulation comes in a number of different R values, which are usually printed prominently on the packaging or backing. Fiberglass batts, for instance, are available in R-11, R-19, or R-21.

Thermal transmittance and resistance are closely related.

$$U = \frac{1}{R}$$ (Equation 10-6)

159   The higher the transmittance, the lower the resistance, and vice versa.

We are not interested in the thermal transmittance per se, but how it changes when more insulation is added. The change in transmittance is designated $\triangle U$ and is given by the following equation[1]

$$\triangle U = \frac{1}{R_o} - \frac{1}{R_o + R_1}$$

(Equation 10-7)

where R_o is the R value of the original section of the building's shell and R_1 is the R value of the insulation that is being added.

Embodied in this expression is an important aspect of the process of insulating: The more insulation you have, the less you gain by adding more. This can be seen by looking at the effect on $\triangle U$ of adding R-11 insulation to areas with different initial thermal resistances.

Table 10-3 Effect of Adding R-11 Insulation to Areas with Different Initial R Values

R_o	$R_o + R_1$	$\triangle U \left(\dfrac{BTUs}{ft^2 \times degrees \times hrs} \right)$
2 (uninsulated)	13	0.42
11	22	0.05
19	30	0.02
31	42	0.01

As a result, the point of diminishing returns can come quite quickly to the process of adding insulation to the home.

A favorite spot to add insulation is the attic. This is the easiest and least expensive place to beef up a home's thermal armor. To determine how much you will save by adding more insulation to your attic, first determine what its existing thermal resistance is. Using Table 10-4 you can estimate R_o for your attic by measuring the thickness of the existing insulation.

EXAMPLE: Ralph now has 2-in fiberglass bats in his attic. He is thinking about adding a new layer of R-11 fiberglass bats. How much will this reduce the heat transmittance?

$$\triangle U = \frac{1}{R_o} - \frac{1}{R_o + R_1}$$

From Table 10-4, $R_o = 8.75$, and R_1 is 11. Thus,

$$\triangle U = \frac{1}{8.75} - \frac{1}{8.75 + 11}$$

$$= 0.11429 - 0.05063$$

$$= 0.06365 \text{ or } 0.064$$

---

[1] The Greek letter *delta*, $\triangle$, is a common mathematical symbol for a difference or change.

Table 10-4 Typical *R* Values for Existing Insulation in the Attic

THICKNESS (INCHES)	R VALUES*		
	Fiberglass Bats	Loose Fiberglass	Loose Cellulose
2	8.75	5.75	9.15
4	12.75	10.55	16.55
6	20.75	15.00	24.00

*With no insulation, *R* value ≅ 1.75.

Determining $\triangle U$ for other parts of the house—windows, doors, walls—is more difficult. For one thing, it is much harder to determine the existing *R* values. Another problem is that the effectiveness of insulating walls depends greatly on the thoroughness of the job. It does not take many air spaces in wall insulation to greatly diminish its insulating value, regardless of the high *R* values that the insulators quote.

Typical values for $\triangle U$ are listed for wall insulation, storm doors, storm windows, and thermopane in Table 10-5.

Table 10-5 Typical $\triangle U$ Values for Various Components of a Building Shell

COMPONENT	$\triangle U \left(\dfrac{BTUs}{ft^2 \times degrees \times hrs} \right)$
Wall insulation blown in	0.16
Storm windows	0.55
Thermopane	0.48
Storm doors	0.16

ANNUAL HEAT-LOSS REDUCTION

With $\triangle U$, the degree-day average for your climate, D, and the dimensions of the area you are thinking of insulating, it is possible to calculate the annual reduction in heat loss (*ARHL*) that would result. If A is the area to be insulated in ft^2, then

$$ARHL = \frac{\triangle U \times A \times D \times 24}{1,000,000}$$ **(Equation 10-8)**

This formula gives *ARHL* in MMBTU.

If the area to be insulated is the attic, multiply A by 0.9 to compensate for the area of the joists, which have a much lower thermal resistance than the insulation.

There are some adjustments that must be made in *ARHL* to account for the following special circumstances:

1. For attic space being insulated for the first time, multiply *ARHL* by 0.7. This compensates for the fact that the temperatures in the attic space

161

will be lower after the insulation is installed. Because the heat flow is proportional to the temperature drop between the inside of the house and the attic space, this means that more heat will flow through the thicker insulation than would otherwise be the case.

2. When adding storm windows, multiply *ARHL* by 1.05. This accounts for the reduction in infiltration losses around the windows.

EXAMPLE: Ralph has determined that $\triangle U$ = 0.064 if he adds the extra insulation to his attic that he feels he can afford. He lives in Salt Lake City, Utah, where the seasonal average is 5,983 degree days. His attic is 30 ft by 40 ft.

In this case, $\triangle U$ = 0.064; A = 30 ft × 40 ft = 1,200 ft^2; and D = 5,983 degree days. Because this is an attic, we must first multiply A times 0.9, which is 1,200 × 0.9 = 1,080. Thus,

$$ARHL = \frac{0.064 \times 1,080 \times 5,983 \times 24}{1,000,000}$$

$$= \frac{9,925,079.0}{1,000,000}$$

$$= 9.925 \text{ MMBTU}$$

EXAMPLE: Pamela gets out her yardstick and measures all the windows in her home in Juneau, Alaska. She finds that she has 22,260 in^2 of window space. The climate there is a severe 9,007 degree days per heating season. How much would she reduce her home's annual heat loss if she installed storm windows?

From Table 10-5, we find that $\triangle U$ = 0.55 for storm windows. D is 0,007. A must be expressed in ft^2 in Equation 10-8. Therefore, divide 22,260 by 144, the number of in^2 per ft^2, to get the area in the proper units:

$$A = 22,260/144 = 154.58 \text{ ft}^2$$

Now we are ready to compute *ARHL*, which is

$$ARHL = \frac{0.55 \times 154.58 \times 9,007 \times 24}{1,000,000}$$

$$= \frac{18,378,387}{1,000,000}$$

$$= 18.378 \text{ MMBTU}$$

We must not forget a final step. Because Pamela is thinking of installing storm windows, these would also cut down on the amount of warm air that leaks out around the casements. So we must multiply *ARHL* by

1.05 to take this into account. The adjusted annual reduction in heat loss is

$$ARHL' = 18.378 \times 1.05$$

$$= 19.297 \text{ MMBTU}$$

ANNUAL REDUCTION IN YOUR HEATING BILL

Now that we have figured *ARHL*, it is a simple step to determine how much you will save in heating bills. We already covered the method to calculate your energy cost on page 155. The annual reduction in your heating bill *ARHB* is

$$ARHB = ARHL \times BTU \ Cost \qquad \text{(Equation 10-9)}$$

EXAMPLE: Ralph has figured that the **ARHL** for additional attic insulation is 9.925 MMBTU. He has an oil furnace and pays $0.40 per gallon for heating oil. From Equation 10-4,

$$BTU \ Cost = \frac{\$0.40 \times 1,000,000}{140,000 \times 0.60}$$

$$= \frac{\$400,000}{84,000}$$

$$= \$4.76 \text{ per } \textbf{MMBTU}$$

and

$$ARHB = 9.925 \times \$4.76$$

$$= \$47.26$$

If Ralph has gotten a low estimate of $275 for installing the insulation, the energy conservation measure should pay for itself in $275/$47.26 = 5.8 years. Actually, as energy costs are rising steadily, the payback period will probably be shorter. At the same time, however, inflation is ever decreasing the value of the dollars you save by this conservation step. If the rate of increase of energy costs equals the inflation rate, then the 5.8-year payback remains valid. If energy costs outweigh general inflation—as many experts predict—then the payback will be sooner. If, on the other hand, the cost of energy rises at a slower pace than inflation, the payback period increases.

EXAMPLE: Our Alaskan homeowner, Pamela, pays an exorbitant $0.60 gal for No. 2 heating fuel. This translates into $7.14 per MMBTU.

How much will she save per year by installing a complete set of storm windows?

$$ARHB = ARHL \times BTU\ Cost$$

$$= 19.197 \times \$7.14$$

$$= \$137.07$$

A WORD OF CAUTION

A number of approximations are used in these formulas and a number of secondary factors are ignored. As a result these figures are far from exact. They only give you "ballpark" estimates. A much more detailed thermodynamic analysis is required to get precise figures. Still, these are accurate enough to give you a pretty good picture of your home's heating performance and how it can be improved.

DID THE INSULATORS DO A GOOD JOB?

Now we have the mathematical tools to check on the job the insulators have done when they installed your new insulation. Suppose you hire someone to come blow insulation into all the walls of your beautiful bungalow. Did they do a legitimate job or were you ripped off? The following example illustrates how you can check.

EXAMPLE: Dan and Dorothy Doe in Philadelphia had insulation blown into the walls of their frame house in October. They have a natural gas and hot water radiator heating system. In September they used 46.1 therms. In November their consumption was 186.7 therms. How good was the insulation job?

To determine this, we first need some basic information. How many degree days were there in September? In November? What was the area that was insulated? From the weather service, Dan learns that there were 123 degree days in September and 562 degree days in November. From the dimensions of his house he calculates the total wall area and subtracts the area of all windows and doors to come up with 1,412 ft² that were insulated. Using Equation 10-2 Dan can calculate the heat loss of his house per degree day before and after the insulating job.

For September,

$$Heat\ Loss = \frac{46.1 \times 100,000 \times 0.6}{123}$$

$$= \frac{2,766,000}{123}$$

$$= 22,487.80\ \text{BTU per degree day}$$

For November,

$$Heat\ Loss\ =\ \frac{186.7 \times 100{,}000 \times 0.6}{562}$$

$$=\ \frac{11{,}202{,}000}{562}$$

$$=\ 19{,}932.38\ \text{BTU per degree day}$$

Thus the insulation made some difference—about a 13% reduction in the heat loss. But is this as much as it should be?

To determine this we must see what this means in terms of $\triangle U$. If it is 0.16 (the typical value listed in Table 10-5) or better, then the job was a good one. If it is much lower than this, it was probably poorly done.

Recall that $\triangle U$ is the reduction in heat loss in terms of BTUs per ft^2 per degree per hr. Therefore, if we multiply it by 24 hr per day and by the area insulated, we get the heat reduction in BTUs per degree day. This is the same form as the heat loss that Dan calculated for September and November. As a result

$$\triangle U \times 24 \times A\ =\ Heat\ Loss\ \text{(Sept)}\ -\ Heat\ Loss\ \text{(Nov)}$$

or

$$\triangle U\ =\ \frac{Heat\ Loss\ \text{(Sept)}\ -\ Heat\ Loss\ \text{(Nov)}}{24 \times A} \quad \textbf{(Equation 10-10)}$$

In Dan's case, then

$$\triangle U\ =\ \frac{22{,}487.80\ -\ 19{,}932.38}{24 \times 1{,}412}$$

$$=\ \frac{2{,}555.42}{33{,}888}$$

$$=\ 0.07541$$

Thus Dan is getting only 47% of the heat loss reduction of a typical installation. Calculating his annual reduction in heating bills, Dan

---

[2] This expression can be generalized to

$$\triangle U\ =\ \frac{Heat\ Loss\ \text{(before)}\ -\ Heat\ Loss\ \text{(after)}}{24 \times A} \quad \textbf{(Equation 10-11)}$$

where the *Heat Loss*(es) are calculated according to Equation 10-2 and are given in BTU per degree day. The interval you use to calculate the *Heat Loss*(es) can be whatever is convenient—the period between 2 fuel oil deliveries, for instance.

also finds that his savings is about 53% less than he anticipated. However, this check gives him grounds for insisting that the installers come back and do a proper job. If they are uncooperative, he may want to engage a lawyer and seek restitution in the courts.

PROBLEMS

1   From September to May, it took 1,732 gal of fuel oil to heat a Concord, New Hampshire, home. Given the degree days from Table 10-2, what is the heat loss for the house?

2   A new townhouse in Buffalo, New York, has electric-resistance heat. Skyrocketing electricity rates have jacked the price in the area to $0.08 per kwh. If the heat loss of the house is 15,000 BTUs per degree day, what is the annual heating cost?

3   If an attic has 2 in of loose fiberglass insulation and another 6 in are added, what is the resulting $\triangle U$?

4   R-20 fiberglass batting is added to an uninsulated attic. What is the change in conductivity?

5   How much does a change in thermal conductivity of 0.22 for a 2,500 ft^2 attic in a 4,900-degree-day climate reduce the annual heat loss?

6   A bungalow is heated with electric-resistance heat. The price of electricity is $0.055 per kwh. The annual reduction in heat loss by increased insulation is 65 MMBTU. What is the annual reduction in the heating bill resulting from the increase in insulation?

11

Lifecycle Costs
of Electric Appliances

Electricity is magical, subtle stuff. How quietly and efficiently it seems to drive our mechanical slaves, the wheels of industry. Yet this genie in a wire does not come to us cheaply. And, as the rest of the labor force, it continually threatens to go on strike if its wages are not raised to keep up with inflation.

Until recently the low cost of petroleum and natural gas kept electrical rates relatively low. Therefore, we did not need or, rather, did not bother to determine the efficiency of the various electrical gadgets we buy and blissfully plug in. Now, though, with electrical costs rising for the foreseeable future, the thrifty shopper has become concerned with the electricity consumption of appliances.

Comparative buying is not an easy task. Appliance manufacturers are not very cooperative in helping the consumer make the best choice. Incomplete labeling and misleading advertising characterize the industry response to the situation. Arthur H. Rosenfeld, an energy expert at Lawrence Berkeley Laboratory and a strong advocate for energy conservation, tells an anecdote that illustrates this fact. As part of his work, he studied the electricity consumption of refrigerators. One Sears model had very poor performance, he discovered. Sometime later the scientist heard that Sears had slightly improved their electrical lemon and were advertising it as having new, improved energy savings. The advertising was factually correct but totally misleading, he says, because even with the improvements it was still only a mediocre performer.

The Association of Home Appliance Manufacturers (AHAM) does sponsor an energy-labeling program. Models tested by the AHAM have a sticker indicating that the association has certified the appliance's energy-use rating. However, a number of manufacturers proudly display this sticker but do not disclose exactly what the appliance's consumption rating is.

Fortunately, groups such as the Consumer's Union do measure the electrical consumption of various appliances as part of their evaluation process. Publications such as CU's *Consumer Reports* are available either at the library or by subscription. The basic information contained in *Consumer Reports* makes it possible to compare different model appliances much more thoroughly than the limited information available from manufacturers.

The basis for a complete financial comparison is *lifecycle costing*— the attempt to estimate the total cost of an appliance over its lifetime. Life-cycle costs include not only the purchase price but also operating costs, repair, and maintenance. Estimating lifecycle costs requires certain assumptions about the price of electricity, water, and whatever else the appliance may need to operate. The biggest uncertainty is what the repair and maintenance costs will be. Even organizations such as Consumer's Union make only a qualitative estimate of these costs—pegging appliances as better than average, average, and below average. This is better than nothing, but still far from satisfactory.

ELECTRICITY COSTS

To estimate lifecycle costs for electric appliances, the first step is to determine how much you currently pay for electricity. Electricity is measured in units of kilowatt-hours, abbreviated kwh. Printed in one of the boxes on your electric bill, you should find a listing of the number of kwh that you used during the billing period. Under the amount column, you will probably find a basic charge, a fuel charge, or fuel adjustment allowance, possibly a state surcharge, and perhaps a city tax. To get an estimate of the electricity rate, divide the amount due by the number of kwh.

$$ER = \frac{Total\ Bill}{kwh} \qquad \textbf{(Equation 11-1)}$$

EXAMPLE: From June 7 to August 7, 1978, Harold used 698 kwh of electricity. The total charge was $37.66. How much was he paying per kwh?

$$ER = \frac{\$37.66}{698}$$

$$= \$0.0540\ per\ kwh$$

Harold was paying $0.054 per kwh. This is an intermediate price: in 1978 electricity costs ranged from $0.035 to $0.10 per kwh.

Electricity costs are rising rapidly, as are other forms of energy. For simplicity's sake, assume that electricity costs are rising at a rate equal to general inflation. In this case, the determination of lifetime operating costs based on current rates is equivalent to a constant-value-dollar calculation.

The actual operating costs will undoubtedly be considerably greater, but the value of the dollars you are paying will be considerably less as well.

REFRIGERATORS

Of all household appliances, energy costs are most significant with refrigerators. According to a Lawrence Berkeley Laboratory study in 1977, the purchase price of refrigerators ranged from $360 to $550, and the total life-time cost of these appliances ranged from $1,400 to over $2,000. The cost of the electricity refrigerators consume over their lifetime accounts for 2/3 to 3/4 of the total cost of the appliance. The Berkeley scientists also discovered that there was no relationship between purchase price and energy consumption: More expensive models were not necessarily more energy efficient than cheaper ones. This fact can be illustrated by plotting the monthly electrical consumption of top-freezer-refrigerators against their purchase price.

If the more expensive refrigerators were more energy efficient, then the points plotted on Graph 11-1 would cluster along a line or curve extending from the upper left-hand corner of the graph to the lower right-hand corner. As you can see, the points are widely scattered: It is possible to get refrigerators for about the same price that have quite different electricity consumption.

Monthly Electric Costs

What do these differences in electricity consumption mean in terms of monthly electric bills? To determine monthly electricity cost, multiply the number of kwh per month for a given model (from Table 11-1) by the electricity cost you determined with Equation 11-1.

$$\textit{Monthly Electricity Cost} = \text{kwh per month} \times \textit{ER}$$

(Equation 11-2)

EXAMPLE: The Admiral KNT1879 uses up 173 kwh of electric current per month. The Hotpoint CTF18HV, on the other hand, consumes only 99 kwh per month. If electricity costs $0.058 per kwh, what will the operating cost of each refrigerator be?

For the Admiral,

$$\textit{Monthly Electric Cost} = 173 \text{ kwh per month} \times \$0.058$$

$$= \$10.03$$

For the Hotpoint,

$$\textit{Monthly Electric Cost} = 99 \text{ kwh per month} \times \$0.058$$

$$= \$5.74$$

So the difference between the 2 refrigerators would be $10.03 − $5.74 = $4.29, or over $50 per year.

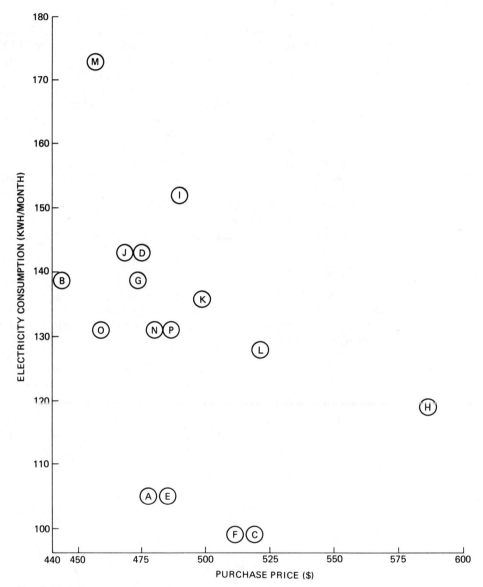

Graph 11-1 Refrigerator Cost and Electricity Consumption in 1978

Table 11-1 Refrigerator Cost and Electricity Consumption

DESIGNATION*	MODEL	PURCHASE PRICE ($)	KWH/MONTH
A	Sears Kenmore 67771	478	105
B	Sears Kenmore 67721	444	139
C	GE TBF18HV	518	99
D	GE TBF18DV	475	143
E	Whirlpool EET171HK	485	105
F	Hotpoint CTF18HV	511	99
G	Whirlpool EET171MK	473	139
H	Amana TC18W	591	119
I	Frigidaire FPC1 170T-7	490	152
J	Hotpoint CTF18EV	468	143
K	Wards Signature 1756	499	136
L	White-Westinghouse RT188T	522	128
M	Admiral KNT1879	457	173
N	Gibson RT17F6	480	131
O	Kelvinator TMK170MN	458	131
P	Wizard Citation 1717	484	131

Source: Consumer Reports, January 1978
*See these designations plotted on Graph 11-1.

Lifecycle Cost

The cost of a refrigerator for its entire lifetime is the sum of its purchase price and its operating cost. The primary operating cost (repair and maintenance will not be included because there are no good estimates) is the price of the electricity it consumes. To calculate this, we must assume a lifetime for the appliance. The design lifetime of refrigerators is typically 20 years, so this figure will be used in the following calculations. Thus

$$Operating\ Cost\ =\ 240\ \times\ Monthly\ Electricity\ Cost$$

(Equation 11-3)

and

$$Lifecycle\ Cost\ =\ Purchase\ Price\ +\ Operating\ Cost$$

(Equation 11-4)

EXAMPLE: Given electricity costs of $0.058 per kwh, what are the lifecycle costs of the Admiral KNT1879 and Hotpoint CTF18HV?
For the Admiral,

$$Operating\ Cost\ =\ 240\ \times\ \$10.03\ =\ \$2,407.20$$

From Table 11-1, the purchase price is $457. Then,

$$Lifecycle\ Cost\ =\ \$457\ +\ \$2,407.20\ =\ \$2,864.20$$

For the Hotpoint,

171

$$Operating\ Cost\ =\ 240\ \times\ \$5.74\ =\ \$1,377.60$$

From Table 11-1, its purchase price is $511. Then,

$$Lifecycle\ Cost = \$511 + \$1,377.60 = \$1,888.60$$

Although the Hotpoint has a price tag $54 higher than the Admiral, over its 20-year life it will be almost $1,000 cheaper to operate. And if electricity costs rise faster than general inflation, the difference in lifetime costs will be even greater. On the other hand, the calculation assumes that you purchase the appliance with cash. If you buy it on an installment plan, you can use Equation 9-14 in Chapter 9 to determine the total real expense of the purchase. Then you can substitute this for the purchase price in Equation 11-4. This will tend to decrease the difference in lifecycle cost, but not by very much.

As you can readily see, the energy efficiency of a refrigerator makes a big difference in the amount it costs you. Besides saving yourself money, purchasing energy-efficient refrigerators can result in major societal and environmental benefits . . . if enough people follow suit. According to Dr. Rosenfeld, if the State of California simply prohibited the sale of inefficient refrigerators, the energy savings that would accrue from 15 years of sales would add up to 600 megawatts—the equivalent of the output of a medium-sized electrical generating plant. If the electricity consumption of new refrigerators could be reduced to range from 50 kwh to 125 kwh per month (a design study by Arthur D. Little concludes this is possible for an additional $50 per unit), the savings in electric power demand over the same time span would amount to 2,200 megawatts, Dr. Rosenfeld has calculated, the equivalent of the output of 2 large nuclear or coal-fired electrical power stations. If you don't like nuclear energy or the pollution created by coal-burning, one of the best methods of fighting is to buy the most electricity-conserving appliances. At the same time you are saving money.

HOT-WATER HEATERS

Another common appliance whose lifecycle cost is substantially more than its purchase price is the hot-water heater. Unlike refrigerators, hot-water heaters come in either natural gas or electric models. As a result, comparisons will be slightly more complicated but no more difficult.

With the purchase price and annual energy consumption listed in Tables 11-2 and 11-3, we can calculate the lifecycle cost of different hot-water heaters. First, we will assume a 20-year lifetime.

If you are considering electric hot-water heaters, you will need to determine the price you are paying for electricity. If you have not already done this, you can do so by using Equation 11-1.

If you are considering gas hot-water heaters, you must first determine the price you are paying per therm for natural gas. You can either get this from your gas bill or from the local gas company. On your gas bill, there should be a listing of the number of therms you have used. Simply divide this into the total bill to estimate the gas rate.

$$GR = \frac{Total\ Bill}{Therms}$$

(Equation 11-5)

Table 11-2 Electric Hot-Water Heaters—All 52-gallon Tanks

MODEL*	PURCHASE PRICE ($)	ANNUAL ENERGY† CONSUMPTION (KWH)
Wards Cat. No. 35170	120	10,040
A. O. Smith KEN52D	169	10,240
Sears Cat. No. 32461	128	10,690
Rheem Rheemglas 10 666J	189	10,310
Jackson Executive LJ05225	117	10,540
Ruud Ruudglas Holiday RH522	189	10,340
A. O. Smith Conservationist PEC52D	235	10,170
Mor-Flo ER52D	130	10,390
Jetglas Jupiter 52JRD2	130	10,580
Bradford SE52DF5	130	10,890

Source: Consumer Reports, March 1976

*See these models plotted on Graph 11-2.

†Based on 100 gallons per day

Table 11-3 Gas Hot-Water Heaters—All 40-gallon Tanks

MODEL*	PURCHASE PRICE ($)	ANNUAL ENERGY† CONSUMPTION (THERMS)
State Geyser G484V	202	494
Rheem Apollo 200 41404	215	512
Jackson Executive W4	107	475
A. O. Smith PGD40	220	494
Wards Cat no 33673	130	501
A. O. Smith Conservationist PGC40	220	459
Ruud Titan 200 RT24044	250	523
Mor-Flo G440S	120	530
Bradford 404S5RN	125	534
Mor-Flor Prestige GDA 440D	140	530

Source: Consumer Reports, March 1976

*See these models plotted on Graph 11-3.

†Based on 100 gallons per day.

EXAMPLE: In March Joanne paid $5.30 for gas. According to the bill, during this period she used 14 therms. What is her unit cost for gas?

$$GR = \frac{\$5.30}{14} = \$0.379$$

Joanne pays $0.379 per therm.

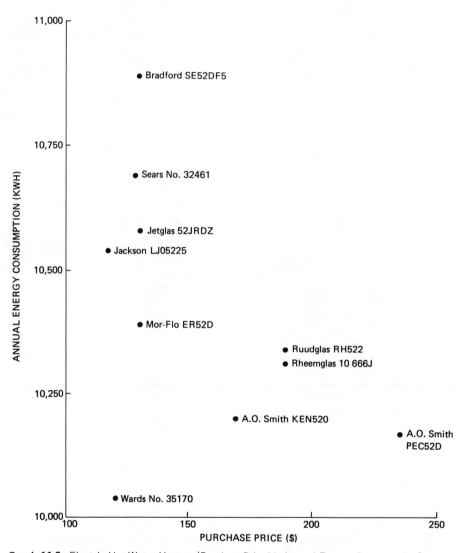

Graph 11-2 Electric Hot-Water Heaters (Purchase Price Vs Annual Energy Consumption)

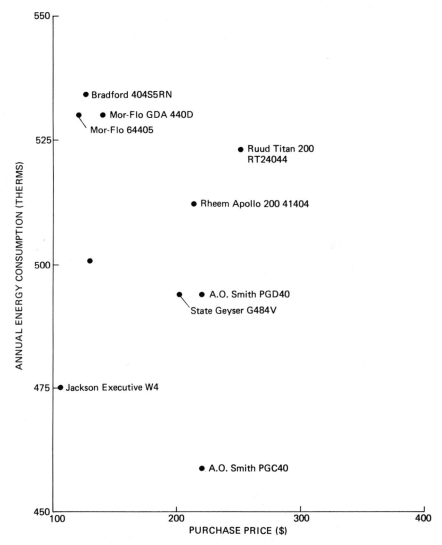

Graph 11-3 Gas Hot-Water Heaters (Purchase Price Vs Annual Energy Consumption)

Operating Cost Very little goes wrong with hot-water heaters. As a result the energy cost over a hot-water heater's lifetime is a good approximation of its total operating cost[1]

For electric hot-water heaters,

$$\textit{Lifetime Energy Cost} = 20 \text{ yr} \times \text{kwh per yr} \times \textit{ER}$$

(Equation 11-6)

where kwh per yr is the annual electricity consumption in kwh, and *ER* is the electricity rate.

For gas hot-water heaters,

$$\textit{Lifetime Energy Cost} = 20 \text{ yr} \times \text{therms per yr} \times \textit{GR}$$

(Equation 11-7)

where therms per yr is the annual gas consumption in therms, and *GR* is dollars per therm.

EXAMPLE: The most energy-efficient electric hot-water heater in Table 11-2 is Wards Cat No 35170 with an annual energy consumption of 10,040 kwh. The least efficient is the Bradford SE52DF5. If the electric rate is $0.056 per kwh, what is the difference in the 2 units' lifetime energy cost?

For the Wards model:

$$\textit{Lifetime Energy Cost} = 20 \times 10,040 \times \$0.056$$

$$= \$11,244.80$$

For the Bradford model:

$$\textit{Lifetime Energy Cost} = 20 \times 10,890 \times \$.056$$

$$= \$12,196.80$$

The difference between the 2 models is $12,196.80 − $11,244.80 = $952.

EXAMPLE: The most energy-efficient natural gas heater in Table 11-3 is the State Geyser G484V with an annual energy consumption of 494 therms. The least efficient is the Bradford 404S5RN with an annual consumption of 530 therms. What is the difference in the lifetime fuel cost of these 2 units if natural gas costs $0.379 per therm?

For the Geyser,

$$\textit{Lifetime Energy Cost} = 20 \times 494 \times \$0.379 = \$3,744.52$$

---

[1] As previously stated, this calculation assumes that energy prices increase at the same rate as general inflation. It is in constant-value dollars.

For the Bradford,

$$\textit{Lifetime Energy Cost} = 20 \times 530 \times \$0.379 = \$4,017.40$$

The difference between them is $273.

The 2 preceding examples illustrate some important points about choosing hot-water heaters. At current rates, electric heaters are substantially more expensive to operate than are natural gas models. If you are limited to electric models or if you feel natural gas is too dangerous, then you should be particularly conscious of the energy efficiency of the unit you buy, because the electricity cost is going to add up to as much as 9,400% of the purchase price.

Lifecycle Cost From here it is simple to determine the lifecycle cost of the various units. It is the sum of the purchase price and the lifetime energy cost.

$$\textit{Lifecycle Cost} = \textit{Purchase Price} + \textit{Operating Cost}$$

(Equation 11-8)

EXAMPLE: Given the energy costs in the 2 preceding examples, determine the lifecycle cost of the Wards Cat No 35170, the Bradford SE52DF5, the State Geyser G484V, and the Bradford 404S5RN.

We have already calculated the lifetime energy cost for these models. All that remains is to look up the purchase prices in Tables 11-2 and 11-3 and plug these into Equation 11-4.

For the Wards Cat No 35170,

$$\textit{Lifecycle Cost} = \$120 + \$11,244.80 = \$11,364.80$$

For the Bradford SE52DF5,

$$\textit{Lifecycle Cost} = \$130 + \$12,196.80 = \$12,326.80$$

For the State Geyser G484V,

$$\textit{Lifecycle Cost} = \$202 + \$3,744.52 = \$3,946.52$$

For the Bradford 404S5RN,

$$\textit{Lifecycle Cost} = \$140 + \$4,017.40 = \$4,157.40$$

So the lifecycle cost of gas hot-water heaters runs about 1/2 to 1/3 that of electric hot-water heaters.

---

1   The Magnum family is thinking about buying the Amana TC18W refrigerator. If the purchase price is $591, its monthly electricity consumption is 119 kwh, and the cost of electricity is $0.076 per kwh, what is the lifecycle cost of this unit?

2   By what percentage would a lower electricity rate of $0.038 per kwh reduce lifecycle cost of the Amana in Problem 1?

3   In Table 11-1, the monthly electricity consumption of the refrigerators varies from a low of 99 kwh to a high of 152 kwh. What does this 35% variation correspond to in the difference in lifetime operating cost with electricity rates of $0.03 per kwh, $0.07 per kwh, and $0.10 per kwh?

4   Using Tables 11-2 and 11-3, determine whether a gas or electric hot-water heater would be cheaper if electricity costs $0.026 per kwh and gas costs $0.87 per therm.

5   At what electricity rate does the lifecycle cost of the Jackson Executive LJ05225 equal that of the Jackson Executive W4 if gas is selling for $0.87 per therm?

6   Emmanuela has a large family and she does about 8 loads of laundry per week, 2 durable-press loads. She is interested in the Maytag A608, but thinks the price is too high. Her second choice is the Whirlpool ADA5800. What is the lifecycle cost of these 2 machines if water costs $0.95 per 100 cu. ft., and she has a gas heater (gas costs $0.77 per therm)? Electricity is running at $0.088 per kwh.

12

Shelter: Renting or Buying

It was over 2,000 years ago that the Roman orator and philosopher Marcus Tullius Cicero asked, "What is more agreeable than one's home?" Even though outward form and structure of human dwellings have remarkably changed since the time of Cicero, the ancient Roman's sentiment still remains strong today.

Buying a house is one of the most important decisions many of us face in our lifetime. This is not only because of the subjective aspects of home buying, but also because it represents the largest personal financial transaction that most people ever undertake. At one time, human shelter was shaped solely by an individual's skill, energy, environment, and the materials available. In today's more complex society, acquiring a home has become more a matter of difficult economic trade-offs and a host of legal considerations. In the last few years, the variety of accommodations in the U.S. has considerably increased because of changes in society. More young people setting up households and elderly people looking for suitable places to live have prompted builders to offer new forms of housing. An example of this is the exceptional growth in condominiums.

There is a need for some method of comparing the costs and returns of housing that takes into consideration its wide variety of types, sizes, ages, locations, and financing. Such a comparison is necessary due to the steady increase in cost of all forms of housing, as is illustrated by the Consumer Price Index for housing in Graph 12-1. Here the ominous upward swing in housing costs that began about 1965 is graphically shown, The two broken lines that extend out to the year 2000 show what will happen to the price of housing if current trends continue.[1]

---

[1]These are mathematical projections of the housing index for the period shown. They do not take other economic factors into account.

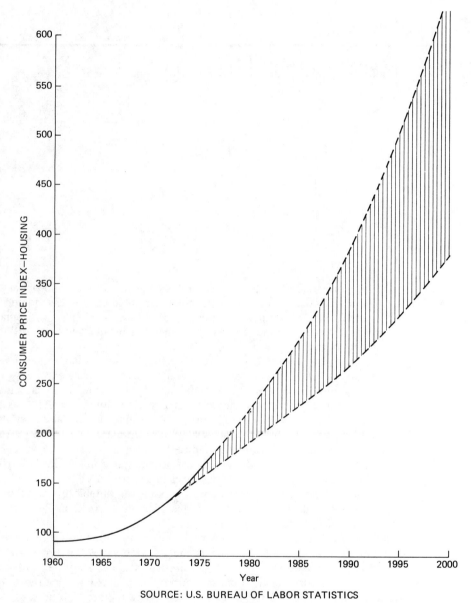

SOURCE: U.S. BUREAU OF LABOR STATISTICS

Graph 12-1 Cost of U.S. Housing. Consumer Price Index for Housing (1960-1976) Projections for Future Value of Consumer Price Index   (Source: U.S. Bureau of Labor Statistics)

An interesting aspect of what has happened to housing prices in the 1970s is their relationship to general inflation. When the housing index is corrected for the general inflation rate, it remains relatively constant. This suggests that, for the nation as a whole, the price of housing is simply keeping pace with inflation, not outstripping it. Of course, there are specific areas—southern California, for example—where the cost of housing has risen considerably faster than general inflation. Such a picture is in general agreement with expert explanations of the mechanics of the housing market. The governing factor in housing prices is the cost of new construction. Older homes tend to sell for 10% to 15% below the value of comparable new homes. Therefore, as inflation drives up the cost of new homes, the selling price for older real estate keeps pace. Because inflation appears to have become ingrown in the U.S. economy, it seems likely that housing costs will continue to rise in the foreseeable future. When this fact is taken together with another inflationary effect, that of decreasing the constant-value costs of long-term borrowing, many people who have considered renting to be their best financial course rather than owning, may find that buying a home is actually the better course.

There are various rules-of-thumb that authorities on the subject of housing finances like to quote. One such rule is that a family or individual should spend a week's pay per month for shelter and that a person should look for a house with a price no more than 2½ times his or her annual income. According to the Bureau of Labor Statistics, however, none of the data available from studies of actual spending support these or any other generalizations about how much a family should pay for their home. In a national survey conducted in 1960 and 1961, the Bureau found that, on the average, Americans paid out 16% of their annual income after taxes on shelter, including utilities. For renters, shelter outlays, including utilities, amounted to 18% of after-tax income. For homeowners, mortgage interest, property insurance, property taxes, maintenance and repairs, and utilities averaged 15% of after-tax income, but when mortgage principal payments were included, the percentage increased to 20%.

Payments on a mortgage principal amount to an enforced savings plan—as long as the value of the property stays constant or increases. Nevertheless, a house is a very inflexible form of investment. Other investments, such as savings accounts or stocks and bonds, make it easier to respond to a change in circumstances or to take advantage of changing rates of return. On the other hand, there are substantial tax benefits given to homeowners. Renters must have some periodic savings plan to offset the financial benefits of home ownership. This requires extra self-discipline, but if the total costs of renting are lower than owning a home, it should be possible. The process of comparing the investment returns from owning and renting has 6 basic steps:

1. Determination of the purchase price and terms of financing for a house you would consider buying.
2. Estimation of your gross monthly expenses for shelter as a homeowner.
3. Estimation of your net monthly expenses for shelter as a homeowner.
4. Estimation of your net proceeds if you were to sell the house at a specified price after a given period.

5. Estimation of the amount of monthly savings required to offset net proceeds from owning if you rent.

6. Estimation of the amount of rent that, in combination with a savings program, would equal your net expense for owning your own home.

Once you have taken these steps you will have a fairly clear picture of the underlying economic trade-offs of owning or renting. It will give you a financial framework on which to base your decision.

This chapter is organized around a series of worksheets, which guide you step by step through the process of comparing buying and renting. You may wish to photocopy them and fill them in as you work out this comparison for your personal situation. Each form has enough space so you can compare purchasing 3 different pieces of property with renting them or with each other. These can be actual pieces of real estate in which you are interested or hypothetical properties in different price ranges to help you determine what you can afford. Alternately, you can compare the same house with different size downpayments or with different interest rates. Or you can evaluate the financial effect of buying in an area with high property taxes or in a community with a more moderate tax rate. Similarly, you can compare the pros and cons of buying a new house with those of an older house.

The basic procedures that are presented can be adapted in a number of different ways in order to fit your particular situation and interests.

FINANCING TERMS—
WORKSHEET A

Item 1. Planning Period. This is your assessment of the length of time you will probably live in a house should you buy it. On the average, Americans occupy a house for less than 5 years before moving. If you are uncertain, use a shorter period rather than a longer one because this will give a more conservative estimate.

A number of experts advise that if you can't stay in one place for more than 3 years you are better off renting. If the length of time you will be able to stay in a house is a major consideration, you may wish to use several different planning periods in the analysis that follows and determine the trade-offs.

Item 2. Sale Price. The price of the property.

Item 3. Capital Outlay to Purchase. This is the lump sum you need to purchase a house. Lack of ready cash is perhaps the greatest obstacle keeping a large number of people out of the housing market. However, extremely low downpayment loans are available, usually at higher interest rates. Besides the downpayment, a purchaser must also pay a number of other costs. These are lumped together under the heading *settlement costs,* and they add up to anywhere from 2% to 10% of the face value of the mortgage, a significant sum of money. The total initial outlay, *TIC* (the total amount of money you need to purchase a house), then, is the sum of the downpayment and settlement costs.

Worksheet A Financing Terms

Property A _____

Property B _____

Property C _____

		A	B	C
1.	Planning Period _____			
2.	Sale price	_____	_____	_____
3.	Capital outlay to purchase			
	a. Downpayment (10%-25% sale price)	_____	_____	_____
	b. Settlement costs (2%-10% P)	_____	_____	_____
	c. Total initial outlay (3a + 3b)	_____	_____	_____
4.	Mortgage			
	a. Principal, P (2 − 3a)	_____	_____	_____
	b. Annual percentage rate, APR	_____	_____	_____
	c. Maturity, T	_____	_____	_____
5.	Monthly cost of debt service			
	a. Mortgage payment, PMT (Equation 9-2)	_____	_____	_____
	b. Mortgage insurance premium	_____	_____	_____
	c. Total to debt service (5a + 5b)	_____	_____	_____

Item 4. Mortgage. This simply lists the salient points of the mortgage loan: principal, annual percentage rate, and maturity. If you go shopping for a lender using Worksheet G, you can pull these figures from that source. If not, you can either get typical values from the officer at your bank or use some approximations.

Item 5. Monthly Cost of Debt Service. The size of the monthly payments of a mortgage is, of course, one of the most important figures. You can get this either from your lender, from mortgage tables, or using Equation 9-2. A lender may demand that you pay mortgage insurance. If this is the case, then you must add the monthly premium to the monthly payment in order to get the Total of Debt Service.

183

Worksheet B Gross Monthly Expenses of Owning a Home

FROM WORKSHEET A

	A	B	C
1. Total to debt service (per month) from Worksheet A			
2. Real estate taxes			
a. Property tax (per month)			
b. Special assessments or levies (per month)			
c. Total monthly real estate tax (2b + 2c)			
3. Homeowner's insurance (per month)			
4. Maintenance and repairs (per month)			
a. For single-family home about 0.07% of property value			
b. Maintenance fee (condominiums)			
5. Fuel and utilities (per month)			
a. Water rate ($ per 100 cu ft)			
b. Monthly consumption U.S. average: 257 cu ft			
c. Average monthly cost			
d. Electricity rate ($ per kwh)			
e. Average monthly consumption (kwh)			
f. Average monthly cost			
g. Natural gas rate			
h. Average monthly consumption (therms)			
i. Average monthly cost			
j. Fuel oil price ($ per gal)			
k. Average monthly consumption (gal)			

FROM WORKSHEET A

	A	B	C
l. Average monthly cost	_____	_____	_____
m. Garbage collection cost	_____	_____	_____
n. Sewerage cost	_____	_____	_____
o. Total fuel and utilities (5c + 5f + 5i + 5l + 5m + 5n)	_____	_____	_____
6. Gross monthly expenses (1 + 2e + 3 + 4 + 5o)	_____	_____	_____

GROSS MONTHLY EXPENSES OF OWNING A HOME—WORKSHEET B

Of course, there are a number of expenses associated with owning a house besides mortgage payments. Worksheet B lists these additional shelter costs. You must have an idea of what these are in your area in order to estimate what your monthly outlay as a homeowner will be. If you are working with an experienced real estate agent, he or she should be able to supply you with representative figures. Or, if you have friends who are homeowners in the area you are considering, they should be able to fill you in on these details.

Item 1. Total to Debt Service. Item 5c from Worksheet A.

Item 2. Real Estate Taxes. Property taxes vary widely from place to place. They are highest in urban areas and lowest in the country. You can get this information from the local assessor's office. If you are considering a condominium, it is a good idea to check the property tax figures supplied by the developers, because there have been a number of cases where buyers have been given misleading figures. Besides determining the base property tax rate, it is a good idea to find out if any special assessments and levies are pending. Many a carefully worked out budget has been upset by an unexpected assessment. These are more likely in newly developed areas than in older, established neighborhoods.

Property taxes have been one of the fastest rising homeowner expenses over the past few years. From 1964 to 1973, property taxes increased by 71% for the nation as a whole. From the spring of 1977 to the spring of 1978, the increase was 6.9%.

Item 3. Homeowner's Insurance. Most American homeowners are under-insured: They have not adjusted their policies to keep up with rising property values. When you take out a mortgage, the lender will undoubtedly insist that you have a certain amount of insurance to protect the property.

Item 4. Maintenance and Repairs. According to the Bureau of Labor Statistics, maintenance and repair costs range from 0.06% to 0.08% of the

185

value of your property per month (¾% to 1% per year). Obviously, the repair and maintenance costs of older houses will tend to be higher, while those for new houses will be lower. Repair and maintenance costs have been rising rapidly: about 7.5% increase from March, 1977, to March, 1978, for instance.

If you are buying an older house with the idea of fixing it up, then your repair and maintenance costs will be considerably higher. Home improvement loans tend to be more expensive than mortgage money. You should consider the situation carefully, and perhaps talk with a few contractors. Chances are that the cost of improvements you wish to make will be substantially higher than you expect.

If you are considering a condominium, repair and maintenance costs will be covered by a set monthly fee. You should check this to see that it is reasonable—some developers keep the maintenance fee too low in order to attract buyers and, as a result, the appearance of the unit gradually deteriorates to the detriment of your resale value.

Item 5. Fuel and Utilities. With the rising cost of energy, home heating has catapulted into a major homeowner expense in most parts of the country. Electric heating (except for the heat pump) is the most expensive, followed by oil and natural gas. For an older house, ask the seller if you can look at the fuel receipts for the last heating season. With this information, you can use the procedures outlined in Chapter 12 to estimate your average monthly heating costs. You should also be able to obtain estimates for your other utility costs from the seller as well.

For a new house, the builder should be able to give you some idea of the price for heating and utilities. More sophisticated contractors will be able to tell you the heat loss per degree day of the structure, so that you can calculate your monthly fuel bills yourself.[2] The developer or real estate agent should also be able to provide you with the cost of other utilities.

Item 6. Gross Monthly Expenses. This is the total amount of money you will pay out each month in order to be a proud homeowner. It is the grand total of the monthly debt service, total monthly real estate tax, homeowner's insurance, maintenance and repairs, total fuel and utilities, and any other shelter-related expenses you may have.

TAX LIABILITY—
WORKSHEET C

Balanced against your gross expenses as a homeowner are the considerable tax breaks that Congress extends to those who put themselves in hock for this officially-sanctioned element of the American dream. Real estate taxes and the interest you pay on the mortgage each year are deductible. To estimate your income tax savings as a homeowner you will need a copy of the current Internal Revenue Service (IRS) income tax tables and rate schedules, or you can use last year's. IRS tables for 1977 are included in Appendix 7.

Item I. Income

A. Total Income. If you have set up a budget along the lines suggested in Chapter 5, then this is the yearly total on the Annual Income Record. It is also the Total Income line on your IRS tax return.

[2]Degree days are explained in Chapter 10.

Worksheet C   Income Tax Liability

I.   Income

    A.   Total income   _____

    B.   Income adjustments   _____

    C.   Adjusted gross income (IA − IB)   _____

II.   As a renter

    A.   For standard deductions use IRS Tables A-D to determine

        1. Estimated annual income tax   _____

        2. Monthly income tax (IIA1 ÷ 12)   _____

    B.   If itemizing use IRS rate schedules (X, Y, or Z) with the following:

        1. Personal exemptions   _____

        2. Itemized deductions   _____

        3. Taxable income
           (IC − IIB1 − IIB2)   _____

        4. Estimated annual income tax   _____

        5. Monthly income tax
           (IIB4 ÷ 12)   _____

III.   As a homeowner

    A.   Personal exemptions   _____

FROM WORKSHEET A

	A	B	C
B. Annual real estate tax From Worksheet B	_____	_____	_____
C. Annual mortgage interest (Equation 9-7)	_____	_____	_____
D. Other itemized deductions	_____	_____	_____
E. Taxable income (IC − IIIA − IIIB − IIIC − IIID)	_____	_____	_____

Using IRS tax schedules X, Y, or Z, determine

	A	B	C
F. Estimated annual income tax	_____	_____	_____
G. Monthly income tax (IIIF ÷ 12)	_____	_____	_____

IV.   Monthly tax savings as homeowner

187   (IIIG − IIA2 or IIIG − IIB5)   _____   _____   _____

B. Income Adjustments. These include business expenses, payments into an individual retirement arrangement (IRA) or Keogh Retirement Plan, and alimony payments. You should not include unusual items, such as moving expenses or forfeited interest penalties, because they are peculiar to only 1 year.

C. Adjusted Gross Income. This is the total income minus the income adjustments.

Item II. As a Renter. Most people who rent will probably use the standard deduction to determine their income tax. These are Tables A-D. Dividing the income tax determined in these tables by 12 gives you the amount of income tax you pay per month. Some non-homeowners, however, have enough personal deductions without those involved with homeowning to make itemizing worthwhile. In this case, use the steps in 2b to determine your taxable income and rate schedules X, Y, or Z to estimate your annual income tax.

Item III. As a Homeowner. Here the procedure is substantially the same as it is for a renter who itemizes. The difference is the hefty amount of added deductions you can use to reduce your taxable income.

C. Annual Mortgage Interest. The annual interest you pay on a mortgage is very large at first, and then it gradually decreases over time. On Worksheet B you established a planning period. If it is relatively short—10 years or less—you can calculate the total interest you will pay during it using Equation 9-7. Divide by the number of years to get an average annual figure. If you intend to keep your home indefinitely, then you may want to average the interest over the first 5 years for this purpose.

D. Other Itemized Deductions. With the large deductions for taxes and mortgage interest now available to you, it is certain that you will be able to take a number of other deductions which, as a renter, were not profitable.

E. Taxable Income. To obtain this, subtract personal exemptions, annual real estate tax, annual mortgage interest, and other itemized deductions from gross adjusted income.

F. Estimated Annual Income Tax. Use your taxable income above with rate schedule X, Y, or Z to determine your annual income tax.

Item IV. Monthly Tax Savings as Homeowner. Subtract the annual income tax per month as a homeowner from the annual income tax per month as a renter to compute the monthly tax savings.

NET MONTHLY EXPENSES
OF OWNING A HOME—WORKSHEET D

This worksheet is self-explanatory. The net monthly expense of owning a home is simply the gross monthly expense minus the tax savings by owning.

Worksheet D Net Monthly Expenses of Owning a Home

From Worksheet A

	A	B	C
1. Gross monthly expenses of owning from Worksheet B	_____	_____	_____
2. Tax savings by owning from Worksheet C	_____	_____	_____
3. Net monthly expense of owning (Item 1 — Item 2)	_____	_____	_____

Worksheet E Net Proceeds from Selling House

	A	B	C
1. Planning period from Worksheet A	_____		
2. Appreciation rate, *A* average: 9% per year	_____		
3. Future market value of house, *FV* (from Equation 12-1)	_____	_____	_____
4. Selling costs average: 8% selling price	_____	_____	_____
5. Amount owed on mortgage (Equation 9-6)	_____	_____	_____
6. Net proceeds from selling (Item 3 — Item 4 — Item 5)	_____	_____	_____

NET PROCEEDS
FROM SELLING A HOUSE—WORKSHEET E

To properly compare your situation as a renter or homeowner it is essential to take into account the (hopefully) increasing value of the house and the growing equity. This can be done by estimating the proceeds you would realize by selling the house at the end of the planning period.

Item 2. Appreciation Rate. At what rate is the market value of your property likely to increase? The national average was about 9% per year from 1970 to 1977. You can get an idea of what a reasonable figure is in your area from local real estate agents. Another source is the Consumer Price Index for Housing if you live in one of the cities where the Bureau of Labor Statistics keeps track of consumer prices. The real estate section of the local news-

189

papers may also give you a good idea of the course property values are taking in different areas.

Item 3. Future Market Value of House. Appreciation works just like compound interest and inflation. Each year the value of the property increases by a certain percentage of its former value. If we let a be the annual appreciation rate expressed as a decimal, FV the future value, and PV the present value, then

$$FV = PV\ (1 + a)^T \qquad \text{(Equation 12-1)}$$

where T is the number of years.

EXAMPLE: An older house in Denver is selling for $42,000. A reasonable estimate of its appreciation rate is 10% per year. What will its market value be in 5 years?

$$FV = \$42,000\ (1 + 0.10)^5$$

$$= \$42,000\ (1.1)^5$$

$$= \$42,000 \times 1.61051$$

$$= \$67,641$$

Item 4. Selling Costs. There are substantial costs involved in selling a house, the greatest of which is usually real estate agency fees. Because this is strictly a hypothetical calculation, it is sufficient to estimate them as 8% of the future market value. For the house in the previous example, the selling costs would total about $67,641 \times 0.08 = \$5,411$.

Item 5. Amount Owed on Mortgage. Chances are you will be selling your house before the mortgage is totally paid off. In this case, you will have to pay back the balance remaining, which you can calculate from Equation 9-6. If you sell too soon, you may have to add prepayment penalties as well.

Item 6. Net Proceeds from Selling. By subtracting selling costs and the amount still owed on mortgage from the future market value you will arrive at the net proceeds from selling the house.

MONTHLY SAVINGS REQUIRED
TO OFFSET NET PROCEEDS FROM OWNING—
WORKSHEET F

Homeowning acts as an enforced savings plan. Therefore, a renter must undertake a major savings or investment program to maintain financial parity with a homeowner. Here we determine the monthly savings required to offset the equity you would build up as a homeowner.

Item 2. Total Initial Outlay. This is the total amount of cash you would invest in a home. Presumably, you have this amount to invest in another way: time certificates, bonds, stocks, and so forth. These have the advantage of being more flexible investments than real estate.

Worksheet F Monthly Savings Required to Offset Net Proceeds From Owning

	From Worksheet A		
	A	B	C
1. Planning period from Worksheet A _____			
2. Total initial outlay from Worksheet A	_____	_____	_____
3. Rate of return from alternative investment, *APR*	_____	_____	_____
4. Final value of alternative investment (Equation 8-2)	_____	_____	_____
5. Interest earned by alternative investment	_____	_____	_____
6. Income tax paid on interest	_____	_____	_____
7. Net value alternative investment (Item 4 — Item 6)	_____	_____	_____
8. Net proceeds selling from Worksheet D	_____	_____	_____
9. Net advantage owning (Item 8 — Item 7)	_____	_____	_____
10. Monthly savings to offset advantage of owning (Equation 8-12)	_____	_____	_____
11. Net monthly expenses of owning	_____	_____	_____
12. Balance for monthly rent and utilities (Item 11 — Item 10)	_____	_____	_____

Item 3. Rate of Return from Alternative Investment. There are a number of different ways you can invest your money. For instance, some savings and loans are offering time certificates with 8% annual interest. Following is a table of the average yields of several types of alternative investments. Depending on your background and interests you can find a variety of different investment plans. Setting up a portfolio is certainly no more difficult or time consuming than finding and buying a home. Large investment houses have become increasingly interested in small investors, and have attempted to tailor plans to suit them.

Item 4. Final Value of Alternative Investment. By investing your present capital at a reasonable rate of return, it will have grown in value by the end of the planning period. Whether you choose to place the money in a

Table 12-1 Yields of Alternative Investments
(% per annum)

PERIOD	U.S. TREASURY NOTES (CONSTANT MATURITIES)		HIGH GRADE MUNICIPAL BONDS (STD AND POOR'S)	CORPORATE AAA BONDS (MOODY'S)
	3-year	10-year		
1972	5.72	6.21	5.27	7.21
1973	6.95	6.84	5.18	7.44
1974	7.82	7.56	6.09	8.57
1975	7.49	7.99	6.89	8.83
1976	6.77	7.61	6.49	8.43
1977	6.69	7.42	5.56	8.02
1978	7.61	7.96	5.60	8.41

Source: Council of Economic Advisors, Economic Indicators.

savings account or in some other form of investment, this will be a compounding process, so you can use Equation 8-2.

Item 5. Interest Earned by Alternate Investment. The total interest is final value minus the total capital outlay.

Item 6. Income Tax Paid on Interest. The interest earned is subject to income tax. On Worksheet D you estimated your tax liability as a renter. From this you can determine what proportion of your taxable income goes to taxes:[3]

$$Tax\ Portion\ (TP)\ =\ \frac{Estimated\ Annual\ Income\ Tax}{Taxable\ Income}$$

(Equation 12-2)

Now, if you multiply the interest earned by *TP*, you will get an estimate of the amount of this interest that goes to the federal government.

Item 7. Net Value of Alternative Investment. The net value of investing your capital is the total initial outlay plus the interest earned minus the income tax paid.

EXAMPLE: George has a taxable income of $11,084. With his wife and 2 children as dependents, he paid $864 last year in income tax. He is considering an investment of $10,000 in Treasury Notes. These notes have a 7.61% annual yield. What will the net value of this investment be after 10 years?

The final value, *FV,* of this investment will be

$$FV\ =\ \$10{,}000\ (1\ +\ 0.0761)^5$$

$$=\ \$10{,}000\ (1.0761)^5$$

---

[3]In the case of renters taking the standard deduction, substitute adjusted gross income for taxable income.

192

$$= \$10,000 \times 1.4429845$$

$$= \$14,429.89$$

The interest earned over this period, then, is

$$Total\ Interest\ =\ \$14,429.89\ -\ \$10,000$$

$$=\ \$4,429.89$$

The proportion of George's income that goes to taxes is fairly low.

$$TP\ =\ \frac{\$864}{\$11,084}$$

$$=\ 0.0780$$

About 7.8% of this interest will go to income tax, assuming that no major changes in George's financial condition or in the tax rates occur during this period.

$$Income\ Tax\ Paid\ =\ \$4,429.89\ \times\ 0.0780$$

$$=\ \$345.53$$

Finally, the net value of the investment will be

$$Net\ Value\ =\ \$10,000\ +\ \$4,429.89\ -\ \$345.53$$

$$=\ \$14,084.36$$

Item 8. Net Proceeds from Selling. This is the bottom line of Worksheet D.

Item 9. Net Advantage of Owning. To a certain extent, the investment of the money you would otherwise have paid out to buy a house offsets the proceeds from selling the home. Therefore, you must subtract the net value of alternative investment from the net proceeds from selling to calculate the net advantage from owning.

Item 10. Monthly Savings Required to Offset Advantage of Owning. Use Equation 8-12 to determine the monthly payments you must set aside to salt away enough money to balance out the net advantage of owning (Item 9 above).

Item 11. Net monthly expense of owning. This was determined on Worksheet D.

Item 12. Balance Available for Monthly Rent and Utilities. Subtracting the monthly savings from the net monthly expense of owning (Item 11) gives the amount you can afford to spend for rent and utilities. If you are a renter, you can compare this with what you are currently paying. Another way of looking at this is as the effective rent you are paying to live in the house.

Worksheet G   Comparing Lenders

LENDER A   _____

LENDER B   _____

LENDER C   _____

		A	B	C
1.	Downpayment (10%-25% appraised value)	_____	_____	_____
2.	Mortgage principal, P	_____	_____	_____
3.	Annual percentage rate, APR Typical variation: ½%-1%	_____	_____	_____
4.	Periodic interest rate, i	_____	_____	_____
5.	Maturity, T National average: new houses— 26.2 yrs; old houses—24.2 yrs	_____	_____	_____
6.	Total number of payments, N	_____	_____	_____
7.	Settlement costs Range from 2%-10% of P	_____	_____	_____
	a. Points	_____	_____	_____
	b. Appraisal	_____	_____	_____
	c. Survey	_____	_____	_____
	d. Title insurance	_____	_____	_____
	e. Homeowner insurance	_____	_____	_____
	f. Credit life insurance	_____	_____	_____
	g. Legal fees	_____	_____	_____
	h. Recording fee	_____	_____	_____
	i. Prepaid property taxes	_____	_____	_____
	_____	_____	_____	_____
	_____	_____	_____	_____
8.	Monthly payment, PMT (Equation 9-2)	_____	_____	_____
9.	Prepayment policy	_____	_____	_____

	A	B	C
10. Late payment policy Typically 4%-6% of *PMT*	_____	_____	_____
11. Total interest, *TI* Absolute dollars (Equation 9-5)	_____	_____	_____
12. Total real interest, *TRI* Constant-value dollars (Equation 9-10)	_____	_____	_____

COMPARING LENDERS— WORKSHEET G

This worksheet is designed to help you compare the financing terms offered by different lenders. In 1975 the Real Estate Settlement Procedures Act (RESPA) became law. This requires lenders to make "good faith" estimates of closing costs on a mortgage. In addition, the lender must give you a full financial disclosure at least one day before the closing. This enables you to shop around for the best mortgage deal available: an effort that could save you thousands of dollars.

The disclosure form is required by the Truth-in-Lending Act. It is provided to you by the lender and must include all financial charges and costs. It is one of the few cases where the borrower is privy to all the financial details of a bank transaction. Most questions can be answered by carefully reading this document.

Item 3. Annual Percentage Rate. As we saw in Chapter 9, small differences in the annual percentage rate (APR) can make a large difference in the amount of total interest paid. While lenders generally give about the same rates, there is often a ½% to 1% variation. Therefore, it is worthwhile to shop around.

Item 4. Periodic Interest Rate. This is the interest rate charged per payment period, as defined in Chapter 9. It is the factor that the bank actually uses in determining the interest you pay. Don't be surprised if the bank officer does not know what you are talking about when you ask for this figure. It should be the annual interest rate divided by the number of payments per year.

Item 5. Maturity. The maturity has a major effect on the total (absolute) cost of a loan. The longer the length of the loan, the more interest you pay. Also, the longer the loan, the greater the effect the differences in percentage points have. However, in times of relatively high inflation, the real cost of longer mortgages sharply diminishes.

Item 6. Total Number of Payments. In some cases, lenders use an odd number of total payments to assure that the APR they quote is in accordance with federal regulations. For instance, Crocker National Bank in California calculates a monthly 20-year mortgage for 237 payments instead of 240.

Item 7. Settlement Costs. It is in this category of costs that the greatest variation can be found among lenders. On a $30,000 mortgage, costs can range from $600 to $3,000. One of the major expenses in this category is the practice of discount points. Lenders use points when money is tight to increase their profit margin. One point is 1% of the value of the mortgage. Under the point system, the lender deducts so many percentage points from the loan at the beginning. Because you must pay back the entire sum rather than the discounted sum, this represents a considerable hike in the effective interest rate. In some cases it is the seller who pays the points. In other cases it is the buyer.

Sometimes lenders will require that a piece of property be appraised before loaning money on it. Appraisals can cost as much as $200. On occasion they prove a wise investment. If the appraised value is below the asking price, it may help you convince the seller to reduce his price.

If you are so inclined, ask the bank if you can shop around for the various types of insurance you will need. Often you can find a better buy.

In certain situations you may have to prepay property tax and assessment fees.

Item 8. Monthly Payments. The amount of the monthly mortgage payments will be provided by the lender. You can check his figures using Equation 9-2. This is also a good check on how well you understand the computational methods the bank is using.

Item 9. Prepayment Policy. Most banks and thrifts demand a stiff penalty if you pay off a mortgage before a certain period of time: frequently in the first 5 to 8 years. In today's mobile society it is quite likely that you will want to pay off a mortgage before this. Because the penalties can be quite stiff—as much as 6 months interest—it is worth looking at the prepayment terms quite closely.

Item 10. Late Payment Policy. If you always pay your bills on time, this will not concern you greatly. Should you occasionally get behind in paying your bills, late payment penalties can greatly increase the cost of the loan. Typical late payment charges range from 4% to 6% of the payment. The most equitable manner for dealing with late payments is to charge the additional interest due on the principal borrowed for an extra period of time, but few lenders have adopted this philosophy.

Item 11. Total Interest. Using Equation 9-5, you can calculate the total interest for the lifetime of the loan in absolute dollars. The lender should disclose this amount to you as well. Of more relevance is the total interest in constant-value dollars, from Equation 9-10. You can use any inflation rate that you feel appropriate in this calculation. I suggest 7% as the best estimate for annual inflation in the 1980s and 1990s.

EXAMPLE: Sam and Hallie have found the house of their dreams for $49,000 in Colorado Springs. They have $10,000 in savings. If Sam's salary is $18,650 a year, how does this purchase compare with renting?

Worksheet A. Sam works for a big company; the most he can count on being in the area is 5 years. They choose this as their planning period. Hallie has visited a number of different banks and thrifts, shopping for the best financing terms. Settlement costs will be about $2,000. This means they can put up $8,000 as a downpayment, so the mortgage principal will be $41,000. The best annual percentage rate available is 9.6%. They would like a 25-year loan.

From Equation 11-6, the monthly payments will amount to

$$PMT = \$41,000 \left[\frac{\frac{0.096}{12}}{1 - \left(\frac{1 + 0.096}{12}\right)^{-300}} \right]$$

$$= \$41,000 \left[\frac{0.008}{1 - (1.008)^{-300}} \right]$$

$$= \$41,000 \left[\frac{0.008}{1 - 0.09158838} \right]$$

$$= \$41,000 \left[\frac{0.008}{0.90841162} \right]$$

$$= \$41,000 \times 0.00880658$$

$$= \$361.07$$

There is no insurance premium required, so the total to debt service per month is $361.07.

The total interest on this loan is

$$(N \times PMT) - P = 300 \times \$361.07 - \$41,000$$

$$= \$108,320.94 - \$41,000$$

$$= \$67,320.09$$

However, in constant-value dollars the total real cost of the loan is less:

$$TRC = PMT \left[\frac{(1 + r_p)^{n+1} - 1}{r_p (1 + r_p)^n} \right] - P$$

Sam uses a 6% annual inflation rate, so $r_p = 0.06/12 = 0.005$.

$$TRC = \$361.07 \left[\frac{(1.005)^{301} - 1}{0.005 (1.005)^{300}} \right] - \$41,000$$

$$= \$361.07 \left[\frac{4.4872 - 1}{0.005 \times 4.4648756} \right] - \$41,000$$

$$= \$361.07 \left(\frac{3.4872}{0.022324378} \right) - \$41,000$$

$$= (\$361.07 \times 156.20592) - \$41,000$$

$$= \$56,401 - \$41,000$$

$$= \$15,401$$

Worksheet B. For this particular house, the property taxes will run about $800 per year, at least for the first year or so. It is in an established neighborhood, so the sewers are in and the streets are paved. There are no large assessments pending. Therefore, the total monthly real estate tax will be $800/12 = $67.

Homeowner's insurance will cost them $390 per year, or $33 per month. They choose a low estimate for repairs and maintenance—¾% of the property value per year (0.06% per month). This amounts to $49,000 × 0.006, or $29 per month.

The home has an oil-fired furnace. They asked the owners of the house next door (which is identical to the one they are considering) what their fuel bills have been. The estimate they got was about $715, or $60 per month.

Their current electricity bills are running about $50 per month and the rates are the same, so they use this figure. Water, they estimate, will be $10 per month, sewage about $15, and garbage collection $15.

Total fuel and utilities, then, amounts to $150.

Gross monthly expenses total $607.07.

Worksheet C. So much for the bad news, the expenses. Now it is time to compute the tax savings. Sam's wages are $18,650 per year. Another $1,250 comes in from interest and stock dividends. So the couple's gross adjusted income is about $19,900. Taking the standard deduction last year, Sam paid $2,886 in income tax, or $240 per month. As a homeowner, he will be able to itemize deductions and reduce his taxable income.

The first step is to determine personal exemptions. In 1977, this amounted to $750 per person, or in this case, $1,500.

Next, the deductions: Real estate taxes will amount to $800.

Sam decides to compute the interest for the first 5 years and average it to estimate the interest he will save. Interest between 2 payment periods is given by formula

$$I_{j-k} = B_k - B_{j-1} + (k - j - 1) \; PMT$$

In this case, $j = 1$, and $k = 60$, so

$$I_{1\text{-}60} = B_{60} - B_0 + (60 \times PMT)$$

However, B_0 is the balance at the zeroth payment, or the principal of the mortgage: $41,000. We know PMT = $361.07. But we must calculate the balance after the sixtieth payment.

$$B_{60} = (1 + 0.008)^{60}\left[\$361.07\left(\frac{(1 + 0.008)^{-60} - 1}{0.008}\right) + \$41,000\right]$$

$$= 1.613\left[\$361.07\left(\frac{0.61997 - 1}{0.008}\right) + \$41,000\right]$$

$$= 1.613\left[\$361.07\left(\frac{-0.38003}{0.008}\right) + \$41,000\right]$$

$$= 1.613\left[\$361.07 \times 0.008 - 47.504 + \$41,000\right]$$

$$= 1.613\,(\$41,000 - 17,152.27)$$

$$= 1.613 \times 23,847.77$$

$$= \$38,466$$

Thus,

$$\begin{aligned}
I_{1-60} &= \$38,466 - \$41,000 + (60 \times \$361.07)\\
&= -\$2,534 + \$21,664\\
&= \$19,130
\end{aligned}$$

Dividing this by 5 gives the yearly average.

Average Annual Interest = $19,130 ÷ 5 = $3,826

This is another healthy deduction. Added to this, Sam figures he has another $650 in medical expenses, state and local taxes, and so forth.

Subtracting personal exemptions, real estate taxes, mortgage interest, and miscellaneous deductions from his gross adjusted income, Sam comes up with a taxable income of $13,124. Looking this income up under Schedule Y, he finds that the tax he would pay in 1977 is $1,380 plus 22% of the amount over $11,200.

$$0.22 \times (\$13,124 - \$11,200) = 0.22 \times \$1,924 = \$423.28$$

Thus Sam would owe a grand total of $1,380 + $423 = $1,803. This is $150.27 per month. Therefore, Sam's monthly tax saving would roughly be $240 - $150 = $90.

Worksheet D. With this monthly tax saving, he can determine what his net monthly expense of owning will be. This is the gross monthly expense from Worksheet C minus the tax savings.

Net Monthly Expense to Own = $607 − $90 = $517

Worksheet E. The next step is to determine the proceeds Sam will realize if he must move 5 years from now. Property in the neighborhood of the house has been appreciating at 9% to 10% over the last few years, he discovers. Nearby, there are a number of $75,000 homes being built, so he is confident that property in this area will continue to appreciate. He decides to use a 9% appreciation rate. Based on this assumption, the future value, *FV*, of the house in 5 years will be

$$FV = \$49,000 (1 + 0.09)^5$$

$$= \$49,000 (1.09)^5$$

$$= \$49,000 \times 1.53862396$$

$$= \$75,393$$

Selling costs will be about 8% of this, so

Selling Costs = $75,393 × 0.08 = $6,031

The amount owed on the mortgage was computed in the course of figuring the annual interest on Worksheet C. It is B_{60}, or $38,466.

Now it is possible to calculate the net proceeds from selling, which is the future market value of the house less the selling costs and the amount owed on the mortgage.

Net Proceeds = $75,393 − $6,031 − $38,466

$$= \$30,896$$

Worksheet F. Sam and Hallie's outlay for the house would be $10,000. Sam knows that he could get at least 7.25% rate of return on this money if he doesn't use it to buy the house. Therefore, the final value of this money after 5 years would be

$$FV = P (1 + APR)^T$$

$$= \$10,000 (1.0725)^5$$

$$= \$10,000 \times 1.41901343$$

$$= \$14,190$$

Dividing his yearly income tax as a renter by his gross adjusted income, Sam finds that the proportion he is paying toward taxes, *TP*, is 0.145. Therefore, the amount of the interest his $10,000 earned that would go to taxes is roughly 0.145 X $4,190 = $608. The net value of this investment would be $14,190 − $608 = $13,582. Deducting this amount from the net proceeds from selling the house, $30,896, gives a net advantage for owning of $17,314.

Because Sam's rate of return on his investments is based on annual yields, he decides to calculate annual payments and then divide by 12 to get the per-month figure. Using Equation 8-12,

$$PMT = \frac{FV \times i}{(1 + i)^{N+1} - (1 + i)}$$

$$= \frac{\$17,314 \times 0.0725}{(1 + 0.0725)^{5+1} - (1 + 0.0725)}$$

$$= \frac{1,255.2650}{1.0725^6 - 1.0725}$$

$$= \frac{1,308.9875}{1.5219 - 1.0725}$$

$$= \frac{1,255.2650}{0.4494}$$

$$= \$2,793$$

Dividing by 12 gives the amount per month: $2,793/12 = $233.

Now, Sam looks back to Worksheet D, and he finds that the net monthly expense of owning is $517. Subtracting the monthly savings he arrives at a figure of $284 per month for rent and utilities.

So for Sam and Hallie, buying this $49,000 house is financially equivalent to paying $284 for rent and investing $233 per month.

PROBLEMS

1   Barbara is a fashion designer living in Los Angeles. She is single, is currently making $19,800 per year, and is looking into buying a condominium. She has $15,000 in savings earmarked for this purpose. Barbara has found that, generally, condominiums in the west L.A. area fall into 2 price ranges: $50,000 to $60,000 and $70,000 to $80,000. To help her select the best class of condominiums for her situation, she decides to analyze the trade-offs of a $55,000 and a $75,000 unit. If

planning period = 7 years
closing costs = 7% of P
annual interest rate = 11%
maturity = 30 years
homeowner's insurance = $220 per year

annual real estate taxes = $12 per $1,000 assessed value

fuel and utilities = $60 per month

maintenance fees = $45 and $65 per month, respectively

appreciation rate = 15% per year

rate of return alternate investment = 12% per year

then what does Barbara's analysis reveal?

2   The Smollets have a small child and $8,000 in savings. They like a small $46,400 house on a nearby tract. But they are not sure if they can afford it on their combined annual income of $16,360. How would this purchase compare with renting if (1) they expect to live there 3 years; (2) they can get a 10.25% loan for 30 years; (3) closing costs are $1,000; (4) insurance would cost them $150 per year; (5) taxes total $40 per month; (6) fuel and utilities run about $75 per month; (7) the appreciation rate in the area has been running at 10% per year; (8) their alternative would be to keep the money in a 7.5% savings account.

3   How would the Smollet's analysis change if they stayed in the house for 6 years instead of 3?

4   Given (1) a house with a sale price of $50,000 per year, an appreciation rate of 10% per year, and real estate taxes of $400 per year; (2) a couple with an income of $14,800 and $6,000 saved in 6.5% savings certificates; (3) other shelter costs totalling $120 per month; (4) a mortgage with 10% down, $1,000 in settlement costs, and a 30-year maturity. How would purchasing this house compare with renting if the interest rate on the mortgage was 9%, 10%, or 11%? Assume a planning period of 5 years.

5   Ronald has only $5,000 saved up. But he can get a loan with 10% down for a $40,000 house if he pays 11¾% annual interest. Settlement costs would amount to $800 for the $35,800, 30-year mortgage. If his taxable income is $11,300, the property tax on the house is $400 per year, and Ronald estimates his other monthly shelter costs as a homeowner to be $125, how does this purchase compare with renting? Use a planning period of 5 years, an appreciation rate of 9%, and a return on alternative investment of 14%.

13

Pros and Cons
of Advanced Calculators

In the Introduction I alluded to the fact that the 4-function calculator is just the beginning of a revolution in consumer computer technology. Today it is possible to get a full-fledged computer for your home for under $600. It is possible to purchase programmable calculators, which are actually limited computers in all but name, for less than $100. Considering the wide variety of computing devices becoming available, a general discussion of the advantages of different types of calculators seems appropriate.

If you have worked through the calculations in this book, you will be acutely aware of the fact that calculating compound interest, the balance of an installment loan after so many payments, or the comparison of renting and buying can be quite involved, even with a 4-function calculator. A measure of the difficulty of doing a given problem on a calculator is the number of keystrokes plus the number digits you must write down. This is not only a measure of the time a problem takes to solve, but also of the likelihood of making an error. For instance, the problem

$$FV = 12,500 \times (1.12)^{10}$$

takes 22 keystrokes to solve with a 4-function calculator and log tables. With a calculator that has a y^x key, on the other hand, the same computation takes only 14 keystrokes. The equation here is that for computing compound interest. Some calculators, such as the Business Analyst by Texas Instruments, are preprogrammed to solve this type of equation. For this problem, you would get an answer with 13 keystrokes—about the minimum possible.

As far as the material covered in this book is concerned, the most useful additional function you can get on a calculator is that of taking a number to a power.

There is an abrupt jump in cost from models that add, subtract, multiply, divide, take a square root, have a percent key and, perhaps, have an addressable memory to the next level: either electronic slide rules or special business calculators. The former can be purchased for less than $10; the latter may cost as much as $40 or more. Both the slide rule and business models have a number of functions that are of little use to most people. However, the pre-programmed financial functions on the business models do have a special virtue. They allow you to explore more easily the implications of changing one or more of the variables involved in financial calculations.

Returning to the example of the future value of a compound savings account, with the preprogrammed calculator you can alter the length of time, for instance, by entering a new number of compounding periods. You do not need to rekey the principal or the interest rate for each computation. This saves a great deal of time when you are making the same computation repeatedly. Suppose, for example, you wish to calculate the future value of a savings certificate with an annual yield of 7% and a principal of $5,000 for 5, 10, and 15 years. With a 4-function calculator and log tables these computations would require about 66 keystrokes. Using a calculator with a y^x key, the number of steps is reduced to 42, and using one with a preprogrammed compound interest function would only take 19 keystrokes.

Programmability

Beyond the realm of functions "hardwired" into calculators are handheld computers that can be rudimentarily programmed. These are now available for under $60. With these machines we really begin to leave the old "adding machine" behind and move into the computer age.

Programming simply means that you can instruct the calculator to execute a sequence of steps over and over again. Essentially, this is done by switching the calculator into a *program* mode and pressing the keys in the same order you would if you were doing the calculation. Then, by switching the calculator back into the *ordinary run* mode and pushing an execute or start key, the calculator can automatically run through the sequence of steps that you programmed.

For instance, imagine that you are faced with the task of multiplying a number of monthly budget figures by 12 in order to get annual estimates. You program the calculator with the keystrokes $\boxed{\times}\boxed{1}\boxed{2}\boxed{=}$. Then you enter a budget figure and push the execute key. The number is automatically multiplied by 12.

Now for a somewhat more difficult example. You want to determine the balance on a mortgage every 5 years through the end of its 30-year maturity. As we have seen, this is a complicated calculation:

$$B_k = (1 + i)^k \left\{ PMT \left[\frac{(1 + i)^{-k} -1}{i} \right] + P \right\}$$

Figuring this 6 times is not only a considerable amount of work, but a considerable duplication of effort. Programmable calculators allow you to avoid this extra work. All you have to do is first instruct the calculator to store the current value for k in one of its memories. Then you keystroke through the computation and each time you come to a k, you instruct the calculator to recall this value from the appropriate memory. Entering the first value for k and pushing the execute key will cause a slight delay, perhaps a flickering of the numbers in the display, and you will be almost magically presented with the value of B_k.

Or, if you prefer, you can write a more general program for B_k, one that will allow you to vary the size of the principal, the interest rate, or the size of the monthly payments, as well as the number of payment periods. To do this, you would store the values of all the variables—k, i, PMT, P—in different memories. Then you would program the calculator to solve the formula by recalling the respective memories when they are encountered in the equation. To determine the balance for different combinations of these variables, simply store the correct values in the appropriate memory registers and push the execute button.

This gives you a general idea of the power of programmability. However, there are some disadvantages. For one thing, it is easy to make a programming mistake, which will invalidate your work. During programming the display carries a number code that corresponds to the keystrokes you are making. You must become quite familiar with this code before you can spot key-punching errors. Another drawback for many programmable models is the fact that there is no way to store a program after you are through with it. Of course, you can document each program you have written to keep for future use by writing down the steps. You will be forced, however, to key it in again with the attendant loss of time and the possibility of error.

Therefore, programmable calculators are only truly valuable for someone whose work involves the repetitive solution of arithmetic problems. This is not the case with most personal financial matters. It is not very often that one has an occasion to solve a compound interest formula 10 times in a row.

This latter problem has been surmounted. In the $200 to $750 range are several *card programmable* calculators. The programs for these machines can be stored on magnetic cards for future use. Calculator companies now provide preprogrammable cards for a wide variety of problems—at a price. The Hewlett-Packard Company, which pioneered the card-programmable, for instance, offers programs in federal income tax computation, real estate investment planning, management of stocks and bonds, marketing and sales forecasting, and diet planning. The card-programmables are true computers. They can execute programs several hundred steps in length. They also have programming capabilities such as skipping to different steps in the program, comparing the value of 2 numbers, performing or not performing a given operation depending on the relationship between them, incrementing or de-crementing values in the memory registers, in short, they perform quite sophis-ticated operations. For instance, it is possible to program one of these cal-culators to perform all the steps involved in comparing renting with buying. All that is necessary is to enter all the salient information: planning period, sale price, total initial outlay, mortgage principal, annual interest rate, matu-rity of the loan, real estate taxes, home insurance, fuel and utilities cost, taxable income as a renter, number of personal exemptions, appreciation rate of the house, and the annual rate of return of alternative investments. Once this is done, the calculator automatically will make the comparison.

The upper end of the card-programmable market overlaps that of the home computer. Radio Shack offers a home computer for $599. There are 2 basic differences between the card-programmable calculator and the home computer: the amount of memory storage and the ability to handle words as well as numbers. The most advanced calculator can store 400 numbers at most; home computers can store thousands of numbers. Home computers are also *alphanumeric*. They can store and manipulate letters and words as well as numbers. Thus a computer can not only help you calculate your budget, it can also store these values under key words. Recipes and telephone numbers can also be stored.

The more expensive home computers can also be programmed to act as word processors, enabling you to write letters and to correct them before printing them. They can even correct your spelling.

In the future, home computers may enable you to tap directly into the computer at the local library to find the reference material you want—for instance, the points of interest in New England for your next vacation—and to make a copy of it (or store it in the computer) for future reference. The same computer could be the brains of a security system for your home. It could also continuously monitor and control your furnace to keep your fuel bills at a minimum, perhaps even signaling when the air filter needs to be changed or if the furnace is out of adjustment. It might be plugged into your microwave oven to facilitate food preparation.

Research now being done suggests that it will be a matter of years before low-cost technology is developed that will enable you to talk directly to a computer (if you use a limited vocabulary). Imagine saying to a computer, "Please add one thousand six hundred twenty-five dollars and fifteen cents, twenty-five dollars and forty cents, four hundred seventeen dollars and ten cents, and three thousand dollars," and seeing $5,067.55 appear on the screen! A National Science Foundation study of the personal computer suggests that such an invention will have a greater impact on current lifestyles than the television had nearly a quarter of a century ago.

As with card-programmable calculators, it is possible to buy extensive libraries of programs for the home computer. To get the maximum use out of these machines, however, you need to learn at least a relatively simple computer language or set of instructions. And writing computer programs is an extremely difficult and demanding task. So flexible is the computer that even experienced programmers are frequently forced to revise their initial programs when they do not work as anticipated. Nevertheless, even the most advanced digital computer employs a machine language similar to that of the programmable calculator. By understanding how one of these calculators operates, you have stepped up the first rung in the ladder toward understanding the computer revolution.

Appendices

APPENDIX 1:
CHECKING ACCOUNT ANALYSIS FORM

BANK _____ AVERAGE NUMBER OF CHECKS
ADDRESS _____ YOU WRITE PER MONTH, _____
DATE _____

GENERAL BANK INFORMATION _____
    COST OF CHECKS: plain, unnumbered _____, plain numbered _____, personalized _____
    scenic _____

TELEPHONE TRANSFERS: yes _____ no _____ charge _____
BAD DEPOSIT POLICY _____ charge _____
TIME FOR DEPOSITS TO CLEAR: local _____ out-of-state _____

SPECIFIC ACCOUNT INFORMATION

Checking account name/description	Certified check charge	Cashier check charge	Traveler's check charge	Safe deposit box charge	Interest on account balance, annual rate	Overdraft charge	Automatic loan rate	Monthly C_M charge	Per check C_C charge	Minimum balance B_{MIN}	Monthly average	Lowest daily balance	Service charge for falling below minimum balance

APPENDIX 2:
LOG/ANTILOG TABLES

FOUR-PLACE LOGARITHMS

FOUR-PLACE

N	0	1	2	3	4	5	6	7	8	9	Proportional Parts								
											1	2	3	4	5	6	7	8	9
10	0000	0043	0086	0128	0170	0212	0253	0294	0334	0374	*4	8	12	17	21	25	29	33	37
11	0414	0453	0492	0531	0569	0607	0645	0682	0719	0755	4	8	11	15	19	23	26	30	34
12	0792	0828	0864	0899	0934	0969	1004	1038	1072	1106	3	7	10	14	17	21	24	28	31
13	1139	1173	1206	1239	1271	1303	1335	1367	1399	1430	3	6	10	13	16	19	23	26	29
14	1461	1492	1523	1553	1584	1614	1644	1673	1703	1732	3	6	9	12	15	18	21	24	27
15	1761	1790	1818	1847	1875	1903	1931	1959	1987	2014	*3	6	8	11	14	17	20	22	25
16	2041	2068	2095	2122	2148	2175	2201	2227	2253	2279	3	5	8	11	13	16	18	21	24
17	2304	2330	2355	2380	2405	2430	2455	2480	2504	2529	2	5	7	10	12	15	17	20	22
18	2553	2577	2601	2625	2648	2672	2695	2718	2742	2765	2	5	7	9	12	14	16	19	21
19	2788	2810	2833	2856	2878	2900	2923	2945	2967	2989	2	4	7	9	11	13	16	18	20
20	3010	3032	3054	3075	3096	3118	3139	3160	3181	3201	2	4	6	8	11	13	15	17	19
21	3222	3243	3263	3284	3304	3324	3345	3365	3385	3404	2	4	6	8	10	12	14	16	18
22	3424	3444	3464	3483	3502	3522	3541	3560	3579	3598	2	4	6	8	10	12	14	15	17
23	3617	3636	3655	3674	3692	3711	3729	3747	3766	3784	2	4	3	7	9	11	13	15	17
24	3802	3820	3838	3856	3874	3892	3909	3927	3945	3962	2	4	5	7	9	11	12	14	16
25	3979	3997	4014	4031	4048	4065	4082	4099	4116	4133	2	3	5	7	9	10	12	14	15
26	4150	4166	4183	4200	4216	4232	4249	4265	4281	4298	2	3	5	7	8	10	11	13	15
27	4314	4330	4346	4362	4378	4393	4409	4425	4440	4456	2	3	5	6	8	9	11	13	14
28	4472	4487	4502	4518	4533	4548	4564	4579	4594	4609	2	3	5	6	8	9	11	12	14
29	4624	4639	4654	4669	4683	4698	4713	4728	4742	4757	1	3	4	6	7	9	10	12	13
30	4771	4786	4800	4814	4829	4843	4857	4871	4886	4900	1	3	4	6	7	9	10	11	13
31	4914	4928	4942	4955	4969	4983	4997	5011	5024	5038	1	3	4	6	7	8	10	11	12
32	5051	5065	5079	5092	5105	5119	5132	5145	5159	5172	1	3	4	5	7	8	9	11	12
33	5185	5198	5211	5224	5237	5250	5263	5276	5289	5302	1	3	4	5	6	8	9	10	12
34	5315	5328	5340	5353	5366	5378	5391	5403	5416	5428	1	3	4	5	6	8	9	10	11
35	5441	5453	5465	5478	5490	5502	5514	5527	5539	5551	1	2	4	5	6	7	9	10	11
36	5563	5575	5587	5599	5611	5623	5635	5647	5658	5670	1	2	4	5	6	7	8	10	11
37	5682	5694	5705	5717	5729	5740	5752	5763	5775	5786	1	2	3	5	6	7	8	9	10
38	5798	5809	5821	5832	5843	5855	5866	5877	5888	5899	1	2	3	5	6	7	8	9	10
39	5911	5922	5933	5944	5955	5966	5977	5988	5999	6010	1	2	3	4	5	7	8	9	10
40	6021	6031	6042	6053	6064	6075	6085	6096	6107	6117	1	2	3	4	5	6	8	9	10
41	6128	6138	6149	6160	6170	6180	6191	6201	6212	6222	1	2	3	4	5	6	7	8	9
42	6232	6243	6253	6263	6274	6284	6294	6304	6314	6325	1	2	3	4	5	6	7	8	9
43	6335	6345	6355	6365	6375	6385	6395	6405	6415	6425	1	2	3	4	5	6	7	8	9
44	6435	6444	6454	6464	6474	6484	6493	6503	6513	6522	1	2	3	4	5	6	7	8	9
45	6532	6542	6551	6561	6571	6580	6590	6599	6609	6618	1	2	3	4	5	6	7	8	9
46	6628	6637	6646	6656	6665	6675	6684	6693	6702	6712	1	2	3	4	5	6	7	7	8
47	6721	6730	6739	6749	6758	6767	6776	6785	6794	6803	1	2	3	4	5	5	6	7	8
48	6812	6821	6830	6839	6848	6857	6866	6875	6884	6893	1	2	3	4	4	5	6	7	8
49	6902	6911	6920	6928	6937	6946	6955	6964	6972	6981	1	2	3	4	4	5	6	7	8
50	6990	6998	7007	7016	7024	7033	7042	7050	7059	7067	1	2	3	3	4	5	6	7	8
51	7076	7084	7093	7101	7110	7118	7126	7135	7143	7152	1	2	3	3	4	5	6	7	8
52	7160	7168	7177	7185	7193	7202	7210	7218	7226	7235	1	2	2	3	4	5	6	7	7
53	7243	7251	7259	7267	7275	7284	7292	7300	7308	7316	1	2	2	3	4	5	6	6	7
54	7324	7332	7340	7348	7356	7364	7372	7380	7388	7396	1	2	2	3	4	5	6	6	7
N	0	1	2	3	4	5	6	7	8	9	1	2	3	4	5	6	7	8	9

* Interpolation in this section of the table is inaccurate.

LOGARITHMS

N	0	1	2	3	4	5	6	7	8	9	Proportional Parts								
											1	2	3	4	5	6	7	8	9
55	7404	7412	7419	7427	7435	7443	7451	7159	7466	7474	1	2	2	3	4	5	5	6	7
56	7482	7490	7497	7505	7513	7520	7528	7536	7543	7551	1	2	2	3	4	5	5	6	7
57	7559	7566	7574	7582	7589	7597	7604	7612	7619	7627	1	2	2	3	4	5	5	6	7
58	7634	7642	7649	7657	7664	7672	7679	7686	7694	7701	1	1	2	3	4	4	5	6	7
59	7709	7716	7723	7731	7738	7745	7752	7760	7767	7774	1	1	2	3	4	4	5	6	7
30	7782	7789	7796	7803	7810	7818	7825	7832	7839	7846	1	1	2	3	4	4	5	6	6
61	7853	7860	7868	7875	7882	7889	7896	7903	7910	7917	1	1	2	3	4	4	5	6	6
62	7924	7931	7938	7945	7952	7959	7966	7973	7980	7987	1	1	2	3	3	4	5	6	6
63	7993	8000	8007	8014	8021	8028	8035	8041	8048	8055	1	1	2	3	3	4	5	5	6
64	8062	8069	8075	8082	8089	8096	8102	8109	8116	8122	1	1	2	3	3	4	5	5	6
65	8129	8136	8142	8149	8156	8162	8169	8176	8182	8189	1	1	2	3	3	4	5	5	6
66	8195	8202	8209	8215	8222	8228	8235	8241	8248	8254	1	1	2	3	3	4	5	5	6
67	8261	8267	8274	8280	8287	8293	8299	8306	8312	8319	1	1	2	3	3	4	5	5	6
68	8325	8331	8338	8344	8351	8357	8363	8370	8376	8382	1	1	2	3	3	4	4	5	6
69	8388	8395	8401	8407	8414	8420	8426	8432	8439	8445	1	1	2	2	3	4	4	5	6
70	8451	8457	8463	8470	8476	8482	8488	8494	8500	8506	1	1	2	2	3	4	4	5	6
71	8513	8519	8525	8531	8537	8543	8549	8555	8561	8567	1	1	2	2	3	4	4	5	5
72	8573	8579	8585	8591	8597	8603	8609	8615	8621	8627	1	1	2	2	3	4	4	5	6
73	8633	8639	8645	8651	8657	8663	8669	8675	8681	8686	1	1	2	2	3	4	4	5	5
74	8692	8698	8704	8710	8716	8722	8727	8733	8739	8745	1	1	2	2	3	4	4	5	5
75	8751	8756	8762	8768	8774	8779	8785	8791	8797	8802	1	1	2	2	3	3	4	5	5
76	8808	8814	8820	8825	8831	8837	8842	8848	8854	8859	1	1	2	2	3	3	4	5	5
77	8865	8871	8876	8882	8887	8893	8899	8904	8910	8915	1	1	2	2	3	3	4	4	5
78	8921	8927	8932	8938	8943	8949	8954	8960	8965	8971	1	1	2	2	3	3	4	4	5
79	8976	8982	8987	8993	8998	9004	9009	9015	9020	9025	1	1	2	2	3	3	4	4	5
80	9031	9036	9042	9047	9053	9058	9063	9069	9074	9079	1	1	2	2	3	3	4	4	5
81	9085	9090	9096	9101	9106	9112	9117	9122	9128	9133	1	1	2	2	3	3	4	4	5
82	9138	9143	9149	9154	9159	9165	9170	9175	9180	9186	1	1	2	2	3	3	4	4	5
83	9191	9196	9201	9206	9212	9217	9222	9227	9232	9238	1	1	2	2	3	3	4	4	5
84	9243	9248	9253	9258	9263	9269	9274	9279	9284	9289	1	1	2	2	3	3	4	4	5
85	9294	9299	9304	9309	9315	9320	9325	9330	9335	9340	1	1	2	2	3	3	4	4	5
86	9345	9350	9355	9360	9365	9370	9375	9380	9385	9390	1	1	2	2	3	3	4	4	5
87	9395	9400	9405	9410	9415	9420	9425	9430	9435	9440	0	1	1	2	2	3	3	4	4
88	9445	9450	9455	9460	9465	9469	9474	9479	9484	9489	0	1	1	2	2	3	3	4	4
89	9494	9499	9504	9509	9513	9518	9523	9528	9533	9538	0	1	1	2	2	3	3	4	4
90	9542	9547	9552	9557	9562	9566	9571	9576	9581	9586	0	1	1	2	2	3	3	4	4
91	9590	9595	9600	9605	9609	9614	9619	9624	9628	9633	0	1	1	2	2	3	3	4	4
92	9638	9643	9647	9652	9657	9661	9666	9671	9675	9680	0	1	1	2	2	3	3	4	4
93	9685	9689	9694	9699	9703	9708	9713	9717	9722	9727	0	1	1	2	2	3	3	4	4
94	9731	9736	9741	9745	9750	9754	9759	9763	9768	9773	0	1	1	2	2	3	3	4	4
95	9777	9782	9786	9791	9795	9800	9805	9809	9814	9818	0	1	1	2	2	3	3	4	4
96	9823	9827	9832	9836	9841	9845	9850	9854	9859	9863	0	1	1	2	2	3	3	4	4
97	9868	9872	9877	9881	9886	9890	9894	9899	9903	9908	0	1	1	2	2	3	3	4	4
98	9912	9917	9921	9926	9930	9934	9939	9943	9948	9952	0	1	1	2	2	3	3	4	4
99	9956	9961	9965	9969	9974	9978	9983	9987	9991	9996	0	1	1	2	2	3	3	3	4
N	0	1	2	3	4	5	6	7	8	9	1	2	3	4	5	6	7	8	9

ANTILOGARITHMS

	0	1	2	3	4	5	6	7	8	9	1	2	3	4	5	6	7	8	9
											Proportional Parts								

	0	1	2	3	4	5	6	7	8	9	1	2	3	4	5	6	7	8	9
.00	1000	1002	1005	1007	1009	1012	1014	1016	1019	1021	0	0	1	1	1	1	2	2	2
.01	1023	1026	1028	1030	1033	1035	1038	1040	1042	1045	0	0	1	1	1	1	2	2	2
.02	1047	1050	1052	1054	1057	1059	1062	1064	1067	1069	0	0	1	1	1	1	2	2	2
.03	1072	1074	1076	1079	1081	1084	1086	1089	1091	1094	0	0	1	1	1	1	2	2	2
.04	1096	1099	1102	1104	1107	1109	1112	1114	1117	1119	0	1	1	1	1	2	2	2	2
.05	1122	1125	1127	1130	1132	1135	1138	1140	1143	1146	0	1	1	1	1	2	2	2	2
.06	1148	1151	1153	1156	1159	1161	1164	1167	1169	1172	0	1	1	1	1	2	2	2	2
.07	1175	1178	1180	1183	1186	1189	1191	1194	1197	1199	0	1	1	1	1	2	2	2	2
.08	1202	1205	1208	1211	1213	1216	1219	1222	1225	1227	0	1	1	1	1	2	2	2	3
.09	1230	1233	1236	1239	1242	1245	1247	1250	1253	1256	0	1	1	1	1	2	2	2	3
.10	1259	1262	1265	1268	1271	1274	1276	1279	1282	1285	0	1	1	1	1	2	2	2	3
.11	1288	1291	1294	1297	1300	1303	1306	1309	1312	1315	0	1	1	1	2	2	2	3	3
.12	1318	1321	1324	1327	1330	1334	1337	1340	1343	1346	0	1	1	1	2	2	2	3	3
.13	1349	1352	1355	1358	1361	1365	1368	1371	1374	1377	0	1	1	1	2	2	2	3	3
.14	1380	1384	1387	1390	1393	1396	1400	1403	1406	1409	0	1	1	1	2	2	2	3	3
.15	1413	1416	1419	1422	1426	1429	1432	1435	1439	1442	0	1	1	1	2	2	2	3	3
.16	1445	1449	1452	1455	1459	1462	1466	1469	1472	1476	0	1	1	1	2	2	2	3	3
.17	1479	1483	1486	1489	1493	1496	1500	1503	1507	1510	0	1	1	1	2	2	2	3	3
.18	1514	1517	1521	1524	1528	1531	1535	1538	1542	1545	0	1	1	1	2	2	2	3	3
.19	1549	1552	1556	1560	1563	1567	1570	1574	1578	1581	0	1	1	1	2	2	3	3	3
.20	1585	1589	1592	1596	1600	1603	1607	1611	1614	1618	0	1	1	1	2	2	3	3	3
.21	1622	1626	1629	1633	1637	1641	1644	1648	1652	1656	0	1	1	2	2	2	3	3	3
.22	1660	1663	1667	1671	1675	1679	1683	1687	1690	1694	0	1	1	2	2	2	3	3	3
.23	1698	1702	1706	1710	1714	1718	1722	1726	1730	1734	0	1	1	2	2	2	3	3	4
.24	1738	1742	1746	1750	1754	1758	1762	1766	1770	1774	0	1	1	2	2	2	3	3	4
.25	1778	1782	1786	1791	1795	1799	1803	1807	1811	1816	0	1	1	2	2	2	3	3	4
.26	1820	1824	1828	1832	1837	1841	1845	1849	1854	1858	0	1	1	2	2	3	3	3	4
.27	1862	1866	1871	1875	1879	1884	1888	1892	1897	1901	0	1	1	2	2	3	3	4	4
.28	1905	1910	1914	1919	1923	1928	1932	1936	1941	1945	0	1	1	2	2	3	3	4	4
.29	1950	1954	1959	1963	1968	1972	1977	1982	1986	1991	0	1	1	2	2	3	3	4	4
.30	1995	2000	2004	2009	2014	2018	2023	2028	2032	2037	0	1	1	2	2	3	3	4	4
.31	2042	2046	2051	2056	2061	2065	2070	2075	2080	2084	0	1	1	2	2	3	3	4	4
.32	2089	2094	2099	2104	2109	2113	2118	2123	2128	2133	0	1	1	2	2	3	3	4	4
.33	2138	2143	2148	2153	2158	2163	2168	2173	2178	2183	0	1	1	2	2	3	3	4	4
.34	2188	2193	2198	2203	2208	2213	2218	2223	2228	2234	1	1	2	2	3	3	4	4	5
.35	2239	2244	2249	2254	2259	2265	2270	2275	2280	2286	1	1	2	2	3	3	4	4	5
.36	2291	2296	2301	2307	2312	2317	2323	2328	2333	2339	1	1	2	2	3	3	4	4	5
.37	2344	2350	2355	2360	2366	2371	2377	2382	2388	2393	1	1	2	2	3	3	4	4	5
.38	2399	2404	2410	2415	2421	2427	2432	2438	2443	2449	1	1	2	2	3	3	4	4	5
.39	2455	2460	2466	2472	2477	2483	2489	2495	2500	2506	1	1	2	2	3	3	4	5	5
.40	2512	2518	2523	2529	2535	2541	2547	2553	2559	2564	1	1	2	2	3	4	4	5	5
.41	2570	2576	2582	2588	2594	2600	2606	2612	2618	2624	1	1	2	2	3	4	4	5	5
.42	2630	2636	2642	2649	2655	2661	2667	2673	2679	2685	1	1	2	2	3	4	4	5	6
.43	2692	2698	2704	2710	2716	2723	2729	2735	2742	2748	1	1	2	3	3	4	4	5	6
.44	2754	2761	2767	2773	2780	2786	2793	2799	2805	2812	1	1	2	3	3	4	4	5	6
.45	2818	2825	2831	2838	2844	2851	2858	2864	2871	2877	1	1	2	3	3	4	5	5	6
.46	2884	2891	2897	2904	2911	2917	2924	2931	2938	2944	1	1	2	3	3	4	5	5	6
.47	2951	2958	2965	2972	2979	2985	2992	2999	3006	3013	1	1	2	3	3	4	5	5	6
.48	3020	3027	3034	3041	3048	3055	3062	3069	3076	3083	1	1	2	3	4	4	5	6	6
.49	3090	3097	3105	3112	3119	3126	3133	3141	3148	3155	1	1	2	3	4	4	5	6	6

| | 0 | 1 | 2 | 3 | 4 | 5 | 6 | 7 | 8 | 9 | 1 | 2 | 3 | 4 | 5 | 6 | 7 | 8 | 9 |

ANTILOGARITHMS

	0	1	2	3	4	5	6	7	8	9	Proportional Parts 1	2	3	4	5	6	7	8	9
.50	3162	3170	3177	3184	3192	3199	3206	3214	3221	3228	1	1	2	3	4	4	5	6	7
.51	3236	3243	3251	3258	3266	3273	3281	3289	3296	3304	1	2	2	3	4	5	5	6	7
.52	3311	3319	3327	3334	3342	3350	3357	3365	3373	3381	1	2	2	3	4	5	5	6	7
.53	3388	3396	3404	3412	3420	3428	3436	3443	3451	3459	1	2	2	3	4	5	6	6	7
.54	3467	3475	3483	3491	3499	3508	3516	3524	3532	3540	1	2	2	3	4	5	6	6	7
.55	3548	3556	3565	3573	3581	3589	3597	3606	3614	3622	1	2	2	3	4	5	6	7	7
.56	3631	3639	3648	3656	3664	3673	3681	3690	3698	3707	1	2	3	3	4	5	6	7	8
.57	3715	3724	3733	3741	3750	3758	3767	3776	3784	3793	1	2	3	3	4	5	6	7	8
.58	3802	3811	3819	3828	3837	3846	3855	3864	3873	3882	1	2	3	4	4	5	6	7	8
.59	3890	3899	3908	3917	3926	3936	3945	3954	3963	3972	1	2	3	4	5	5	6	7	8
.60	3981	3990	3999	4009	4018	4027	4036	4046	4055	4064	1	2	3	4	5	6	6	7	8
.61	4074	4083	4093	4102	4111	4121	4130	4140	4150	4159	1	2	3	4	5	6	7	8	9
.62	4169	4178	4188	4198	4207	4217	4227	4236	4246	4256	1	2	3	4	5	6	7	8	9
.63	4266	4276	4285	4295	4305	4315	4325	4335	4345	4355	1	2	3	4	5	6	7	8	9
.64	4365	4375	4385	4395	4406	4416	4426	4436	4446	4457	1	2	3	4	5	6	7	8	9
.65	4467	4477	4487	4498	4508	4519	4529	4539	4550	4560	1	2	3	4	5	6	7	8	9
.66	4571	4581	4592	4603	4613	4624	4634	4645	4656	4667	1	2	3	4	5	6	7	9	10
.67	4677	4688	4699	4710	4721	4732	4742	4753	4764	4775	1	2	3	4	5	7	8	9	10
.68	4786	4797	4808	4819	4831	4842	4853	4864	4875	4887	1	2	3	4	6	7	8	9	10
.69	4898	4909	4920	4932	4943	4955	4966	4977	4989	5000	1	2	3	5	6	7	8	9	10
.70	5012	5023	5035	5047	5058	5070	5082	5093	5105	5117	1	2	4	5	6	7	8	9	11
.71	5129	5140	5152	5164	5176	5188	5200	5212	5224	5236	1	2	4	5	6	7	8	10	11
.72	5248	5260	5272	5284	5297	5309	5321	5333	5346	5358	1	2	4	5	6	7	9	10	11
.73	5370	5383	5395	5408	5420	5433	5445	5458	5470	5483	1	3	4	5	6	8	9	10	11
.74	5495	5508	5521	5534	5546	5559	5572	5585	5598	5610	1	3	4	5	6	8	9	10	12
.75	5623	5636	5649	5662	5675	5689	5702	5715	5728	5741	1	3	4	5	7	8	9	10	12
.76	5754	5768	5781	5794	5808	5821	5834	5848	5861	5875	1	3	4	5	7	8	9	11	12
.77	5888	5902	5916	5929	5943	5957	5970	5984	5998	6012	1	3	4	5	7	8	10	11	12
.78	6026	6039	6053	6067	6081	6095	6109	6124	6138	6152	1	3	4	6	7	8	10	11	13
.79	6166	6180	6194	6209	6223	6237	6252	6266	6281	6295	1	3	4	6	7	9	10	11	13
.80	6310	6324	6339	6353	6368	6383	6397	6412	6427	6442	1	3	4	6	7	9	10	12	13
.81	6457	6471	6486	6501	6516	6531	6546	6561	6577	6592	2	3	5	6	8	9	11	12	14
.82	6607	6622	6637	6653	6668	6683	6699	6714	6730	6745	2	3	5	6	8	9	11	12	14
.83	6761	6776	6792	6808	6823	6839	6855	6871	6887	6902	2	3	5	6	8	9	11	13	14
.84	6918	6934	6950	6966	6982	6998	7015	7031	7047	7063	2	3	5	6	8	10	11	13	15
.85	7079	7096	7112	7129	7145	7161	7178	7194	7211	7228	2	3	5	7	8	10	12	13	15
.86	7244	7261	7278	7295	7311	7328	7345	7362	7379	7396	2	3	5	7	8	10	12	13	15
.87	7413	7430	7447	7464	7482	7499	7516	7534	7551	7568	2	3	5	7	9	10	12	14	16
.88	7586	7603	7621	7638	7656	7674	7691	7709	7727	7745	2	4	5	7	9	11	12	14	16
.89	7762	7780	7798	7816	7834	7852	7870	7889	7907	7925	2	4	5	7	9	11	13	14	16
.90	7943	7962	7980	7998	8017	8035	8054	8072	8091	8110	2	4	6	7	9	11	13	15	17
.91	8128	8147	8166	8185	8204	8222	8241	8260	8279	8299	2	4	6	8	9	11	13	15	17
.92	8318	8337	8356	8375	8395	8414	8433	8453	8472	8492	2	4	6	8	10	12	14	15	17
.93	8511	8531	8551	8570	8590	8610	8630	8650	8670	8690	2	4	6	8	10	12	14	16	18
.94	8710	8730	8750	8770	8790	8810	8831	8851	8872	8892	2	4	6	8	10	12	14	16	18
.95	8913	8933	8954	8974	8995	9016	9036	9057	9078	9099	2	4	6	8	10	12	15	17	19
.96	9120	9141	9162	9183	9204	9226	9247	9268	9290	9311	2	4	6	8	11	13	15	17	19
.97	9333	9354	9376	9397	9419	9441	9462	9484	9506	9528	2	4	7	9	11	13	15	17	20
.98	9550	9572	9594	9616	9638	9661	9683	9705	9727	9750	2	4	7	9	11	13	16	18	20
.99	9772	9795	9817	9840	9863	9886	9908	9931	9954	9977	2	5	7	9	11	14	16	18	20
	0	1	2	3	4	5	6	7	8	9	1	2	3	4	5	6	7	8	9

7 PLACE
LOGARITHMS

N.	0	1	2	3	4	5	6	7	8	9	d.
1000	000 0000	0434	0869	1303	1737	2171	2605	3039	3473	3907	**434**
1001	4341	4775	5208	5642	6076	6510	6943	7377	7810	8244	**434**
1002	8677	9111	9544	9977	*0411	*0844	*1277	*1710	*2143	*2576	**433**
1003	001 3009	3442	3875	4308	4741	5174	5607	6039	6472	6905	**433**
1004	7337	7770	8202	8635	9067	9499	9932	*0364	*0796	*1228	**432**
1005	002 1661	2093	2525	2957	3389	3821	4253	4685	5116	5548	**432**
1006	5980	6411	6843	7275	7706	8138	8569	9001	9432	9863	**431**
1007	003 0295	0726	1157	1588	2019	2451	2882	3313	3744	4174	**431**
1008	4605	5036	5467	5898	6328	6759	7190	7620	8051	8481	**431**
1009	8912	9342	9772	*0203	*0633	*1063	*1493	*1924	*2354	*2784	**430**
1010	004 3214	3644	4074	4504	4933	5363	5793	6223	6652	7082	**430**
1011	7512	7941	8371	8800	9229	9659	*0088	*0517	*0947	*1376	**429**
1012	005 1805	2234	2663	3092	3521	3950	4379	4808	5237	5666	**429**
1013	6094	6523	6952	7380	7809	8238	8666	9094	9523	9951	**429**
1014	006 0380	0808	1236	1664	2092	2521	2949	3377	3805	4233	**428**
1015	4660	5088	5516	5944	6372	6799	7227	7655	8082	8510	**428**
1016	8937	9365	9792	*0219	*0647	*1074	*1501	*1928	*2355	*2782	**427**
1017	007 3210	3637	4064	4490	4917	5344	5771	6198	6624	7051	**427**
1018	7478	7904	8331	8757	9184	9610	*0037	*0463	*0889	*1316	**426**
1019	008 1742	2168	2594	3020	3446	3872	4298	4724	5150	5576	**426**
1020	6002	6427	6853	7279	7704	8130	8556	8981	9407	9832	**426**
1021	009 0257	0683	1108	1533	1959	2384	2809	3234	3659	4084	**425**
1022	4509	4934	5359	5784	6208	6633	7058	7483	7907	8332	**425**
1023	8756	9181	9605	*0030	*0454	*0878	*1303	*1727	*2151	*2575	**424**
1024	010 3000	3424	3848	4272	4696	5120	5544	5967	6391	6815	**424**
1025	7239	7662	8086	8510	8933	9357	9780	*0204	*0627	*1050	**424**
1026	011 1474	1897	2320	2743	3166	3590	4013	4436	4859	5282	**423**
1027	5704	6127	6550	6973	7396	7818	8241	8664	9086	9509	**423**
1028	9931	*0354	*0776	*1198	*1621	*2043	*2465	*2887	*3310	*3732	**422**
1029	012 4154	4576	4998	5420	5842	6264	6685	7107	7529	7951	**422**
1030	8372	8794	9215	9637	*0059	*0480	*0901	*1323	*1744	*2165	**422**
1031	013 2587	3008	3429	3850	4271	4692	5113	5534	5955	6376	**421**
1032	6797	7218	7639	8059	8480	8901	9321	9742	*0162	*0583	**421**
1033	014 1003	1424	1844	2264	2685	3105	3525	3945	4365	4785	**420**
1034	5205	5625	6045	6465	6885	7305	7725	8144	8564	8984	**420**
1035	9403	9823	*0243	*0662	*1082	*1501	*1920	*2340	*2759	*3178	**420**
1036	015 3598	4017	4436	4855	5274	5693	6112	6531	6950	7369	**419**
1037	7788	8206	8625	9044	9462	9881	*0300	*0718	*1137	*1555	**419**
1038	016 1974	2392	2810	3229	3647	4065	4483	4901	5319	5737	**418**
1039	6155	6573	6991	7409	7827	8245	8663	9080	9408	9916	**418**
1040	017 0333	0751	1168	1586	2003	2421	2838	3256	3673	4090	**417**
1041	4507	4924	5342	5759	6176	6593	7010	7427	7844	8260	**417**
1042	8677	9094	9511	9927	*0344	*0761	*1177	*1594	*2010	*2427	**417**
1043	018 2843	3259	3676	4092	4508	4925	5341	5757	6173	6589	**416**
1044	7005	7421	7837	8253	8669	9084	9500	9916	*0332	*0747	**416**
1045	019 1163	1578	1994	2410	2825	3240	3656	4071	4486	4902	**415**
1046	5317	5732	6147	6562	6977	7392	7807	8222	8637	9052	**415**
1047	9467	9882	*0296	*0711	*1126	*1540	*1955	*2369	*2784	*3198	**415**
1048	020 3613	4027	4442	4856	5270	5684	6099	6513	6927	7341	**414**
1049	7755	8169	8583	8997	9411	9824	*0238	*0652	*1066	*1479	**414**
1050	021 1893	2307	2720	3134	3547	3961	4374	4787	5201	5614	**413**

N.	0	1	2	3	4	5	6	7	8	9	d.

7 PLACE
LOGARITHMS

N.	0	1	2	3	4	5	6	7	8	9	d.
1050	021 1893	2307	2720	3134	3547	3961	4374	4787	5201	5614	413
1051	6027	6440	6854	7267	7680	8093	8506	8919	9332	9745	413
1052	022 0157	0570	0983	1396	1808	2221	2634	3046	3459	3871	413
1053	4284	4696	5109	5521	5933	6345	6758	7170	7582	7994	412
1054	8406	8818	9230	9642	*0054	*0466	*0878	*1289	*1701	*2113	412
1055	023 2525	2936	3348	3759	4171	4582	4994	5405	5817	6228	411
1056	6639	7050	7462	7873	8284	8695	9106	9517	9928	*0339	411
1057	024 0750	1161	1572	1982	2393	2804	3214	3625	4036	4446	411
1058	4857	5267	5678	6088	6498	6909	7319	7729	8139	8549	410
1059	8960	9370	9780	*0190	*0600	*1010	*1419	*1829	*2239	*2649	410
1060	025 3059	3468	3878	4288	4697	5107	5516	5926	6335	6744	410
1061	7154	7563	7972	8382	8791	9200	9609	*0018	*0427	*0836	409
1062	026 1245	1654	2063	2472	2881	3289	3698	4107	4515	4924	409
1063	5333	5741	6150	6558	6967	7375	7783	8192	8600	9008	408
1064	9416	9824	*0233	*0641	*1049	*1457	*1865	*2273	*2680	*3088	408
1065	027 3496	3904	4312	4719	5127	5535	5942	6350	6757	7165	408
1066	7572	7979	8387	8794	9201	9609	*0016	*0423	*0830	*1237	407
1067	028 1644	2051	2458	2865	3272	3679	4086	4492	4899	5306	407
1068	5713	6119	6526	6932	7339	7745	8152	8558	8964	9371	406
1069	9777	*0183	*0590	*0996	*1402	*1808	*2214	*2620	*3026	*3432	406
1070	029 3838	4244	4649	5055	5461	5867	6272	6678	7084	7489	406
1071	7895	8300	8706	9111	9516	9922	*0327	*0732	*1138	*1543	405
1072	030 1948	2353	2758	3163	3568	3973	4378	4783	5188	5592	405
1073	5997	6402	6807	7211	7616	8020	8425	8830	9234	9638	405
1074	031 0043	0447	0851	1256	1660	2064	2468	2872	3277	3681	404
1075	4085	4489	4893	5296	5700	6104	6508	6912	7315	7719	404
1076	8123	8526	8930	9333	9737	*0140	*0544	*0947	*1350	*1754	403
1077	032 2157	2560	2963	3367	3770	4173	4576	4979	5382	5785	403
1078	6188	6590	6993	7396	7799	8201	8604	9007	9409	9812	403
1079	033 0214	0617	1019	1422	1824	2226	2629	3031	3433	3835	402
1080	4238	4640	5042	5444	5846	6248	6650	7052	7453	7855	402
1081	8257	8659	9060	9462	9864	*0265	*0667	*1068	*1470	*1871	402
1082	034 2273	2674	3075	3477	3878	4279	4680	5081	5482	5884	401
1083	6285	6686	7087	7487	7888	8289	8690	9091	9491	9892	401
1084	035 0293	0693	1094	1495	1895	2296	2696	3096	3497	3897	400
1085	4297	4698	5098	5498	5898	6298	6698	7098	7498	7898	400
1086	8298	8698	9098	9498	9898	*0297	*0697	*1097	*1496	*1896	400
1087	036 2295	2695	3094	3494	3893	4293	4692	5091	5491	5890	399
1088	6289	6688	7087	7486	7885	8284	8683	9082	9481	9880	399
1089	037 0279	0678	1076	1475	1874	2272	2671	3070	3468	3867	399
1090	4265	4663	5062	5460	5858	6257	6655	7053	7451	7849	398
1091	8248	8646	9044	9442	9839	*0237	*0635	*1033	*1431	*1829	398
1092	038 2226	2624	3022	3419	3817	4214	4612	5009	5407	5804	398
1093	6202	6599	6996	7393	7791	8188	8585	8982	9379	9776	397
1094	039 0173	0570	0967	1364	1761	2158	2554	2951	3348	3745	397
1095	4141	4538	4934	5331	5727	6124	6520	6917	7313	7709	397
1096	8106	8502	8898	9294	9690	*0086	*0482	*0878	*1274	*1670	396
1097	040 2066	2462	2858	3254	3650	4045	4441	4837	5232	5628	396
1098	6023	6419	6814	7210	7605	8001	8396	8791	9187	9582	395
1099	9977	*0372	*0767	*1162	*1557	*1952	*2347	*2742	*3137	*3532	395
1100	041 3927	4322	4716	5111	5506	5900	6295	6690	7084	7479	395
N.	0	1	2	3	4	5	6	7	8	9	d.

LOGARITHMS

N.	0	1	2	3	4	5	6	7	8	9	d.
1100	041 3927	4322	4716	5111	5506	5900	6295	6690	7084	7479	395
1101	7873	8268	8662	9056	9451	9845	*0239	*0633	*1028	*1422	394
1102	042 1816	2210	2604	2998	3392	3786	4180	4574	4968	5361	394
1103	5755	6149	6543	6936	7330	7723	8117	8510	8904	9297	394
1104	9691	*0084	*0477	*0871	*1264	*1657	*2050	*2444	*2837	*3230	393
1105	043 3623	4016	4409	4802	5195	5587	5980	6373	6766	7159	393
1106	7551	7944	8337	8729	9122	9514	9907	*0299	*0692	*1084	393
1107	044 1476	1869	2261	2653	3045	3437	3829	4222	4614	5006	392
1108	5398	5790	6181	6573	6965	7357	7749	8140	8532	8924	392
1109	9315	9707	*0099	*0490	*0882	*1273	*1664	*2056	*2447	*2839	392
1110	045 3230	3621	4012	4403	4795	5186	5577	5968	6359	6750	391
1111	7141	7531	7922	8313	8704	9095	9485	9876	*0267	*0657	391
1112	046 1048	1438	1829	2219	2610	3000	3391	3781	4171	4561	390
1113	4952	5342	5732	6122	6512	6902	7292	7682	8072	8462	390
1114	8852	9242	9632	*0021	*0411	*0801	*1190	*1580	*1970	*2359	390
1115	047 2749	3138	3528	3917	4306	4696	5085	5474	5864	6253	389
1116	6642	7031	7420	7809	8198	8587	8976	9365	9754	*0143	389
1117	048 0532	0921	1309	1698	2087	2475	2864	3253	3641	4030	389
1118	4418	4806	5195	5583	5972	6360	6748	7136	7525	7913	388
1119	8301	8689	9077	9465	9853	*0241	*0629	*1017	*1405	*1792	388
1120	049 2180	2568	2956	3343	3731	4119	4506	4894	5281	5669	388
1121	6056	6444	6831	7218	7606	7993	8380	8767	9154	9541	387
1122	9929	*0316	*0703	*1090	*1477	*1863	*2250	*2637	*3024	*3411	387
1123	050 3798	4184	4571	4958	5344	5731	6117	6504	6890	7277	387
1124	7663	8049	8436	8822	9208	9595	9981	*0367	*0753	*1139	386
1125	051 1525	1911	2297	2683	3069	3455	3841	4227	4612	4998	386
1126	5384	5770	6155	6541	6926	7312	7697	8083	8468	8854	386
1127	9239	9624	*0010	*0395	*0780	*1166	*1551	*1936	*2321	*2706	385
1128	052 3091	3476	3861	4246	4631	5016	5400	5785	6170	6555	385
1129	6939	7324	7709	8093	8478	8862	9247	9631	*0016	*0400	385
1130	053 0784	1169	1553	1937	2321	2706	3090	3474	3858	4242	384
1131	4626	5010	5394	5778	6162	6546	6929	7313	7697	8081	384
1132	8464	8848	9232	9615	9999	*0382	*0766	*1149	*1532	*1916	384
1133	054 2299	2682	3066	3449	3832	4215	4598	4981	5365	5748	383
1134	6131	6514	6896	7279	7662	8045	8428	8811	9193	9576	383
1135	9959	*0341	*0724	*1106	*1489	*1871	*2254	*2636	*3019	*3401	382
1136	055 3783	4166	4548	4930	5312	5694	6077	6459	6841	7223	382
1137	7605	7987	8369	8750	9132	9514	9896	*0278	*0659	*1041	382
1138	056 1422	1804	2186	2567	2949	3330	3712	4093	4475	4856	381
1139	5237	5619	6000	6381	6762	7143	7524	7905	8287	8668	381
1140	9049	9429	9810	*0191	*0572	*0953	*1334	*1714	*2095	*2476	381
1141	057 2856	3237	3618	3998	4379	4759	5140	5520	5900	6281	381
1142	6661	7041	7422	7802	8182	8562	8942	9322	9702	*0082	380
1143	058 0462	0842	1222	1602	1982	2362	2741	3121	3501	3881	380
1144	4260	4640	5019	5399	5778	6158	6537	6917	7296	7676	380
1145	8055	8434	8813	9193	9572	9951	*0330	*0709	*1088	*1467	379
1146	059 1846	2225	2604	2983	3362	3741	4119	4498	4877	5256	379
1147	5634	6013	6391	6770	7148	7527	7905	8284	8662	9041	379
1148	9419	9797	*0175	*0554	*0932	*1310	*1688	*2066	*2444	*2822	378
1149	060 3200	3578	3956	4334	4712	5090	5468	5845	6223	6601	378
1150	6978	7356	7734	8111	8489	8866	9244	9621	9999	*0376	378
N	0	1	2	3	4	5	6	7	8	9	d.

LOGARITHMS

N.	0	1	2	3	4	5	6	7	8	9	d.
1150	060 6978	7356	7734	8111	8489	8866	9244	9621	9999	*0376	378
1151	061 0753	1131	1508	1885	2262	2639	3017	3394	3771	4148	377
1152	4525	4902	5279	5656	6032	6409	6786	7163	7540	7916	377
1153	8293	8670	9046	9423	9799	*0176	*0552	*0929	*1305	*1682	377
1154	062 2058	2434	2811	3187	3563	3939	4316	4692	5068	5444	376
1155	5820	6196	6572	6948	7324	7699	8075	8451	8827	9203	376
1156	9578	9954	*0330	*0705	*1081	*1456	*1832	*2207	*2583	*2958	376
1157	063 3334	3709	4084	4460	4835	5210	5585	5960	6335	6711	375
1158	7086	7461	7836	8211	8585	8960	9335	9710	*0085	*0460	375
1159	064 0834	1209	1584	1958	2333	2708	3082	3457	3831	4205	375
1160	4580	4954	5329	5703	6077	6451	6826	7200	7574	7948	374
1161	8322	8696	9070	9444	9818	*0192	*0566	*0940	*1314	*1688	374
1162	065 2061	2435	2809	3182	3556	3930	4303	4677	5050	5424	374
1163	5797	6171	6544	6917	7291	7664	8037	8410	8784	9157	373
1164	9530	9903	*0276	*0649	*1022	*1395	*1768	*2141	*2514	*2886	373
1165	066 3259	3632	4005	4377	4750	5123	5495	5868	6241	6613	373
1166	6986	7358	7730	8103	8475	8847	9220	9592	9964	*0336	372
1167	067 0709	1081	1453	1825	2197	2569	2941	3313	3685	4057	372
1168	4428	4800	5172	5544	5915	6287	6659	7030	7402	7774	372
1169	8145	8517	8888	9259	9631	*0002	*0374	*0745	*1116	*1487	371
1170	068 1859	2230	2601	2972	3343	3714	4085	4456	4827	5198	371
1171	5569	5940	6311	6681	7052	7423	7794	8164	8535	8906	371
1172	9276	9647	*0017	*0388	*0758	*1129	*1499	*1869	*2240	*2610	370
1173	069 2980	3350	3721	4091	4461	4831	5201	5571	5941	6311	370
1174	6681	7051	7421	7791	8160	8530	8900	9270	9639	*0009	370
1175	070 0379	0748	1118	1487	1857	2226	2596	2965	3335	3704	369
1176	4073	4442	4812	5181	5550	5919	6288	6658	7027	7396	369
1177	7765	8134	8503	8871	9240	9609	9978	*0347	*0715	*1084	369
1178	071 1453	1822	2190	2559	2927	3296	3664	4033	4401	4770	369
1179	5138	5506	5875	6243	6611	6979	7348	7716	8084	8452	368
1180	8820	9188	9556	9924	*0292	*0660	*1028	*1396	*1763	*2131	368
1181	072 2499	2867	3234	3602	3970	4337	4705	5072	5440	5807	368
1182	6175	6542	6910	7277	7644	8011	8379	8746	9113	9480	367
1183	9847	*0215	*0582	*0949	*1316	*1683	*2050	*2416	*2783	*3150	367
1184	073 3517	3884	4251	4617	4984	5351	5717	6084	6450	6817	367
1185	7184	7550	7916	8283	8649	9016	9382	9748	*0114	*0481	366
1186	074 0847	1213	1579	1945	2311	2677	3043	3409	3775	4141	366
1187	4507	4873	5239	5605	5970	6336	6702	7068	7433	7799	366
1188	8161	8530	8895	9261	9626	9992	*0357	*0723	*1088	*1453	365
1189	075 1819	2184	2549	2914	3279	3644	4010	4375	4740	5105	365
1190	5470	5835	6199	6564	6929	7294	7659	8024	8388	8753	365
1191	9118	9482	9847	*0211	*0576	*0940	*1305	*1669	*2034	*2398	364
1192	076 2763	3127	3491	3855	4220	4584	4948	5312	5676	6040	364
1193	6404	6768	7132	7496	7860	8224	8588	8952	9316	9680	364
1194	077 0043	0407	0771	1134	1498	1862	2225	2589	2952	3316	364
1195	3679	4042	4406	4769	5133	5496	5859	6222	6585	6949	363
1196	7312	7675	8038	8401	8764	9127	9490	9853	*0216	*0579	363
1197	078 0942	1304	1667	2030	2393	2755	3118	3480	3843	4206	363
1198	4568	4931	5293	5656	6018	6380	6743	7105	7467	7830	362
1199	8192	8554	8916	9278	9640	*0003	*0365	*0727	*1089	*1451	362
1200	079 1812	2174	2536	2898	3260	3622	3983	4345	4707	5068	362
N.	0	1	2	3	4	5	6	7	8	9	d.

1983

JANUARY

S	M	T	W	T	F	S
						1
2	3	4	5	6	7	8
9	10	11	12	13	14	15
16	17	18	19	20	21	22
23	24	25	26	27	28	29
30	31					

FEBRUARY

S	M	T	W	T	F	S
		1 (32)	2 (33)	3 (34)	4 (35)	5 (36)
6 (37)	7 (38)	8 (39)	9 (40)	10 (41)	11 (42)	12 (43)
13 (44)	14 (45)	15 (46)	16 (47)	17 (48)	18 (49)	19 (50)
20 (51)	21 (52)	22 (53)	23 (54)	24 (55)	25 (56)	26 (57)
27 (58)	28 (59)					

MARCH

S	M	T	W	T	F	S
		1 (60)	2 (61)	3 (62)	4 (63)	5 (64)
6 (65)	7 (66)	8 (67)	9 (68)	10 (69)	11 (70)	12 (71)
13 (72)	14 (73)	15 (74)	16 (75)	17 (76)	18 (77)	19 (78)
20 (79)	21 (80)	22 (81)	23 (82)	24 (83)	25 (84)	26 (85)
27 (86)	28 (87)	29 (88)	30 (89)	31 (90)		

APRIL

S	M	T	W	T	F	S
					1 (91)	2 (92)
3 (93)	4 (94)	5 (95)	6 (96)	7 (97)	8 (98)	9 (99)
10 (100)	11 (101)	12 (102)	13 (103)	14 (104)	15 (105)	16 (106)
17 (107)	18 (108)	19 (109)	20 (110)	21 (111)	22 (112)	23 (113)
24 (114)	25 (115)	26 (116)	27 (117)	28 (118)	29 (119)	30 (120)

MAY

S	M	T	W	T	F	S
1 (121)	2 (122)	3 (123)	4 (124)	5 (125)	6 (126)	7 (127)
8 (128)	9 (129)	10 (130)	11 (131)	12 (132)	13 (133)	14 (134)
15 (135)	16 (136)	17 (137)	18 (138)	19 (139)	20 (140)	21 (141)
22 (142)	23 (143)	24 (144)	25 (145)	26 (146)	27 (147)	28 (148)
29 (149)	30 (150)	31 (151)				

JUNE

S	M	T	W	T	F	S
			1 (152)	2 (153)	3 (154)	4 (155)
5 (156)	6 (157)	7 (158)	8 (159)	9 (160)	10 (161)	11 (162)
12 (163)	13 (164)	14 (165)	15 (166)	16 (167)	17 (168)	18 (169)
19 (170)	20 (171)	21 (172)	22 (173)	23 (174)	24 (175)	25 (176)
26 (177)	27 (178)	28 (179)	29 (180)	30 (181)		

JULY

S	M	T	W	T	F	S
					1 (182)	2 (183)
3 (184)	4 (185)	5 (186)	6 (187)	7 (188)	8 (189)	9 (190)
10 (191)	11 (192)	12 (193)	13 (194)	14 (195)	15 (196)	16 (197)
17 (198)	18 (199)	19 (200)	20 (201)	21 (202)	22 (203)	23 (204)
24 (205)	25 (206)	26 (207)	27 (208)	28 (209)	29 (210)	30 (211)
31 (212)						

AUGUST

S	M	T	W	T	F	S
	1 (213)	2 (214)	3 (215)	4 (216)	5 (217)	6 (218)
7 (219)	8 (220)	9 (221)	10 (222)	11 (223)	12 (224)	13 (225)
14 (226)	15 (227)	16 (228)	17 (229)	18 (230)	19 (231)	20 (232)
21 (233)	22 (234)	23 (235)	24 (236)	25 (237)	26 (238)	27 (239)
28 (240)	29 (241)	30 (242)	31 (243)			

SEPTEMBER

S	M	T	W	T	F	S
				1 (244)	2 (245)	3 (246)
4 (247)	5 (248)	6 (249)	7 (250)	8 (251)	9 (252)	10 (253)
11 (254)	12 (255)	13 (256)	14 (257)	15 (258)	16 (259)	17 (260)
18 (261)	19 (262)	20 (263)	21 (264)	22 (265)	23 (266)	24 (267)
25 (268)	26 (269)	27 (270)	28 (271)	29 (272)	30 (273)	

OCTOBER

S	M	T	W	T	F	S
						1 (274)
2 (275)	3 (276)	4 (277)	5 (278)	6 (279)	7 (280)	8 (281)
9 (282)	10 (283)	11 (284)	12 (285)	13 (286)	14 (287)	15 (288)
16 (289)	17 (290)	18 (291)	19 (292)	20 (293)	21 (294)	22 (295)
23 (296)	24 (297)	25 (298)	26 (299)	27 (300)	28 (301)	29 (302)
30 (303)	31 (304)					

NOVEMBER

S	M	T	W	T	F	S
		1 (305)	2 (306)	3 (307)	4 (308)	5 (309)
6 (310)	7 (311)	8 (312)	9 (313)	10 (314)	11 (315)	12 (316)
13 (317)	14 (318)	15 (319)	16 (320)	17 (321)	18 (322)	19 (323)
20 (324)	21 (325)	22 (326)	23 (327)	24 (328)	25 (329)	26 (330)
27 (331)	28 (332)	29 (333)	30 (334)			

DECEMBER

S	M	T	W	T	F	S
				1 (335)	2 (336)	3 (337)
4 (338)	5 (339)	6 (340)	7 (341)	8 (342)	9 (343)	10 (344)
11 (345)	12 (346)	13 (347)	14 (348)	15 (349)	16 (350)	17 (351)
18 (352)	19 (353)	20 (354)	21 (355)	22 (356)	23 (357)	24 (358)
25 (359)	26 (360)	27 (361)	28 (362)	29 (363)	30 (364)	31 (365)

APPENDIX 4

Savings Account Analysis Form

Name	Lender A	Lender B	Lender C
Annual percentage rate, *APR*			
Annual Yield			
Periodic percentage rate, *PPR*			
Compounding periods per yr			
Crediting period dates			
Maturity			
Early withdrawal penalty			
When will they refuse to allow withdrawals?			
Grace Days			
For deposits			
For withdrawals			
Computing method			
Day-in-day-out (BEST)			
Other			

Solutions

1   a. $(17 \times 24) \div 5.5 + 215.7 - 16.6 = 273.28181$
    b. already in correct order; total $= 3,030.08$
    c. $(44 + 55) \times 2,100 \times 44.7 = 9,293,130$
    d. cannot be suitably rearranged; total $= 2,541$

2   a. upper limit: $5 \times 150 = 750$
       lower limit: $5 \times 100 = 500$
       total: 581
    b. upper limit: $1 \times 5 \times 5 \times 5 \times 5 = 625$
       lower limit: $1 \times 1 \times 1 \times 1 \times 1 = 1$
       total: 120
    c. upper limit: $1 \times 100 \times 1 \times 1000 \times .1 = 10,000$
       lower limit: $1 \times 10 \times .1 \times 100 \times .01 = 1$
       total: 120
    d. lower limit: $\dfrac{100}{10 + 25 + 25 + 20 + 20} = \dfrac{100}{100} = 1$

       upper limit: $\dfrac{150}{5 + 20 + 20 + 15 + 10} = \dfrac{150}{70} = 2.1$

       total: 1.5243902
    e. upper limit: $100 - 10 - 0 - 10 - 0 = 80$
       lower limit: $100 - 20 - 10 - 20 - 10 = 40$
       total: 60

SOLUTIONS TO PROBLEMS IN CHAPTER 3

1   2,997.80;   17,650.056;   151

2   a. 330 mi
    b. 3,400 km
    c. 40,320 ft = 7.636 mi

3   11,000%;   5.5%;   0.1%;   155%

4   0.04;   0.125;   1.00;   0.0003

5   $51.75

6   $18,750.00

7   16.666667%

8   −9.0909091%

9   $85.66; $4,368.66

10 a. 0.13561397
    b. 316.75

11 12,350,000;   87,650,000;   150.5;   0.0056;   13,440,000;   2,257

12 100,000;   456;   0.008;   5.05;   75.8;   1,410

13 a. 36,000
    b. 1.58
    c. 4,775

SOLUTIONS TO PROBLEMS IN CHAPTER 4

1   Error is in the subtraction of check 179. The balance should be $1,121.34.

2   The register balance is correct.

3   First checking account: $3.25 per month
    Second checking account: $4.75 per month
    The 2 are equal for a person who writes 10 checks per month.

4   Average balance; $802.46
    Monthly yield: $3.71

SOLUTIONS TO PROBLEMS IN CHAPTER 6

1   a.   3.2494
    b.   −2.6576

    c. 5.1992

    d. 1.4419

    e. 1.2989

    f. 9.0878

2   **a.** 119.8

    b. 0.1729

    c. 882,100

    d. 0.00098400

    e. 10.1

    f. 1.005

3   Normal: 1,718.4;   Log: 1718

4   23,250

5   0.0000001

6   34,590

7   1.105

8   0.8870

9   3-term: 1.10471021   6-term: 1.10471263

10   1.03044681

11   1.21664333

12   5-term: $160.58

SOLUTIONS TO PROBLEMS IN CHAPTER 7

1 $0.48

2   333.33

3   8.01%

4   3%

5   16.88%

6 $17,331; $17,658; $17,985

7 $41,225

8 $29,289

9 $905

10 $15,069

SOLUTIONS TO PROBLEMS
IN CHAPTER 8

1   $7541.94;   14,220.22

2   4.6 years

3   $4,625

4   $66.60

5   $81

6   $9,665.81; $5,198.02

7   $64.71

8   After 5 years: $26,803; $27,425; $28,708
    After 10 years: $28,735; $30,085; $32,963

9   $19,181; $26,855

10 $213,384; $75,281

11 $181,200

SOLUTIONS TO PROBLEMS
IN CHAPTER 9

1   12.5%

2   $805.13

3   $438.07

4   72 months

5   $113,176

6   $56,860; $31,495

7   $336.72

8   $30,168; $15,370

9   12.5%

10 11.04%

SOLUTIONS TO PROBLEMS
IN CHAPTER 10

1   22,911 BTU/DD

2   $2,435.51

3   0.1257

4   0.4546

5   64.68 MMBTU

6    $1,047

SOLUTIONS TO PROBLEMS
IN CHAPTER 11

1    $2,761.56

2   39.30%

3    $ 712.80; $1,094.40
     $1,663.20; $2,553.60
     $2,376.00; $3,648.00

4   Electric heaters would have the lowest lifecycle cost: Jackson Execu-
     tive W4–$8,372;   Wards No. 35170–$5,340.

5   3.92¢ / kwh

6   Maytag–$9,386;   Whirlpool–$12,248

SOLUTIONS TO PROBLEMS
IN CHAPTER 12

1

Sale Price Condo	$ 35,000.00	$ 75,000.00
Mortgage Payment	399.98	619.01
Gross monthly expense as Homeowner	578.31	847.34
Monthly tax savings as Homeowner	211.50	152.04
Net monthly expense as Homeowner	460.80	670.38
Future value condo	146,301.00	199,501.00
Net advantage Homeowner	50,070.00	00,054.00
Monthly savings to offset home owning	453.70	658.09
Balance remaining for rent/utilities	7.11	12.30

2   The purchase of this home is financially equivalent to putting $200.06
     per month in a savings plan and paying $249.36 per month for rent and
     utilities.

3   In this case, the purchase would be equivalent to putting $277.91 in
     savings and paying $172.17 for rent and utilities per month.   /

4

	Monthly Savings	Rent/ Utilities
9% mortgage	$319	$115
10% mortgage	314	145
11% mortgage	310	191

5   Monthly savings: $122.35
     Rent incl. utilities: $315.56

Index